SELECTED SERMONS
OF
CANON ORVILLE E. WATSON

Orville E. Watson.

SELECTED SERMONS
OF
CANON ORVILLE E. WATSON

EDITED BY
LACY LOCKERT
*Formerly Assistant Professor of English
at Kenyon College*

PRINTED FOR KENYON COLLEGE
by
THE PARTHENON PRESS
Nashville, Tennessee

SELECTED SERMONS OF
CANON ORVILLE E. WATSON

COPYRIGHT 1955
BY KENYON COLLEGE

To The Memory Of Orville E. Watson
(1857 - 1951)

Lighten our darkness, we beseech thee, O Lord.

When God said light should be, no sudden torch
Kindled the chaos to one heavenly flame,
But only across the endless dark there came*
The finger-tips of stars, that in the arch
Themselves created waved as from a porch
To night-bound stumblers. Cosmos is the name
Of the little light, much darkness where these same
Faint stars alone bear fires that blaze and scorch.

Hail, holy light! God lifts a candle high
Above our heads and makes the dark half-plain,
And stays his hand a while and lets us spy
Into a world of shadowed things, and then
Takes it away; but when we vainly cry
Our light is quenched, replies, *My stars remain.*

Philip W. Timberlake
Gambier, May, 1952

Foreword

ORVILLE ERNEST WATSON—known to many generations of Kenyon students as Canon Watson—was born in
Westfield, Ohio, on December 1, 1857, the son of a country
doctor. He grew up in the neighboring village of Cardington, and was graduated from Cardington High School in
1877. In the autumn of that year he entered Ohio Wesleyan
University at Delaware, Ohio, and was graduated from that
institution in 1882, having remained out of college for one
year because of ill health. While he was at Ohio Wesleyan
he became a member of the Methodist Church.

For some time after his graduation he worked as a bank
clerk in Cardington; but in 1889 he was confirmed in the
Episcopal Church by Bishop William A. Leonard, of the
Diocese of Ohio, and in the late autumn of that year entered the General Seminary, in New York, as a candidate for
orders. The following year Bishop Leonard recalled him
to Ohio, where he carried on his studies at Bexley Hall,
the theological school of Kenyon College, in Gambier. He
was ordained to the diaconate on June 26, 1892, and to
the priesthood on June 25, 1893. After becoming a deacon
he went to Trinity Cathedral, in Cleveland, and served as a
minor canon there until 1903.

In 1903 Canon Watson was appointed Professor of New
Testament Instruction in Bexley Hall. In this position he
remained for forty years, until his retirement from active
teaching in 1943. He spent the rest of his life in Gambier.
He died there on May 17, 1951, and is buried in Lakeview
Cemetery, in Cleveland.

During Canon Watson's tenure at Bexley he served
several times as acting chaplain of Kenyon, and in some
years he taught one or two classes there. No one else in
the history of these institutions was so long connected with

9

them or was so generally and greatly revered and loved. His influence on both undergraduates and theological students was very notable, and their frequent visits to his rooms in Bexley Hall, where he lived among his many books and musical recordings, were much-prized occurrences at the time and treasured memories thereafter. His influence had a wider range through the sermons—of remarkable quality —that he preached, not only in the college chapel but in churches elsewhere in Ohio.

The manuscripts of some one hundred and twenty-five of these sermons were among his effects at the time of his death. This volume contains what are thought to be the best and most characteristic of them. The date of each is given wherever known either precisely or approximately; when it is not absolutely certain, it is enclosed in parentheses. Three sermons which seem especially appropriate to begin the book are placed first; the others are in as nearly chronological order as possible.

Naturally, certain favorite ideas of Canon Watson find expression in more than one sermon. There has been no attempt to avoid such repetition; the contents of the volume have been selected solely on the basis of merit. On that basis a few sermons have been included which definitely "date." Most of these were in connection with the First World War, to which his reactions were intense and are worthy of record as very characteristic of him. He himself would surely have wished his position at that time to be recalled in any memorial of him, though he later would not have eulogized France as he did in his sermon on Honor.

Last of all comes a fragment of a long manuscript— several times too long for a sermon—entitled "The Servant of Yahweh," which deals with the development of the Messianic idea among the ancient Hebrews. The first few pages of this manuscript are very much superior in quality to the rest of it (which has many interlined changes and alternative readings, suggesting that its author was never satisfied with it as a whole) ; and as these opening pages of it reach the end of one sub-division of its theme, they can be taken alone and, so taken, form a very suitable and indeed brilliant finale to the volume.

In the choice of the sermons and in the problems that arose in editing them, I have been aided by the advice of Dr. Philip W. Timberlake of Kenyon College, who is the Chairman of the book's Publication Committee, and by that of others; but the final decision in all cases has been mine, as the responsible Editor of the volume. I have persuaded Dr. Timberlake, overcoming his considerable diffidence, to allow me to use his fine sonnet "To the Memory of Orville E. Watson," published in *The Kenyon Alumni Bulletin* for the summer of 1952, as an appropriate opening of the book.

Canon Watson's sermons were made available by the late W. Ray Ashford of Kenyon College, whose devoted care of him during his last years won the admiration of all the friends of both. It is most regrettable that Dr. Ashford did not live to see the completion of this book, in which he was so greatly interested.

LACY LOCKERT

Nashville, Tennessee
January 15, 1955.

Contents

CHAPTER 1

The First Commandment

"God spake these words and said: 'I am the Lord thy God; thou shalt have none other gods but me.'"

THROUGH A VOLCANO'S mouth these words were uttered in thunder—so it is recorded—as if the God who spoke them sat on his throne to speak them, wearing his official robes of smoke and fire. And the thunder-trumpets of Mount Sinai proclaimed these words in seventy languages—so it is recorded—seventy being the number of all the languages on the earth. With such emphasis and completeness this first and primary law is published to the whole human race: "I am the Lord thy God; thou shalt have none other gods but me."

But it is in the soul of men—so men are made—to demand the reason for any claim addressed to their support or sympathy. When a traveler stops at our tent-door, we desire to see his letters of introduction or recommendation before we start relationships with him; and we will look, perhaps, for his name in some specialized list, a *Blue Book* or *Bradstreet* or *Who's Who*. And if this care has proved advisable in the intercourse of men, how much more reason there is for caution when the stranger is a god clothed with mystery and armed with power. For, from all that we learn of gods in our classical books, it would appear that there is a certain hazard in our choice of Olympian associates, whether for purposes of business or more intimate acqaintanceship.

Therefore, when we hear this commandment read, as given us from Mount Sinai, "I am the Lord thy God, thou

shalt have none other gods but me," it surely will not be ir-
religious but altogether in harmony with something deep
in our human nature, if we shall answer and say, "Why and
wherefore, O Lord?" It surely will not be presumptuous if
we shall answer and say, in the very words of Saint Paul,
"Who art thou, Lord?"

It is a proper question to ask, but God seems to answer
this question, as he seems to answer all questions, by leading
us to find out for ourselves. And the way thereof is long. For
men began to ask this question, "Who art thou, Lord?"
when they began to make flint knives, and they imagined
they saw an answer in every strange thing, and to every
such answer they gave a god-name. They saw his strength
in the strong wild beasts, and they saw the print of his feet
in the changing seasons, and they saw his anger in the storm.
And so, we find the names of gods in all the seventy dialects
of men: Zeus and Apollo and Thor, Venus and Astarte and
Isis, the great god Pan and old Silvanus and the sister
nymphs, with many and many another, gods of every high
hill and every bright fountain and every green tree. But no
one of them all possesses the right or claims the right to say,
"Thou shalt have none other gods but me." Indeed, the
God whom we seek has no name, as we know names. We do
not even call him Jehovah; for Jehovah is the name of the
god of the Jews. We simply call him God, which is merely
to give him the generic name of all gods, distinguished only
with a capital G.

And yet all these many names of many gods express the
endless endeavor of ages of men to get some answer to their
question, "Who art thou, Lord?"—listening at nature's
key-holes and spying in nature's kitchen—especially in
nature's kitchen, their food supply. All these names were
such answers as they dreamed they heard to their inevitable,
primeval question, "Who art thou, Lord?" And when they
gave the first watch of the night to the red planet Mars, or
when they gave the day's high noon to Ammon-Ra, sailing
across the blue in his golden boat, they were brought to

16

a dead standstill in their search by the mere appearance of things.

It was a shepherd—so we read—a shepherd keeping his sheep in the solitude, to whom at last was revealed the name of God—at least the only name of God that men may know. Springtime it must have been, when the trees and shrubs were in full blossom, making another, lovelier Sinai with fire of crimson and smoke of white. And when the shepherd, gazing on this mystery of life, asked his hereditary question, "Who art thou, Lord?" a still, small voice in his soul replied with a name which is no name: "I am that I am," it said. And the shepherd put off his shoes from his feet as he cried out in the exultation of his great discovery:

"God is that which is behind all seeming. God is the Reality of things! And the very ground on which I stand is holy ground!"

"I Am That I Am," or simply "I AM,"—this is the ultimate name, as it is the ultimate conception of God. And Rudyard Kipling puts this name into another form when he calls him, "The God of Things as They Are."

It is very plain to see that such a God, the God of Reality, has full authority to say, "I am the Lord thy God," and full right has he to say, "Thou shalt have none other gods but me." For to learn the existence and scope of Things as They Are is not only the real business of every human soul born into the world, but it is the real business of the whole human race. The story of all human achievement is the story of the progressive discovery of Things as They Are. It is the passion both of Science and of Philosophy to know Things as They Are. And so it is the sublime aspiration of Religion to know the God of Things as They Are.

Born into a world of Things that Seem, we have it as our absolutely necessary task to learn the reality behind them; for it is Things as They Are, and not Things as They Seem, that determine results. It matters nothing that a flame of fire seems to our opening eyes to be a bright flower; we cannot reach out and pick it on that seeming. It matters nothing that foretold Effects often seem to have lost remembrance of

17

their related Causes; we dare not stake our happiness on such forgetting. It matters nothing that Satan puts on disguise and appears to us as an Angel of Light; it is with reality that we actually make our contracts and find, maybe, that we have signed away our souls.

It is Things as They Are that absolutely rule the world. And so the God of Things as They Are is the only God whom we can consistently serve and worship, no matter what name men call him by. For any other god is a god of Things as They Seem, and so he is a false god who will lead us into confusion. That is why every lie is inherently a blasphemy and a treason. Nor is it a matter of choice for us. We may "cling to shadows and dote on dreams," we may "plant a false self in the midst of our life and build around a world that seems"; sooner or later all shams break down and force us to acknowledge realities. The God of Things as They Are *is* the Lord our God. No use to ignore him or rebel. He compels our ignorance to serve him, and he bends our waywardness to obey.

And this submission to the God of Things as They Are, is our great hope in a world of deceiving appearances. Every veil of seeming that we pierce through reveals something that takes its place in a mysterious unity of Truth. And so certain facts in our world which seem to us most calamitous, may, in their turn, dissolve into realities with nothing in them to make us afraid. The waste, the loss, the failure of life, may all be gathered up into precious forms in the hands of the God of Things as They Are; and the inexorable face of Death itself may break, when we behold it as it really is, into something that blooms into light, like an aspect of the spring.

The Lord our God is the God of Things as They Are; but he has yet another name.

When Pompey the Roman took possession of Jerusalem and added it to the trophies of the gods of Rome, it is recorded of him that when he entered the city he had a curiosity to see the God of the Jews. He could not have conceived it to be difficult, for every other temple that he knew had a statue of its divinity set up in an inmost shrine, visible to all who came. So Pompey the Roman went up into the Temple to look upon the God of the Jews. To be sure, his worshipers seemed to guard him with a strange reserve. Not only was the inmost shrine of the Temple, which was called the Holy of Holies, hidden behind a great curtain stretching from side to side and from ceiling to floor, but no man was allowed ever to enter the dark room behind it where the Lord God of the Jews was supposed to dwell; no man save one, and he was the high priest, and he came but once, on a specified day, every year.

Such a prohibition might hold for Jews, but not for a Roman, and so Pompey strode down the length of the Holy Place, in which none but priests might walk, and he drew aside the folds of the heavy, forbidden curtain, beyond which none but the high priest might go, and he passed within. Perhaps the priests who watched him had not warned him, holding back a safe distance and hoping to see him struck dead. But no thunderbolt fell as he stood gazing round in the light of the torch held high. What fell upon Pompey was astonishment, for there was nothing to see. The Holy of Holies was empty. There was no God there.

And yet the Holy of Holies had not always been empty. A thousand years before, when the Temple was built on Zion Hill, a sacred object stood in the Holy of Holies—the Holy of Holies was made for it. And during four hundred years this sacred object stood in the Holy of Holies, until the Babylonians came and destroyed Jerusalem and burned the Temple and carried away all the sacred things in it, including, perhaps—for we hear of it no more—the most holy thing on account of which the Holy of Holies had been built. This Most Holy Thing which stood in the midst of the Most Holy Place was a chest; simply a chest, but a chest regarded with the utmost awe and reverence because it represented the presence of the Hebrew God among his people.

This chest is called in history the "ark." It was a box some four feet in length, plated with gold, and having its gold-covered lid over-shadowed by the wings of two symbolic cherubim. But a box is important only on account of what it is made to hold; and whatever is wrought upon it of beauty or of art simply emphasizes that importance, the importance of holding something of great worth. The ark, therefore, represented the presence of God, not in itself, but in that which it contained. The ark was made rich with gold, and guarded by cherubim, and curtained with darkness, and set in the place where men were wont to erect the statues of their gods, all because of that which was preserved inside the ark, something which guaranteed the presence of God in the midst of his people.

So now it remains to ask, what was the sacred object which was kept inside the ark? What was the ark made to contain? The answer will be significant. Down in Egypt arks were constructed to hold the image of a god. But not so the ark of the Hebrews. If by some special privilege you could have lifted the lid of the ark of the Hebrews and looked within—the two golden cherubim watching you all the while—you would have found no god lying asleep in his acacia coffin. No, but what you would have discovered is far more wonderful, when you come to consider it. What you would have found therein was simply two slabs of stone. But upon these two slabs of stone were letters carved. And if you could have deciphered these carven letters, it is very familiar words you would have read: for it was the Ten Commandments that were cut into the stone.

Here were a people who knew, as they were taught, that their God dwelt in the inner dark room of their Temple, and the priests, day in and day out, kept in operation the most elaborate apparatus of worship. Altar fires blazed, and incense-smoke arose, and psalms of praise were chanted, and silver trumpets blew; but the center of all this ritual, as far as anyone could see, was only a box containing a list of rules governing the daily conduct of men. The center of worship, as far as anyone could see, was the moral law.

Pompey the Roman found the Temple chamber empty, the dark chamber which had been built for God to dwell within;

20

but into the dark heart of Israel Pompey could not see, nor could he dream that that was the only place in which to look.

For the inner chamber of the Temple represents the heart of Israel; more, it represents the dark heart of all mankind, made for God to dwell within. And the golden ark, watched by sleepless cherubim, is that strange cell planted like a seed in the heart of humanity, whose life-germ is a strange impulse to do something we call right. And this life-cell men have named the Conscience. The Ten Commandments, then, given from the Mount Sinai of ten thousand years of human experience, flaming with divine meanings, represent the right direction impressed upon the Conscience, to guide its groping impulse upward toward the light.

And so close is this relationship between the light that we call God and the upward impulse we call Conscience, that the Presence of God among his people was identified, in old Israel, with the developed accomplishments of Conscience, the moral law, controlling the sources of human action. But Conscience, with its ceaseless endeavor, is universal; so that the God who claims the exclusive loyalty of men is altogether justified in his demand when he declares: "I am the Lord thy God—the God of Things that are Right. Thou shalt have none other Gods but me."

So these are the two names of the God who claims our sole allegiance: "The God of Things as They Are," and "The God of Things that are Right." And manifestly our real allegiance to such a God, and our real worship of him, will be in the passion for justice among men, and the passion for harmony of life, and the passion for truth—truth both in its utter wideness and truth in its manifold implications in our works and days. The man cannot go far wrong, nor ultimately wrong, who has these passions in his soul.

And such a God cannot be denied nor ignored, because we cannot deny nor ignore things as they are and things that are right. We cannot deny nor ignore the multiplication table when we deal with figures, nor can we deny nor ignore

21

the law of gravitation when we walk in slippery places. We are only warned to act in co-operation with them. And so in human life it is at our own peril that we deny or ignore that which is True and that which is Right. Any voice that is a friendly voice will urge us to co-operation with that which is Right and that which is True. And so the Lord our God is a friendly God, not because he gives us hope that he himself will break his own laws for us, but because he calls us to face facts and heed realities, and puts upon us responsibility for results when we dally with that which is wrong and build upon that which is false. It is just because he is a God of love that he has said:

"I am the Lord thy God; thou shalt have none other gods but me. For I am the God of Things as They Are, and I am the God of Things that are Right."

And so he invites us into his very heart of love when he calls us to realities; or, rather, he invites us to realize that we dwell already in the very heart of God when we begin to see things as they are. We dwell in the very heart of God, and the currents of life, around us and within, are his very thoughts unfolding in the processes of some vast and cosmic logic. That mysterious throb in the cells of all organic being, repeated in the beat of our own hearts, and re-echoed in all music, is measured again in the swing of seasons and tides and worlds, and again in the waves of light which break in starry foam on the very edge of time. The rhythm of the universe is the heart of God beating there.

Our own hearts beat because God's heart beats; and that is why, as we become capable of knowing things as they are, we grow capable of knowing things that are right, and so seeing that they are beautiful. For the Lord our God is the God of the True, the Beautiful, and the Good. To know God is to learn to know the True, the Beautiful, and the Good.

Is it matter of wonder, then, that he should say to us, should say to all the world, "I am the Lord thy God; thou shalt have none other gods but me? For I am the God of

Things as They Are; and I am the God of Things that are Right."

And is there anything left but this for us to answer: "Lord, have mercy upon us, and incline our hearts to keep this law?"

Kenyon College Chapel
May 10, 1925.

Chapter 2

The Gate Beautiful

"A certain lame man was laid daily at the Gate of the Temple which is called Beautiful, to ask alms of them that entered into the Temple."

Acts iii:2.

THERE IS A field of France, in the midst of which an ancient gate-way stands. It is an old Roman gate-way, all that now remains of a town which once was there. You pass through it from the open field on one side to the open field on the other. Strange, you seem to have entered nothing, although you have passed through a gate. But one cannot think of a gate except as an entrance into an enclosed space. So this gate-way must open at least—your thought demands it—into some place whose walls and roofs invisibly enclose invisible interiors. You look up at the gate, upon whose weather-beaten pilasters the moss and lichens have wrought mosaic-patterns, and upon whose architrave above, tufts of grass and wild flowers have found crevices in which to root—patient Nature claiming this work of man as again her own. It is the Gate Beautiful—what else can it be? you say, and it opens into the Temple of Nature, all the green field and the blue sky on the one side being the porch of it, and all the green field and the blue sky on the other side being the sanctuary.

The Gate Beautiful: an old story stirs in your memory at the name, and this ancient archway takes significance. You have entered through it into a region of thought. You have entered through it into a New Testament story.

It was under the Beautiful Gate of the Temple at Jerusalem that a lame beggar once lay, and the story of him is one

24

of those vivid and clear-cut stories of the Bible that we learn in our childhood, and that remain ever after in the picture galleries of our memories, a part of the permanent furniture there. The story of Joseph sold into Egypt, the story of Samson grinding blind in a mill, the story of David with his sling against the giant Goliath, the story of Daniel in the lions' den: these dramatic little stories stand side by side in our memory with the parables of our Lord, each one, like them, meaning much more than itself. That is their value: each one represents a fact or feature of universal human life, recurring perpetually in every land and every time.

Among such stories and parables lives the story of the lame man at the Gate Beautiful. Every day he was carried to the Temple and laid on the steps of the Gate Beautiful, to beg of the people going in. This was his daily life, to lie on the steps of the Gate Beautiful and beg, until, one morning, Saint Peter and Saint John came up that way.

"Give a poor lame man a penny," he asked of them as he asked of all.

"Silver and gold have I none," Saint Peter answered, "but what I have, that give I unto thee. In the name of Jesus Christ, arise and walk."

And the lame man arose, with the help at first of Saint Peter's hand; he arose and walked. And then, through the Gate Beautiful he went into the Temple, walking and leaping and praising God.

This story may be classed with the parables; stories in which the meaning is much more than the story; stories in which the persons acting may be taken to represent ourselves, maybe, and the things they do and the things that happen to them, may be taken to represent things that happen to us and are done by us. Look at this story so, and behold, the lame man assumes the face and figure of a composite photograph; he becomes the whole human race. It is true, is it not? We all of us spend our lives with our hands stretched out, begging for the things that we want from the days as they pass by. How many multitudes of men

25

are forever stretching out their hands for money; and that is all they ask of life. How many multitudes of people are forever stretching out their hands for amusement and pleasure, and that is all they ask of life.

But it is not desire, of itself, which discredits human nature; for all growth is but the reaching out after that which is desired by the body or the soul. To "hunger and thirst after righteousness" is to win one of the Beatitudes of our Lord. It is what human nature asks for in its lameness, which makes its occupation beggary. Instead of asking to be cured and made able to walk, it sits under the Gate Beautiful and asks of the passing days and years nothing but pennies. Living men with immortal souls beg of Life nothing but pennies.

And it is under the Gate Beautiful that we sit to follow this abject employment. For the world in which we live is the Beautiful Gate; it surely is very beautiful, and above all things it is, we know, a place of constant entry and departure, greeting and farewell. What better name could we devise for the world, with the blue arches and cloud-buttresses of its vault, and with the infinite arabesques of beauty upon its walls, and with the eager processions of life forever passing through—what better name than the Beautiful Gate? How many times do we see people stop to look at flowers or trees, or across the valley to the East, and say to themselves or to us, "How beautiful is Gambier Hill!" And yet it is nothing new; every year presents its changing seasons, not only on Gambier Hill but on every hill, and it is always a wonder and a miracle. Beauty seems to be one of the most emphasized, the most insistent, aspects of creation. Look through telescopes at the stars and there is beauty; look through microscopes at the dust and beauty is there; always beauty. Look into the history of men, and there is always to be seen the impulse and the endeavor to make something beautiful, and to carve or paint patterns of curve and color and meaning upon the tools men used and the clothes they wore and the houses they lived in. The world

26

is flooded with beauty as with light; the world in which we live is the Beautiful Gate.

But a gate must necessarily open into something; that is why it is a gate. So into what does the Gate Beautiful open —under which we sit begging for pennies? In other words, what does universal beauty mean? What revelation has it, which we are slow to learn? Men usually try to account for its purpose in terms of utility or pleasure; but there is a mystery in beauty far wider than that. Such explanation is like cutting up the embroidered curtains of the tabernacle to make towels and ribbons. No, just as the Beautiful Gate of the Bible opened into the Temple, so the Gate Beautiful of Nature opens into something analogous. The Book of the Revelation of Saint John the Divine declares that a door was seen opened in heaven. Truth to say, it has never been shut; and the universal beauty of earth is the light of heaven shining through, to guide the race of men, if they would only see, up its golden stair.

Many men and women today are trying to get glimpses into the world beyond by means of ouija boards and mediums and spiritualistic cabinets. "We need the evidence," they say, "to give us faith in immortality." Just as, two thousand years ago, the scribes and Pharisees demanded signs from heaven, in such wise the lame beggars of materialism sit under the Gate Beautiful today, begging for pennies, and painfully fishing them out from the gutters and the garbage-cans of this earth.

It was a young poet, a few years ago, who looked up instead of down, and out instead of in, and forward instead of back; and this is what he saw in beauty:

"I cannot die who drink delight
    From the cup of the crescent moon;
And hungrily, as men eat bread,
Love the haunted nights of June.
I cannot die—for is there not
    Some shining, strange escape for me

27

Who find in Beauty the bright wine
Of immortality?"

This is the evidence which he finds, in the very home of all mankind, to give us faith in immortality. This is the secret hidden in Beauty, which gives to it its strange unearthly power over the souls of men: immortality, to which something immortal in the soul of man responds, just as the one right tone, when rightly sung, sets the strings of a harp sympathetically to singing. Recall how many soldiers in the World War who never had sung before, were moved to write poetry when face to face with death. Immortality is the inner meaning of Beauty, that mysterious meaning which has always puzzled the intellect while it enraptured the hearts of men. Immortality is the inner meaning of Beauty, immortality and the things involved in it, moral order and living truth and heavenly joy. So that Beauty, clothed with wings and winds and fire, is the gracious Presence everywhere made visible to men, the gracious Presence of the Holy Spirit, the Revealer and the Comforter, the Lord and the Giver of Life.

We see, oftentimes, this motto inscribed over the doors of studios, "Art for Art's sake"; which means, "Beauty for beauty's sake"; which means, when all is done, "Beauty for pleasure's sake." And this is the same as to say, "A gate is for the gate's own sake; its end is to lead nowhere." It is true that people will gather beneath the Beautiful Gate, thinking that it was specially built to give them a place in which to beg. And it is true that one poor beggar will scorn another poor beggar for begging copper pennies while he himself begs for silver or for gold; but it is not Saint Peter nor Saint John who will mark the difference between the two.

We live in a land at present very much occupied in amusing itself, and all Beauty is conscripted to serve this agreeable end. Not only Beauty, but also Life itself, is practically held to be for pleasure's sake. But not even pleasure is for pleasure's own sake. Nothing exists for its own sake; everything exists for the sake of something beyond itself. An individual exists for the sake of adding that which is unique in himself to a society of men; and a society of men exists for the sake of the Kingdom of Heaven. Gates open into farther gates, and stairs lead up to farther stairs, until we arrive at the climax of Saint Paul's magnificent declaration, that all the universe exists for the sake of the praise of the glory of God.

The great hymn of creation, celebrating the beauty of it in terms of its meaning, is the "Benedicite," which we used to sing through the season of Lent. It begins with a universal sweep: "O all ye works of the Lord, bless ye the Lord, praise him and magnify him forever." And then it runs through a kind of roll-call of creation: the Angels and Heavens and Powers of the Lord; the Sun, the Moon and Stars; Showers and Dew and Winds and Fire; Winter and Summer; Ice and Snow; Nights and Days; Lightnings and Clouds; Mountains and Hills; Seas and Floods; Beasts and Birds and all the Green Things upon the Earth—they all are addressed as performing in their manifold operations one great oratorio to the Creator of them all. And the perfect obedience to the laws of their being, the perfect rhythm from the smallest cell to the widest orbit, the perfect form for the perfect thought—it all is visible to our eyes as Beauty. And we, in looking upon these beautiful things, shall not only be doing what is fitting for us as ourselves a part of creation, but we shall also be doing what is for our own best growth and happiness, by joining in that universal song to the praise of the glory of God. A thing of beauty will be to us a joy forever, only as we make the enjoyment of it an act of worship, that is, a sacrament, an outward visible sign of an inward spiritual grace.

And, indeed, the "Benedicite" rises to this very thought; for after the roll-call of Nature follows the roll-call of humanity: "O ye children of Men, ye Servants of the Lord, ye Spirits and Souls of the Righteous," and then "ye holy and humble Men of heart, bless ye the Lord, praise him and

29

magnify him forever." The climax of creation is the holy and humble Men of heart, just as the climax of beauty is the Beauty of Holiness. The supreme beauty in the world is the beauty of soul, displayed in human living; and the whole world acknowledges this when it bows in admiration, if not in submission, at the foot of a Cross upon which a Man dies for men. The way of the perfect life is very simple, for it is traveled by the humble of heart, none else. And yet it is a proud way, for it is the way of the Cross, and it is a prouder thing to give than to receive. To swear the loyalty of our service to the most beautiful human life we know, which is that of our Lord Jesus Christ; like him to conquer all selfishness; to perform all duty; to have "good-will to all that live, letting unkindness die"; striving "to hinder not but help all things both great and small"; with courage to meet the trials of life and the threats of death—this is the way of the Cross, and it is also the way of the Beauty of Holiness and the hope of everlasting life.

When the lame man was no longer lame; when he looked up and saw that the Gate Beautiful was not a place in which to beg, but the entrance into a better kind of life, he rose and entered in through the Beautiful Gate; through the Gate Beautiful he went into the Temple, walking and leaping and praising God. It was into the Temple he went.

(1920)

Chapter 3

What Is Christianity?

*"Henceforth I call you not servants . . . but I have
called you friends."*
*"Ye are my friends if ye do those things which I
command you."*

John xv:15, 14.

AS I WALKED one day on Gambier Hill, I met a group
of students who were busy discussing a matter. And when
I asked them the subject of their debate, they told me that
they were trying to settle upon an answer to a very perplexing question. It was a question which had been proposed to them in the class-room, and they found it hard to
answer. The question was this: "What is Christianity?" And
this question asked of them I carried home to ask of my-
self, "What is Christianity?"

It does not seem to be an impertinent question, when
we recall the claims which Christianity makes upon the
whole world. And when we recall the fact that we, most of
us, are even enrolled as followers and champions of Christianity, it does not seem to be an impertinent attitude in us,
that we should ask ourselves just what we think we are.

If it be agreed that it is fitting to ask this question, it still
does not seem to be so very easy to answer. Men have waged
cruel wars to prove that Christianity is a religion of peace, and
they have burned each other at the stake to prove that it is
a religion of love. They have embalmed it in books to prove
that it is a religion of intellect, and they have enthroned it in
Bedlam to prove that it is a religion of spirit. They have endeavored to murder everything human in themselves in order to prove that it is a religion for humanity, and they

31

have allied it with every license and lawlessness in order to prove that it is a religion for those whose souls are truly free. They have made of it a whip of scorpions for the enslavement of thought, and at the same time they have found in it the divine secret of liberation from the enslavement of matter. Sometimes it has been largely hell, and sometimes it has been largely heaven; but never has paradox been too bold to serve in the processes of man's definitions of Christianity.

All this simply means that it is something too wide for definition, and men play along the edges of it, like children, dreaming their own dreams in the aspects of it, imagining archangels in the clouds above and devils in the depths below, while they launch the toy sail-boats of their own manufacture upon its mysterious tides.

But all this is not enough to discourage the human mind in its innate love of inquiry, and men still ask each other, "What is Christianity?" And I think, for all practical living, an answer may be found in the words of the Founder of Christianity when he called his disciples his friends. It was when he sat with them at their Last Supper together, and he was leaving to them his intimate farewell thoughts. "Henceforth I call you not servants," he said, "but friends; ye are my friends if ye do whatsoever I command you." The relation between himself and them was a relation of friendship. Christianity then is the friendship between heaven and earth.

Now friendship is absolutely the closest bond between human beings that human beings can know, or can imagine, on this earth. Ties of blood are strong, but they are strong especially because of the opportunities that they afford for the development of closer ties of friendship. Ties of blood are, after all, external ties, accidental ties. They belong among outside things; they belong to environment, along with country, climate, race, social class, and physical body. A father and a son may be total strangers to each other. It often happens that even a mother cares more for the glamour of society than for her own child. Two brothers may have nothing in common but their common surname. A man and wife may live in two entirely different worlds, worshiping different gods. That people pass the days in the same house, doing the same work, eating the same food, talking the same talk, never means, necessarily, that the bond that holds them together is anything more than the bond of circumstance. Our social ties are, indeed, the most precious things we know in life; but they are precious because through them friendship is usually allowed its perfect work. When father and son, man and wife, brother and brother, are friends as well as partakers in a social relationship, then life is at its richest, its highest, its most divine level. The mere outward form of union has now its living soul.

And that suggests exactly the reason why friendship is the closest bond on earth. It is because it is necessarily a thing of mind and soul. If mind and soul are not involved in a partnership, then that partnership is a poor affair, held together by conventionalities; but if mind and soul are at all concerned, then the association begins at once to incline towards friendship.

So when two human beings are drawn together because they like the same work, or the same games, or the same food, or the same fashions, this surface intercourse is not a friendship; but when they are attracted together because they love the same interior qualities, the same ideals of loyalty, beauty, truth, or some unknown and unnamed element of soul, still inward and still spiritual, then friendship begins at once to strike a root into the soul of life, and to lift a flower into its vibrant air.

So friendship is based upon the best that is within us. It is impossible to found a friendship upon partnership in evil things; it may exist alongside of evil things, but if so it is exposed to the deadliest hazards. There appears to be little honor among thieves, in spite of the proverb. One of the most pathetic and tragic features in the history of crimes is the wearisome monotony with which comrades in wicked deeds betray each other.

Christianity, then, is a friendship between heaven and earth; a relationship established between the best that is in us and the best that is outside. And this friendship, this relationship, may be thought of as taking three lines of direction. The first will be the direction of nature. The second will be the direction of other people, the direction of society. And the third will be the direction of something mysterious, above and around as well as within—the direction of God.

The first aspect of this friendship is the answer to the question which men ask of Nature, always: "Is the universe friendly to man?" That is inevitably the foremost question which is asked by a human being, for it is important to him above all others. The hills and rivers, animals and birds, trees and flowers, clouds, sunshine, and rain—all these things seem perfectly at home on the earth. They may be subject to continuous conflict and change, but no doubt there is of their status: they belong to the earth, they are a part of nature, they cannot be disinherited. But man, on the contrary, has always been in doubt of the Power that made him and placed him here. He has always been afraid of it; he has always tried to conciliate it and to propitiate it, in every slavish way. The taint is in our blood. We always have a suspicion that our title-deeds to earth are defective, and that we are foundlings in the house of God. We are forever in fear lest we shall be forgotten, or left behind, or ejected, or in some other way lost out of creation. Why this is so, is another matter; we all of us know the coward fact.

But the religion which stands for friendship between heaven and earth denies all real foundation for this fear. It asserts that we are as much a part of nature as any tree or flower or star. We belong to this earth, and since we have something within us that is not of earth, we belong also to another sphere than earth—the invisible source out of which time flows, and life, and beauty, and truth. But it is the same source in which the earth itself was born.

34

We cannot, then, be forgotten, or left behind, or lost out of creation. Our title-deeds are good for some estate, somewhere, in the plan by which the world was made—by which we, too, were made, contrived so cunningly to fit into the world, and yet not quite to fit! We, too, are subject to continuous conflict and change, indeed, but that will not alarm us—being friends with the Great Cause of Change. Sparrows fall, but they are not unnoticed by the Father who made them. Towers fall on eighteen men of Siloam, but that tragedy is not outside of law and order. A man is born blind and sits begging by the way—but he is there only awaiting some good purpose of God.

Feeling sure of our status in nature, we shall find it more reasonable to live in harmony with laws of nature, as the trees and the animals do; and, being friends with the Lord of Nature, we shall be the more eager to prove that we are worthy of such a proud relationship. In the language of Christianity we shall pray: "Our Father who art in heaven . . . thy will be done—on earth!"

Christianity as a friendship between heaven and earth may now be thought of under a second aspect, that of a society consciously carrying out the fundamental ideals of friendship in its social processes and activities. Perhaps society began as a mere compromise for self-protection; primitive men found it expedient to tolerate each other to a degree, rather than to fall easily a prey to things more intolerable than themselves. At any rate, whatever the beginning, other impulses soon appeared and developed to extend and intensify the gregarious habit among the human kind. And society has grown to be now an extraordinarily intricate and complicated structure: a woven web of alliances and truces and compromises, all of which may not have, necessarily, any principle in them deeper than calculated selfishness. As a matter of fact, of course, there are many party and tribal loyalties and enthusiasms, as well as ethical loyalties, to relieve the blank ugliness of a society so selfishly constituted. But that it still is ugly no one can deny; the strongest bonds of society still are selfish ones. The various divisions of society are really shaped to a system of never-ending war, although under legal regulations, the system named competition. The principle of it, indeed, is the principle of nature, and under the rule of nature our physical life belongs. But when men adopt the methods of nature, the fact of failure among men has a significance beyond nature, and raises an issue which the trees and animals do not know.

For the religion that stands for friendship between heaven and earth, must take up the cause of human failure on earth. The divine law of competition is not divine enough to blot out divine friendship. And a society which asserts that divine friendship, must allow no human failure within its boundaries which society can prevent. Society must act as the agent of Divine Friendship, and be the friend of every human being in its membership. The Christian rule specifies that every member must treat every other member as he himself would be treated. And it distinctly forbids all things that would tend to destroy unity and harmony in our ideal society. No angry thought, still less an angry word; no evil thought, still less an evil deed. No resistance to violence, still less retaliation for a wrong. No harsh criticism, no duplicity, no self-assertion, no greed.

Do these commandments of the religion of friendship astonish us, perplex us, repel us? Do they imply conclusions so antagonistic to our notions of social structure, that we feel driven back upon some theory of mistake in the way these commandments have been handed down to us, or some theory of figurative language, or some theory of changing times? Or do we simply ignore them, without a theory?

Very well: we may shrink from the application of the teaching, but we cannot retreat beyond the fact that our Christianity, if it means anything at all, means a society of friends, in all that the word "friend" can mean; and, moreover, the fact that Christianity aims at the ultimate extension of such a society to include all mankind. It is a magnificent vision; but that is what we ought to mean when we pray Christianity's typical prayer: "Our Father who art in heaven . . . thy Kingdom come—on earth!"

Christianity as a friendship between heaven and earth may now appear under a third aspect: that of an individual soul establishing relations of intimacy with a personal ideal, and realizing the Presence of God within itself. The most important and significant possession of any human being is the picture, within him, of the human being that he or she would like to be. For this ideal picture which a man cherishes of the man that he would like to be, is a revelation and measure of himself. It is impossible to imagine a man without this inner picture, this ideal of some kind. It is a part of his humanity, whether it be a picture of Sir Galahad or a soldier or a merchant prince, or a picture of a champion prize-fighter. It represents the qualities which he conceives of as the best qualities to possess. It has gradually taken shape in his soul, a composite photograph of all the characters he has found to admire, in books or in life, colored with innumerable tiny strokes added by words or acts which day after day and year after year he has taken note of as praiseworthy in the persons who said and did them. It is the most sacred thing about a man, the picture of the man he would like to be. The picture may be dim; it may be framed in despairs; but there it hangs in his soul, the aim of his most passionate desire, or the mockery of his lost opportunities, or the torment of his impotence. But still—there it hangs!

It is a heavenly thing, this picture within the soul of a man, because it infallibly represents the best the man knows. The man's ideal man is the most vital fact about him, and so we shall expect the religion that stands for friendship to take account of this innermost self of a man, and to make him better friends with himself. Christianity, the religion of friendship, is pre-eminently the religion that does this. To bridge the gulf between the ideal and the actual, to draw the inner vision outward and make it influential in the man's life, this is of the very essence of Christianity. It takes whatever ideal the man already has, and so transfigures it with heroic qualities, human and divine, and so charges it with personality and life, that the man is said to have a new self created within him. For it breathes into him the hope that this is what he actually may become. It inspires him with the resolve to make the great endeavor. It divulges to him the secret of the method by which it may be attained—which is to stake all his life upon the hazard, and to start out at once and be the new man he would like to be. In the language of Christianity this method is named "faith," and the aim of it is named "salvation." Or, in the language of Christianity taught us by Saint Paul, Christ is born, Christ is formed, Christ comes to dwell, within the human soul.

This, then, is one answer to the question, "What is Christianity?" It is not a theological answer, which you may find in plenty of books. It is simply a way of approach. It is Christianity looked at from one angle, as the religion of friendship between heaven and earth; between this world and the invisible world which holds this world in its arms. The first article of its creed is that the Universe is not hostile, but friendly to us men, and our welfare is inherent in its purposes. The second article is that humanity is destined to become a society of friends, and it is an obligation laid upon our hearts and wills to help in its accomplishment. And the third article is that the revelation of a Perfect Man has been planted in the center of our souls, and salvation consists in making friends with him, and, at last, in becoming one with him.

But one might ask what is Christianity with the doctrine of the Sacraments left out? Yet they are here. For baptism is a pledge of friendship; and the Holy Communion, the partaking of a common food together, has in all ages and countries been counted the sign and covenant of friendship.

Or one might ask what is Christianity with the doctrine of the atonement left out. Yet it is here. For Christianity is, above all other religions, a religion of *at-one-ment,* which means friendship, between God and man.

Or some old-fashioned Christian might ask what is Christianity with a hell left out. But, alas, it too is here—in our unresponsiveness to friendship. For all our worst woes arise out of disloyalty to friendship, and as the old prophet Hosea expressed it, "Judgment springeth like hemlock in the very furrows of our fields." So intimate, after all, we are with hell.

Religion is most religious when it is most completely blended with our daily lives; it is least religious as it is most unrealized. So that every morning ought to mean for us a resurrection, and every day one of the Seven Days of Creation, and every meal a Holy Communion, and all beauty the light of Eden, and every night a blessed death. Every earthly thing ought to have for us a higher meaning, for truly such a meaning is its very soul.

And so friendship, which is the most heavenly thing we know, comradeship in the things that are most worth while, friendship is the promise and the beginning of associations which shall bind us to Eternity. We shall render all friendship still more sacred and still more wonderful by thinking of it so. A blissful thing it is to walk with our friend without fear and to talk with him without reserve; but an ungrateful thing in us it is, if, for this blessed friendship's sake, the whole world is not made more fair; if we shall not walk more fearless everywhere, and feel that forever a friendly ear —a heavenly Ear—is listening to our every thought. And for friendship's sake we shall extend the rule of friendship, and learn to search for what is good in every human being with whom we have to deal, knowing that so, and only so, shall we find ground for friendship wherever we may look, and friends wherever we shall walk.

And, last of all, the passionate desire to be worthy of such a miracle as friendship, will impel us to stop oftentimes and look anxiously within our own souls, to see what may perhaps be there to hinder or restrain a capacity for friendship. Whatever we find there in our thoughts and hearts to shame us, will surely be the enemy of those precious ties which we desire to last. And whatever we find there to be proud of, because it seems to us to be something good, will, for friendship's sake, reveal a meaning that it did not show before. Whatever is good within us is hidden and ineffective until it responds to something good outside of us. It cannot abide alone. We never truly live until we have found a friend. And earthly friendships, when they have their due result, must make us friends of God.

March 19, 1916.

CHAPTER 4

St. Matthias' Day

"That he might go to his own place."
Acts i:25.

THESE WORDS ARE very simple and colorless in themselves. They might be understood to mean, "He went home," and then they would arouse in our minds dear and beautiful associations. But in the connection in which they stand in the book of Acts, they take on a most fearful and mysterious suggestion; as gray vapors around a setting sun oftentimes flame out suddenly in lurid red, revealing the ominous outlines of a thundercloud.

For these words, "That he might go to his own place," are spoken of Judas Iscariot, the traitor. It is furthermore declared that he "by transgression fell, that he might go to his own place"; as if it were over a precipice that he went— as if it were by plunging down a precipice that he went home—to his own place. The standing-point from which he thus by transgression fell, was the ministry and apostleship in the Church of our Lord Jesus Christ. From this ministry and apostleship Judas by transgression fell, that he might go to his own place.

In such a setting, these are not pleasant words to meditate upon. Indeed, to pause and think upon them at all, is like seeing that door open again which Bunyan's Pilgrim Christian saw opening in the side of the hill, from which came forth smoke and flames of fire, and sounds of wailing and gnashing of teeth. We may not adopt these figures of speech; but surely the place of Judas Iscariot, his own place, can hardly be less dark than our shuddering imagination might

41

paint, approached as it was by him over a bridge of such transgression, and entered as it was by him through such a doorway of despair, opening there on the hillside of Akeldama, the Field of Blood.

Through that door Judas hurled himself into his own place. But what does that mean—his own place? It is a peculiar expression, used purposely, and with no superficial significance. His own place must have been such a place as exactly corresponded to the shape of his soul; which exactly reflected the color of his mind; and which exactly expressed the affections of his heart. And when he, in the terrifying darkness which fell upon him from the shadow of the cross, found earth no longer endurable on account of the remorse which seemed to turn the old familiar world into a Gehenna, a place of burning, and when he fled wildly away from that world and plunged headlong into his own place, what could he find there but the very heart and source of the gloom from which he had so madly run away?

For he had not escaped from his own self. He was in his own place. The very thing which he had fled from, his own inward state, he had now shut himself irrevocably into, when the gate of life had clanged behind him with its strong spring-lock.

So little had he escaped from what he fled from, that it was now the very landscape round about him, immeasurable deserts, and iron mountains, and leafless trees, to picture forth his dry and selfish heart. So little had he escaped from what he fled from, that it was now his only companionship, specters made up out of the memories of his scheming mind, arrayed in the winding-sheets and grave-clothes of vain regrets. So little had he escaped from what he fled from, that it was now the very sky over his head, heavy with the clouds of his soul's despair, and analogous to the blessed roof of earth's sweet weather only because of a rain that fell— though here it was the rain of the bitter tears of shame. And the fearful thing about all this picture is that it is not mere fancy; some such place must have been the own place of Judas, because it was the inside of himself.

Through that dark doorway, in that Field of Blood, Judas hurled himself into his own place. And although we may shudder at the mysterious and awful fate into which that door was the entrance, yet the real strength and the real stress of its import will be a personal one. Somewhere, there is a door leading into *our* own place. Toward that door every road we travel tends. Whether we turn aside to the right hand or to the left, every path we take but leads us back to the main highway of which the destination is that door. There it waits, locked and barred, until you come, or until I come, with the key. And unto it we are sure to come at last, to unlock the door which no one can undo but ourselves, and to pass through the opened door unto our own place. For each one of us there waits the place that is our very own.

How can we fail to wonder what this our own place is like? With inevitable doubtings and with tremulous hopings we wonder what our own place is like. But we are never so far away that we cannot get some glimpses, as through telescopes, of this region all our own. For, as "the Kingdom of Heaven is within you," so also is the kingdom of hell.

Suppose that it were possible, this day, to retire within ourselves, and to shut out all the external objects of sense, just as we can retreat into some inner room of our houses and shut ourselves away from the outside world. Suppose that it were possible for us to stop the outer eye from seeing and the outer ear from hearing, and to break off all the senses from power of responding to material things. Our consciousness would then be left in a world entirely made up of what we really are and what we really have within ourselves. Such a condition is a difficult one to realize, because this outside world of ours seems so very much to be everything, and not to be able to see and hear and feel seems to leave us so utterly in the dark and void. But let us do the best we can to imagine ourselves as existing entirely in our inner world, the world of our thoughts and feelings, with everything else cut off. No sun, no moon, no stars, no beauty of nature, no round of work and pleasure,

43

no face of relative or friend; nothing but what we are in ourselves, nothing but what we have stored up in our own soul. Does it seem dark, or are there pillars of fire? Does it seem empty, or are there gracious Presences of comfort? Does it seem cold, or is there something like a warm heart throbbing there? Whatever it seems to be, let us examine it with intensest interest, for it is a glimpse into our own place.

Let us ask ourselves, first, whether we can feel the Presence of God there? Is the Fatherhood of God a thing so real to us, so vital in our every-day life, that we still should realize it and trust in it, were the outside world to be done away? Is the love of our Lord Jesus a thing so daily felt in our hearts that we still might be warmed with the warmth of it, were the objects of all other affections to be beyond our reach? Is the movement of the Holy Spirit in our souls a thing so buoyant there with upward aspirations, that we still should know it as brooding over the waters of our darkness and promising a new creation, were all visible nature to be but the memory of a beautiful order blotted out? Is God, in other words, a living God in our own place? We can answer this only by trying to measure how far we know him to be a living God in our thoughts, as we live our lives from day to day. If we can feel God's Presence, independent of the visible universe which is "the garment we see him by," then there will be light in our own place, rosy dawns in the obscurity, and the hope of a fuller day.

Let us ask ourselves, next, what is the prevailing weather of our souls? What is the general character of our thoughts? We may have our flying doubts and our flurries of passion and our seasons of despondency, but, on the whole, do we keep a courageous front against these moods so hostile to our peace, and do we keep an eye of hope lifted toward the sky? Or is it the desire to be good and the resolve to be unselfish and kind and true which is the rarer thing in our days, and are our thoughts more like a monotonous muddy stream of bargaining and self-seeking and complaint and suspicion and ill-will? The answer to this question will reveal to us, in a degree, what kind of a place our own place is, or at least is like to be.

Just think of it a moment. Should we be willing to enter permanently into a place where our only company would be the thoughts that we have every day? Would they be uplifting, or even interesting, to associate with? Would they be fair white thoughts, fit to fly in the sunshine, or would they be twisting, hissing, earthy ones, fit only to crawl in the dark? Should we be willing to live in a place where the only beauty we could see would be the beauty of things we ordinarily select for our satisfaction and our pleasure? Should we be willing to abide in a place where our only sky would be the spiritual outlook towards higher things which we have this day? Would such a place be very attractive or satisfactory or even tolerable to us? Yet such a state of soul, whatever it may be, the inside of us, with all the affinities which belong to it, this is our own place.

This is the point that I want to make: that we are busy, each one of us, all our lives long, in creating an inner world. To the making of this inner world not only our deeds and words contribute, but also our thoughts—in fact, especially our thoughts, for words and deeds are but the expression of thoughts, the crystallization of interior states. Day by day we build and build and build; desire upon desire; thought upon thought, purpose upon purpose; act of will upon act of will; so that streams of mental movements become tendencies, and tendencies become settled moods, and settled moods and chronic attitudes become characters; and lo! at last we have an entire inner world rounded fully out within us, distinct and individual of its own kind, a heaven or a hell. Its real nature does not clearly appear in this life, because it is hidden behind a material shell, the shell of our every-day existence. But death breaks this enclosing shell finally, and then the inner world which we have all the time been building at once stands forth revealed. We enter fully into that which we really are. The law of liberty allows us to be as good or as bad as it is in our nature to be. We go into our own place.

So far we have been thinking of our own place as the state into which we enter when we have passed out of our physical bodies into a spiritual state; into that state, namely, which is the outcome of our life here. But in truth that law of gravitation which tends to draw us into our own place operates perpetually, even on earth and in this earthly life. Internal states of soul are forever struggling to work outward, and interior attitudes of will are continually tending to make themselves visible in external results. Every day we see the positions of men shifting in relation to one another; changing in the power they hold in business concerns, changing in the influence they wield in the community. Men work upward in wealth and honor; men sink down into poverty and loss. Never ceasing are the currents of adjustment and readjustment, and all on account of this effort of the internal and spiritual to show itself in the external and material; that each may go to his own place.

It was through no sudden transition that Judas by transgression fell. The tragic end of him, seen by man, was but the final plunge of a gradual descent begun long before. He must have given a better promise once. When our Lord called him to be one of his disciples, there must have been good qualities apparent in him, some teachableness, some winsomeness, some capacity for righteousness, making him seem fit to become an apostle in the founding of the Kingdom of God. So he entered on his training to become a witness for Jesus Christ. But whatever response of spirit he had at the first seems gradually to have died away; perhaps because he grew to see only with the physical eye; to look always for material results; to be on the side of majorities. Perhaps he had his own temptation in the wilderness, and when the devil showed him the glory of the world and said, "All this will I give *thee,* if thou wilt fall down and worship me," Judas gave the homage and reached for the bribe. Alas, poor Judas! all that he received of that promised glory was thirty small pieces of silver, being so cheated in his bargain as those who make contracts with Satan always are.

There is something terrifying in this fact, that Judas the

traitor and the suicide was one of the twelve disciples, one
of those most closely associated with Jesus. It should serve to
remind us that we, in the midst of influences meant for
health, may be making them elements of poison in our lives
instead of elements of strength. To attend the church serv-
ices, to listen to God's holy Word, to partake of the Holy
Communion—these things may be making us only the blinder
and deafer and deader, just as to be with Jesus only made
Judas worse. To see signs and wonders means nothing,
unless we see God in them. So men see and hear in different
ways; they have pretty much the same environment, the
same temptations, the same joys—but men build different
things out of them. The same materials go to make heaven
or hell.

For there was another man, all this time, who had been
a witness of the same things which Judas saw, and, a little
farther off, had listened to the same words which Judas
heard. This man's name was Matthias.

Matthias was not one of the twelve disciples; he had not
been chosen by Jesus to make one of that favored number.
He stood farther off, unnoticed by any Gospel writer. But
he had seen, from the edge of the crowd, the baptism at the
Jordan and what came to pass thereafter. He had listened to
the Sermon on the Mount. He had seen the blind and the
deaf and the lame restored. He had seen the multitude
fed. He, too, had beheld the final tragedy of the Cross. But to
him all these things had more meaning. He was a witness
not only of physical signs and wonders, but he was also a
witness of Divinity revealed in the life of a man. And so
this power of recognition enabled him to assimilate some
higher truth in all he saw and heard; enabled him to breathe
into his soul more and more of the spirit of his Lord, and
so, from the outskirts of the crowd drew him nearer and
nearer to him. He had the same environment that Judas had;
he saw the same things, he heard the same divine words. But
they saw and heard in different ways. Their seeing and
hearing contributed to opposite ends. The same materials
built heaven and hell. The soul of the one man grew

47

brighter and brighter with light within, and the soul of the other grew all the darker for the light without. So, when the Day of Judgment arrived, Judas sank naturally down into the outer darkness, his own place; while Matthias rose as inevitably into his own place, into that ministry and apostleship from which Judas by transgression fell. For when, we are told, the disciples in the upper room lifted a voice of prayer and said, "O Lord, who knowest the hearts of all, show to us whom thou wilt choose to occupy this empty place," the lot which was given in answer fell upon Matthias, and he was numbered with the eleven apostles. So he came, thus, into his own place, an apostle's place, with a martyr's death at the end, and a martyr's crown.

We often hear people complain of the place in which they live, blaming it for their failure in life. It is not their own place, so they think. They would be better Christians, perhaps, if they had better surroundings and better Christians with whom to associate. But every such complaint is a confession of poverty of soul. For the place where one really lives is the place within one's self. The Kingdom of Heaven is within us. Whether the world shall seem to us like a swallow's nest built in the altar of the Lord of Hosts, or whether it shall seem like a storm-tossed boat on Lake Galilee, all depends upon the steadfastness of our own faith, and the beauty of our own hope, and the vitality of our own love.

Trinity Cathedral.

CHAPTER 5

Pray Without Ceasing

"Pray without ceasing."
1 Thess. v:17.

WHEN WE OPEN the letter of Saint Paul to the Thessalonians and read these words, "Pray without ceasing," we may do one of two things: we may interpret them as a rather strong expression meaning simply, "Pray whenever you have leisure for it, pray as much as you have time for"; or we may believe that Saint Paul meant exactly what he said, but that he had a conception of the nature of prayer which made ceaseless prayer a possibility.

To pray without ceasing. If prayer is the taking of a certain bodily posture and the repetition of a certain form of words, then ceaseless prayer becomes indeed a heavy task upon human ability. Nevertheless in Christian history the actual bearing of this burden has not been unattempted. There are Chapels of Perpetual Adoration and Supplication, where every hour continually, in watches relieving one another, day and night, year in and year out, a human heart lies beating before God's altar in ceaseless praise and prayer.

In the far-off East the same injunction has been impressed in some strange way upon souls not Christian, and there the problem of ceaseless prayer has been solved more frankly. Many a pious Buddhist's method of prayer, so we read, is to make a praying-machine and attach it to a water wheel or to a wind-mill, whereby written prayers are run off from a cylinder continuously, so that the ingenious petitioner may go off to work or to sleep with the contented consciousness that ceaseless prayer is being made in his behalf while he is otherwise engaged.

49

We smile pityingly at this crude heathen idea of prayer, thinking over it perhaps as we settle ourselves in church, perhaps kneeling down to say our litany with thoughts still beside the Ganges to wander off thence in associated directions, among pagodas and minarets and palm-trees; to the Vale of Cashmere, the Suez Canal, and the Nile, among pyramids and sphinxes and Pharaohs; thence to darkest Africa and thence to darkest America, and thence into the luxuriant gardens of our daily interests—and all the time our minds are thus roving our lips are saying, "Good Lord, deliver us. We beseech thee to hear us, good Lord." Has not such prayer something in its quality which brings us very close to that poor Buddhist repeating his one hundred thousand sacred words by the aid of his whirling prayer-wheel?

Or, the last thing at night, when we go through that most intimate ritual by which we tie up, as it were, the raveled strings of the day, giving thanks for its pleasures and for its deliverance from known and unknown dangers, and handing over all its imperfections to God, for him to fill out and make good, commending ourselves and our loved ones to the care of watching angels while we sleep—how often we say the too familiar words with our lips, while our mind, which we have sent back over the day to take a hurried account of its value before presenting it to God, loiters over the engrossing details of business or of pleasure, forgetting its errand, so that we sink to sleep with a dissatisfied sense that the clearness of our petitions has someway been blurred—as it has, indeed; the fine note of our prayer's meaning made indistinct by the sound of the wind blowing through the sails of our praying-machine.

How much of all praying this day and every day is of that sort; praying which is merely of the knees and of the lips; praying which is merely of the husk and the shell; praying from which we arise with our hearts still hungry and with our souls still dry! Whenever we repeat prayers while our restless thoughts are wandering away from the meaning of our words, we are in very truth fellow-worshipers along with the Buddhist whom we scorned for his praying-machine.

50

The fact is that we only half believe in prayer; and so, performing an action which has but a half-vitality to our consciousness, the mind feels itself quite capable of doing two things at once, keep a prayer going and at the same time conduct an independent line of thought or fancy.

Now the reason why we only half believe in prayer, is partly because we have come to doubt its results in that field of our existence in which we ordinarily feel the deepest interest, the field we see and hear and touch, the field in which we eat and sleep and work and play.

It has always been a field of uncertainty and tragedy, full of unexpected treachery and hostility; and it has been man's ultimate recourse from time immemorial, to direct entreaty toward the Unknown out of which things spring. We instinctively pray whenever we get into trouble. And so we still cling tenaciously to prayer, and we still use the old terms of confidence with regard to prayer. We still affirm with desperate emphasis, because we are so anxious that it should be true, that prayer can heal the sick and move mountains and raise the dead. But probably we all have had at least one crisis in our life when we strenuously and passionately set ourselves to wrestle in prayer against some dark angel invading our happiness; only to find ourselves helpless in such a struggle, beaten back and trodden down and overwhelmed, seeing our enemy work his evil will on what we held most dear. We all find it out sooner or later, that, bringing every last fiber in our being to its utmost tension in our endeavor to reach that faith in prayer which, we are told, will turn back death and disaster, we are compelled to face that which we thought we could not face, and to bear that which we thought we could not bear. And perhaps it was then that we learned to pray for the only thing left for which to pray,—courage to face that which we cannot escape, and strength to endure what we cannot avert. Like the magic sword Excalibur, the sword of the faith which we desired seems to be meant for none but King Arthur to wield.

Passionate human nature, ever hungry for more than it has, and yet with the robbers Time and Death continually

51

stealing away its most precious possessions, lays hold upon a certain promise of Christ as a kind of talisman in its precarious world. "Ask and it shall be given you": that is the simple magic formula which men would like to use as an Aladdin's lamp to get all their desires fulfilled. We are not past that notion yet, that Prayer ought to be a sort of Aladdin's lamp for us, whereby to obtain the thousand things we want. And, as this notion of prayer fails us, as fail it must, the danger is that in our disappointment at not finding prayer to be what we had dreamed, the Adversary of Souls will pass by with a cry of "New Lamps for old," like the magician in the ancient Arabian story, and delude us into giving up a value which we do not understand.

"I will prove to you that your old lamp, Prayer, is of no worth," said he a while ago, perhaps you all have read of it; "I will prove to you that your old lamp, Prayer, is of no worth. Listen. You will choose one ward of a hospital to pray for systematically in all the churches, and another ward you will choose to leave out of your prayers entirely. We will keep a careful record and make accurate statistics, counting how many of the sick get well in each ward and how many do not, and so shall we find out exactly what is the value of prayer."

"And I will give you," said the cunning Adversary of Souls, "a bright new lamp in place of the old; and that bright new lamp is Science, a Knowledge of Law. Look, I throw upon this great white screen the invisible causes of your diseases, so that you can behold them as plainly as the dogs that kill sheep or the snakes that kill men. This germ produces cholera, and nothing else; and this, tuberculosis, and nothing else; and this, typhoid fever, and nothing else. To destroy them we search out the agents naturally fatal to these germs, letting loose upon each kind its own particular enemy. And as little as you would turn to prayer instead of to your shot-gun when rabbits devastate your garden, so little would the scientist expect a great Hand to appear across his white screen in answer to prayer and begin to crush pneumonia germs between its fingers. You do not fall to praying when typhoid fever breaks out, you purify the water supply."

"And now look," continues the Adversary of Souls; "see on the white screen how the molecules of matter march in regular companies and regiments and armies, throwing themselves with the utmost precision into various drill-figures as they pass in review, each word of command obeyed always in one certain way and no other. If you know how to command, you shall move the forces of nature as you will. Study nature, learn nature's laws, guide nature's winged feet, and so shall the currents of air and ether, riches and pleasure and power, follow the road your finger points out to them. This is the bright new lamp of Science which I will give you —in exchange for the old."

So speaks the Adversary of Souls, and his speech is very seductive and his lamp is very bright and new; but we shall say to him, if we are wise: "Get thee behind us, Satan; you have no right to bargain with us. The bright new lamp of Science is not yours to give; you have stolen it, indeed. We are the heirs of all the ages, and to us shall belong both the new and the old."

For the prayer of faith has its miracles, and it has them today. Even on the physical plane it is the prayer of faith, faith in truth, which nerves the mind of the scientist and opens the secrets of nature to him. But, apart from this, did you never see hungry men and women fed by multiplied bread in the wilderness, so that they took up patiently again and went on with the heavy burdens which despair had made them throw down? Did you never see sick souls healed, deaf ears made to hear and blind eyes made to look up? Did you never see storms of wind and wave calmed to peace upon the Galilee of men's hearts? Did you never see souls called forth from the tomb of sin, bound in the grave-clothes of passion, and made to live again? If you have seen such things, you have seen what is legitimately claimed for prayer today and always; you have seen greater miracles than those spectacular ones which are the natural man's desire. And this leads us to the true nature of prayer.

Someone with a poet's thought once said: "Every plant comes up with folded hands." The seed-germ has felt within itself an impulse and aspiration, so to speak, which impels it upward out of the dark earth in which it finds itself, and in which, indeed, it must keep itself rooted. It belongs not below in the gloom, but above in the light; and those folded hands enclose between them what promise and prophecy of leaves rustling wide in wind and sunshine, or shivering ecstatic in star-light and rain; promise and prophecy of flowers and fruit, of humming bees and nesting birds: all shut up, in possibility, between those folded hands.

Now let us imagine the plant's career somewhat within its own control; that it might choose to wind about, all roots, below in the dark, or fulfil its destiny by pushing up into the air and sunlight where its proper sphere is, and we have something analogous to our own state. We wake to find ourselves buried in the earth, subject to strong conditions of matter. But we feel now and then, great as may be the downward pull of sense upon our wills, that something inside us wants to grow upward. Then is our chance; let us seize upon that blind emotion, that uncertain groping, that flickering spark; let us breathe it into a flame, direct it upward into a definite conscious reaching, strengthen it into a tendency and a growth;—and here we have real prayer, something worthy of our divine origin; not the abject and cringing supplication of slaves, nor the incantations of superstition, nor the dead forms of conventionality; but that aspiration of beings made in the image of God to return to their ineffable source—which to quench utterly is perhaps the unpardonable sin against the Holy Ghost.

Prayer is the asking for satisfaction of need; and the plant with its folded hands as it comes up, expresses so the normal attitude of its life. It is continually asking, continually holding itself open to the reception of those things which are necessary to its well-being and growth, praying for food from the air and the rain and the sunshine. It has the hunger and thirst first of all; then comes the opening out of all its pores to receive what it prays for, and just what it needs flows into it as easily as gravitation.

It should be so with us. Our growth upward should be as simple and easy as that of the plant; and it would be so, only we have such an unaccountable love for the dark underground place where we begin to grow, this earth-life of ours, and the upward aspiration and growth seem so strangely put within our own choice and power. Above this is another sphere entirely, to which we really belong far more than to the changing aspects of this dark world. Above us, just through the thinnest crust of surface, is the kingdom of the skies, with its free wide spaces, its winds and its sun. And up into that kingdom of the skies we were meant to grow. It is our proper atmosphere, in which we were meant to expand all our capacities and capabilities, to blossom and bear fruit in forms hidden from us in God's own thought.

And this reaching upward to the place where we belong; this active passivity, so to speak, by which we yield ourselves to God's purpose for us; this attitude of soul so like the plant's asking for the things of its inmost need; this open receptivity of mind and heart, which allows the living dews of God to sink into the very growing center of our being; this hunger and thirst after righteousness; this continual upholding of our souls to God, like a cup to be filled with the water of life; all this is that prayer which we may pray without ceasing. For whatever we do, in the house or on the Middle Path, at work or at rest, alone or among our fellows, we may do with an ever-abiding underlying reference to that ideal life toward which all our conscious effort is made to tend; until we are like the flame which must burn upward continuously—it cannot do anything else.

This is the prayer which we may pray without ceasing; Saint Paul expressed it in another way when he admonished us to do all things to the glory of God. And in the same strain Martin Luther declared that the Christian's life ought to be one long Lord's Prayer.

It was only the other day that I heard a student lament that he finds it so hard to pray because he finds it so hard to feel that God hears his prayer. He thought that something unique was the matter with him: but the experience is universal. We all know its bitterness. No one who prays but often feels that his prayers have no wings, falling back as soon as uttered like lead upon the heart from which they rise.

The thought of reassurance is surely this: that God must hear the prayer which he himself inspires. Our very thought of God is communion with him. We could not say, "Our Father who art in Heaven," if we did not first hear the still, small voice in our souls, "My children, who are on earth, speak to me."

CHAPTER 6

Hallowed Be Thy Name

OUR LORD'S PRAYER is our pattern prayer. "After this manner pray ye," he said as he gave it to us. And so Christians from the beginning have loved to repeat after him the model-prayer which fell from his lips there on the mountainside; in lonely cells and public halls, in deserts and catacombs, from hearts full of gladness and from souls full of sorrow, stammered out amid sobs and tears, reiterated mechanically on strings of beads, chanted in great cathedrals to the thunderous bass and the woven harmonies of wonderful music,—for two thousand years, almost, we have been saying our Lord's Prayer after him.

Yet I think that this is hardly what he meant, that we should take his very words and keep on saying those literal words forever. "After this *manner* pray ye," he said; that is, when you pray, make your petitions of this sort, and say them in this way. Pray these same sentences, if you will, but when you pray your own prayers from your own heart, let them harmonize with these of mine.

We have been praying his Prayer for nearly two thousand years now, making it the introduction, night and morn, to our own heart's petitions. Often enough have we said it, loving to say it because he gave it to us, we Christians who love our Lord, but have we been praying "after this manner," as soon as we strike off into prayers of our own?

With this thought in mind, let us examine our typical prayer, petition by petition. We have a thousand things to pray for, each one of us. More than any other one thing are we a palpitating bundle of desires. Suppose that we should open the doors of our nature and say to all the elements which make up that nature, "Pray! ask for whatever you want!" Instantly

the caged lions and tigers and serpents and swine of our
animal part would set up their clamor of appetite; and the
desires and ambitions and affections of our mind would
raise voices of importunate pleading; and, finally, distinct
amid all this uproar, a still, small voice would make itself
felt rather than heard, perhaps, the voice of Conscience and
heavenly aspiration, the white doves which fly through the
upper airs, the spiritual plane, of our nature. There are a
thousand things to ask for, but, out of this thousand, what
has our Lord chosen? Let us count them. After the address
at the beginning, the attitude of relationship which we take
first of all—after the words "Our Father who art in heaven"
—there are just six petitions. There are just six requests
chosen out of a thousand to be offered up to God. And not
one of these six, as we shall see later, has reference to our physical well-being; the lions and tigers and serpents and swine
in us are all left out of account—perhaps because they may
be trusted to look after themselves; and the warrior of ambition in us, and the angels of love in us, and the goodness
of beauty in us, the muses and the arts, they, too, are all left
out of account; they, too, may be trusted to take for themselves all they ought to have; but the voice of the Son of man
in us says, "Father, hallowed be thy name; thy kingdom
come, thy will be done." And the voice of the Spirit in us,
in its heavenly hunger, says, "Give me this day my real
bread, the heavenly bread." And the voice of Conscience
in us says, "Forgive me my transgressions." And the voice
of our Conscious Weakness says, "Lead me not into temptation." And then all the voices in our nature fall together into
one tonic chord and say, "For *thine,* not the Evil One's, is
the kingdom and the power and the glory."

Now the first three petitions, "Hallowed be thy name, thy
kingdom come, thy will be done," are not only similar in
substance, but they also appear to be balanced over against the
last three petitions, and appear to be joined together in construction with the expression, "in earth as it is in heaven,"
which belongs to all three and to each one of the three;
so that they, in meaning, read thus: "Hallowed be thy name,

in earth as it is in heaven; thy kingdom come, in earth as it is in heaven; thy will be done, in earth as it is in heaven."

God's name! it is written in earth as well as in heaven; for the skies declare the glory of God, and the firmament showeth his handiwork. God's name is written in earth as well as in heaven. But in heaven his name is hallowed, reverenced, held sacred, because all the eyes in heaven can read that name. It is in earth that his name is not hallowed, further than in a vague, imperfect, stupid way; and the reason of this is that, having eyes, we see not, and we do not know how to read God's name.

So, in the prayer, "Hallowed be thy name, in earth as it is in heaven," we really mean, "Let thy name be read in earth as it is in heaven! Let thy true Self be known of men." That is the inner soul of the prayer. The hallowing, the reverencing, the praising of the great name of God, is the result of reading the name of God, of knowing God, and follows as a matter of course. As soon as veils are lifted and the outer glories of God's nature are really seen a little, though dimly and as in a glass, what can every knee inevitably do but bow?

But what is God's name? what is any name? A name is properly the sign of some distinguishing quality, of some peculiar character or special mark belonging to the object which bears the name. Originally all names meant something, and were not given haphazard, as now—just as Ohio meant "beautiful river," and Philadelphia meant "brotherly love," and the name of Jesus meant "savior." So God's name means "good"; it is everything in nature which expresses his character to us. When we dig down into the rocks, there is God's name of forethought, written in strange hieroglyphics of delicate fern-leaf and foot-print and wave-mark. When we open all the ponderous volumes of science, there is God's name of wisdom written in ten thousand languages. Then in what gorgeously illuminated letters it is printed across the manuscript of nature, in the red and blue and green and white of the seasons and the sunsets, and the rivers and the mountains and the Milky Way! How shines his name of power in the constellations of mighty suns which hang poised in space upon his word alone, interrelated most marvelously! How God's dread name of judgment burns through all the palimpsests of history! How ineffably is God's fair name of love wrought in purple and gold through all the life of Christ! Everywhere about us is God's name written, and we spell at it slowly and haltingly with grammar and dictionary and all sorts of philological tools; often with mistakes and misreadings and shadows of meanings; stumbling and stammering and hesitating over the letters as we try to spell them; but even these fragments of God's name which we so imperfectly delve out, how they transform our lives! God's name is spelled with the letters of wisdom and power and beauty and truth and love, and it is as these qualities grow to be appreciated and loved and desired by ourselves, as elements of our own characters, that God's name begins to be hallowed upon earth.

This is the reason why this petition is set at the head of all our petitions, to be prayed first of all; because without it all other petitions are empty and void. We grow to be like that which we love and admire; the features of our souls will reflect the light which they gaze upon, be it fire of hell or the white candles of the Lord. That is why it is all-important that we should hold sacred the best things. That is why it is first of all important that we should set highest in our affections that concentration of all good and all truth and all beauty, which we mean by the Name of God. When a man finds himself growing cold toward the good and unresponsive to higher things, and God receding into the dim and far-off distance— ah, then is the time for him to flee for his life, to pray with all agonizing for something to open within him to respond to the nature of God, and for eyes with which to read his holy Name.

To know God and to love what he is—this is what it is truly to hallow his name; this is what we are striving to make dominant in our lives, the preference of all things good to all things evil, insisted upon until it becomes a second nature; this it is to be growing into his likeness, by loving and admiring and holding sacred that which he is, growing into his likeness as the little pool of water may reflect the whole sky and be made blue and beautiful by it.

When we awake in that likeness, it shall be made manifest, without a doubt, for it could not be hid. And it must have been the external revealing of that inward divine likeness of the souls of the redeemed to the nature and character of God, which Saint John told of in symbol when he described the one hundred and forty-four thousand in heaven as having God's Name, his ineffable Name, written upon their foreheads.

CHAPTER 7

Forgive Us Our Trespasses

"Forgive us our trespasses as we forgive those who trespass against us."

WHEN WE WERE praying our Lord's Prayer this morning, if we had stopped to think of the words which have grown so familiar to us, if we had paused to mean them utterly before we spoke them, how many of us, I wonder, after we had said from our hearts, "Forgive us our trespasses," would have shrunk from saying the completing half of the petition? Upon the reluctant lips of how many of us, I wonder, would the words have died unspoken, "As we forgive those who trespass against us"? How many of us, after looking into our own hearts, would dare to ask to be judged ourselves as we judge others?

Perhaps someone has injured us, deeply wronged and hurt us; betrayed our trust; abused our confidence; defrauded us of our right; taken advantage of a chance to overreach us; has misrepresented and slandered us and alienated friends from us, or in some other way has dealt us a blow to wound our affection or our pride.

Does our resentment over the wrong take the form of outward acts of retaliation in our purpose? Will we hurt him in return as soon as we can—even though we intend only to sting him in some polite and refined way which yet will cut him to the quick? Being Christians, perhaps we have fought down this desire to return evil for evil, and to make him smart for our smart; but does the remembrance of our wrong smoulder in our heart, burning there under the surface, biting into our soul its painful complaint and protest?

Can we, with this bitter water stagnating in the shade of

the Upas-tree of such remembrance, ask God to forgive thus
our transgressions against him? Suppose that in the Heart of
the Universe there should remain smouldering the continual
red remembrance of our sins. With the harp in our hands, our
fingers must tremble on its strings; with the song of the
redeemed on our lips, the notes must break and faint in a
flight of joy too high for them; the very golden pavement on
which we walk must burn the soles of our feet as we tread
it, like a lava-crust,—if we bear into heaven the knowledge
that, though our sins have been pronounced forgiven, yet hot
within God's heart there burns the perpetual remembrance
of those sins. If we have been wronged, let us think twice and
be sure of ourselves, before we pray to be forgiven as we forgive.

But the feeling in our hearts may not be so emphasized.
We may own that precious gift of invulnerability against
slight or hurt or wrong. We may practise, both in external
action and in internal attitude, that first law of court-life,
"never to take offense." We may hold that proud principle of
self-defense which declares, "No words can offend me if I do
not hear them; no arrow but fails of its aim if I do not feel
it enter my heart." We may live in obedience to all this, and
yet we may harbor an aversion to some of our fellow-creatures,
not on account of what they do to us personally, but on account of offense which they give to our sense of propriety, to
our taste, to our estheticism. Anything which makes a wall of
separation within us between our sympathy and our fellow-
men is covered by the words of our text.

Suppose that the Soul of the Universe, while it forgave us
our transgressions, yet drew away in aversion from us. Shall
we be so posted in the etiquette of heaven that the angels
will never dream that we have come from earth? Will the
robes of our righteousness be so unsullied that a seraph might
not shrink in passing us lest his white robes might brush
against ours? Will our tongues, educated on earth, so know the
language of the skies that we shall make no mistakes in celestial grammar and pronunciation? Will our culture and our
refinement, and our artistic feeling and our literary taste, ad-

mit us on equal terms into the heavenly circles of the blest?

Ah, well may we blush and stammer and shiver with deadly cold, if God only feels toward us as we feel toward our fellowmen, and we enter into his Kingdom, forgiven indeed, but knowing that he is drawing his garments away from contact with our ignorance and awkwardness and imperfection. If we feel a sense of separateness between ourselves and any class or any individual of our human kind, let us look anxiously into what that feeling means, before we venture to pray to be forgiven as we ourselves forgive.

For let us examine this petition which we are putting up. It is not that we say, "Forgive us our trespasses," and then add a second half subordinately and as an afterthought, "May we forgive those who trespass against us"; but the two parts are correlated and made proportionate: "as we forgive others, so forgive us." It is one prayer; it means one thing. We acquiesce in a law of balance; we agree that the one shall determine the other. There must be in the nature of things a close and vital relation between the two parts, since we find it so expressed in our typical prayer.

Theology has far too long taught us to look upon redemption in a mercantile way: our sins kept account of in some celestial ledger, mounting up to a sum which bankrupted us from the very first entry, but which our Lord Jesus Christ volunteers to pay, drawing a red line across the account so balanced, so that we ascend free into glory.

Alas for that crude and false conception! Our sins are indeed kept account of, with a rigid accuracy which we cannot imagine—for the account is so rigidly kept that our sins become bone of our bone and flesh of our flesh and soul of our soul, and never may we believe that we shall not pay the uttermost farthing. The deadly power of them is not that they bind us to punishment and penalty, but that they bind us to love of sinning. How we struggle and strain, how we wrestle and run; like serpents we pull them off from our limbs while they wind around our throats, and tear them away from our throats while they wind around our limbs—we cannot get rid of sin because sin sits ruler on the throne of life. We sin simply because we prefer to sin. That is why the word *forgive* is not adequate to express what is really meant here. "Put away from us," we really mean to say, "that which makes us commit trespasses." And then that is our redemption, complete and safe and sure, which Christ came down to earth to reveal to us, and suffered upon the cross to illustrate and seal for us—that redemption which consists in our receiving Christ into our very nature, until every fiber of our being chooses the good as its own proper possession and element always; and then are we forgiven indeed! And more than forgiven indeed, for then are we freed from the bonds of sin because then we are freed from sinning.

Nature never forgives; break her laws and though it may be long before she arrests you, yet her police will have her handcuffs on your wrists at last, and you wake up in her prisons, from which you come not forth until you have served your time. Let a child meddle with nature's poisons, and not all that child's loveliness and innocence awakens nature's mercy; it is death to touch them, so reads the law, and that is the end of it. Push your boat into nature's Niagaras, and it is not your ignorance of cataracts which will save you; the current catches you up and swirls you away. Kindle fires where fire finds fuel, and it is no outcome of black ruin which deters nature one instant in her rush of destruction. Nature seems to have no exceptions to her law of cause and effect.

Now our danger is that we put sin and its results outside the realm of nature, and dream that there God may forgive where nature will not—forgetting that we are not sinning outside nature's domain, but inside, subject to all her laws and to her unforgivingness. Then when we turn from nature to God, we are not turning from a harsh sovereign to a milder one. Nature is God's visible working, after all, and what God shows us is not how we may escape the results of the stones which we have unwittingly set rolling down the mountainside—they will go to the bottom. But he takes away from us the disposition which urges us and drives us and flatters us and persuades us and deceives us into sinning.

There has been much discussion in the world as to the basis

and essence of sin, as, for instance, whether it lies in the violation of an abstract rightness, or whether it is rather relative and accidental, and lies in doing whatsoever interferes with man's development into that perfect stature of manhood to which he is destined. But this, at least, is true: that whatever is sin does interfere most fearfully with man's development. Sins are sometimes classified into sins against God and sins against ourselves and sins against our neighbor. But we see, when we stop to think of it, that those sins which are called sins against God are sins whose results are immediately apparent in the hindrance of our progress, our own and our neighbor's. To love God with all our soul and heart and mind; to keep his worship dissociated from worship of matter; to keep one day perpetually sacred to higher things among days given to earthly ones;—the observance of all these commandments is of the most vital importance to the welfare of humanity, and to its progress towards its goal; so that no more are they sins against God than they are sins against ourselves and our neighbor.

And so woven together are the destinies of all men that no one can simply sin against himself. It is impossible for him to do a single wrong thing without its affecting someone besides himself. He cannot even suffer alone. Pythagoras, back in the old Greek dawn, had surely a flash of inspiration from God when he said that if there be but one suffering soul in the universe, all other souls will be affected with suffering until that one suffering soul shall be restored to health.

This combining of individuals into a race until the race itself is conceived of as an individual; this interdependence of men in a vast system of unity; this salvation of a *people,* under the gorgeous Jewish symbols; this Kingdom of Israel, this new Jerusalem, this Kingdom of the Skies;—we have hardly begun to realize it yet, so absorbed we have been in our fear lest our own little individual lights shall be blown out in the tempest of wrath which the old theologians loved to paint. Let us recollect ourselves; our own salvation is included in the salvation of the race, the salvation of the race embraces our own—through what strange, far ways we may not dream.

But let us remember that with all that our Lord was, he was also the representative, the epitome, of the human race, as it exists in God's idea. Men, in as much as there is anything good in them, in all times and ages, as it was and is and shall be, make up a whole, which Christ himself called his Body. All history, then, becomes the record of the development of his Body. We need to remind ourselves of that far more than we do. The holiness of the human race is something never to forget. Whelmed in struggle and in darkness and in chaos as it is, there is yet so much of the Divine appearing sublimely in its ambitions,—there are such deeps, there are such heights, forever suggested and a little revealed in its hopes and despairs,—that we can well believe, especially when he himself says it, that within it the soul of Christ is striving to take possession of his own.

And so appears the sin of not forgiving those who trespass against us; so appears the relation between forgiving and being forgiven. To hold our hearts hard and shut against any other human being is to take the side of that power which is trying to keep Christ out of his own Body, the human race. By so much we are rebelling against humanity, we are delaying the day of its perfect unity, by so much we are postponing the time of its deliverance from its own transgressions. By so much we are rebelling also against our own Higher Self; we are delaying the day of our perfect incorporation in the Body of Christ; we are postponing the time of our own deliverance; we are denying ourselves those blessings which shall flow more and more abundantly and gloriously upon the whole race in its process of redemption, as men shall more and more fully and understandingly pray: "Forgive us our trespasses as we forgive those who trespass against us."

CHAPTER 8

The Second Commandment

"God is a Spirit, and they that worship him must worship him in spirit and in truth."

John iv:24.

IT TAKES A long time for men to learn this. And naturally; because we live in a world which we can know only through our five senses, and not through our five senses are we able to perceive what is spirit. So we want symbols which we can see, in order to grasp what is unseen. Perhaps we represent it by a dove, floating in the upper air; or perhaps by fire, so mysterious and yet so full of power. Or we may want an audible sound, like the blowing wind, to suggest to us the still, small voice.

This desire of human nature is vividly illustrated by our first lesson set for this day by our Church. Moses, who had led the Israelites out of the comparative security of Egypt into the unknown perils of the wilderness, had gone up into Mount Sinai and had been away now for a long while. The people, lost without his guidance, turned to religion— such crude religion as they were familiar with. "Make us a god to follow," they said to Aaron, "for that man Moses, we know not what has become of him."

So Aaron gathered the people's ornaments of gold, and he melted the gold and beat it out and fashioned it into the shape of a calf, a symbol of vigorous life, a symbol natural and common among the pastoral tribes. The people now had a visible object to concentrate their worship on, a focus for their prayers. "This is the god that brought you up out of the land of Egypt," so Aaron assured them. And he issued a proclamation, "Tomorrow there shall be a great feast to Jehovah." Apparently the calf was to represent Jehovah. So on the next day they offered burnt-offerings on the altar they built, and they brought peace-offerings and sat down to their religious feast; after which they rose up to dance, always a part of religious ceremonial among primitive races.

Then Moses came down from the mountain, and when he saw the golden calf and the people dancing before it, he was moved to great fury. And he took the golden calf and he melted it in the fire, and he ground it to powder, and he scattered it on the water and made the people drink of it. And that was not the worst that Moses did to punish them.

Now the people's sin was disobedience against the Second Commandment: "Thou shalt not make to thyself any graven image, nor the likeness of anything in earth or sky; thou shalt not bow down to it nor worship it."

We may imagine—we do imagine—that this commandment, important as it may have been once for warning people with image-making proclivities, is now rather like an ancient fort on an obsolete frontier, so that the rusty old cannon have no longer an enemy to point at. Then why should *we* repeat it still, one might ask, any more than another old command, "Thou shalt not offer children to Moloch"? But we do offer children to Moloch, in certain places, and so perhaps we still make and worship graven images, without knowing what we do.

Anyone who has read Edmund Gosse's interesting autobiography, *Father and Son,* may recall how the boy got to pondering over the lines of a familiar hymn:

> "The heathen in his blindness
> Bows down to wood and stone."

And he asked his father whether bowing down to wood and stone was something very bad, and he was assured by his father that it was as bad as bad could be. The boy, very curious, then inquired what consequences might be expected to follow if anyone should actually bow down before wood and stone. The father could not inform his son exactly, but he impressed upon him, in vague but awful terms, that God's wrath must certainly fall heavily on any man who committed that which is to be held the very worst of sins.

The father's mysterious hints of spectacular doom only served to whet the boy's curiosity; so, one day when he was alone, he placed a chair upon the dining-room table, and then, kneeling down, he said his prayers to it. The dreadful thing was done, and he waited to see what would happen. Out of the window he could look up into the sky, as blue and serene as before. The silence was broken by no crash of thunder. Just nothing happened. And yet something had happened. In that hour a skeptic was born.

But the father's literalness is the literalness of human nature, and whole races of men have interpreted the Second Commandment in the same way, allowing the inner principle of it to evaporate while jealously guarding the outer shell of words. The Jews developed a prejudice against images of any kind so thorough that they were ready to start a war over the presence of Roman eagle-standards in their city of Jerusalem. And among the Arabs a beautiful art grew up, Arabesque art, due to the suppression imposed by this Second Commandment.

But in the West the Second Commandment has had a different history. In very many Christian churches a pious Jew or Mohammedan might well suppose that the Second Commandment there is either openly defied or quietly ignored; for in them images of wood or of stone are common, with many people bowing down before them, busily repeating prayers. If one were to question these worshipers, no doubt that they would protest that they are not worshiping the images, but something true that the images represent; the images enable them to realize more vividly something invisible that is true.

But the Second Commandment makes no such distinction. It allows no images, even if intended to represent Jehovah. The images the early Jews were impelled to make, some of them, at least, would have stood for Jehovah, but this was not permitted them. No statue of Jehovah, no more than of Jupiter, could be erected in the Holy of Holies. And intelligent pagans, had they been asked, would have explained that they did not offer sacrifices to statues, but to forces and qualities of divinity in nature that the statues made definite for them: power and wisdom and life and love.

So what is the matter with graven images? Not necessarily are they the symbols of false gods. Jeroboam's golden bull, which he set up at Bethel, was a symbol of Jehovah himself. Where is the plague-spot in idolatry?

It seems to be this: that a material symbol of divinity is not only very inadequate, but it tends to fix that inadequate conception in the minds of the worshipers; more than that, a symbol by its very inadequacy may be misleading— just as a triangle used to represent the Trinity inevitably suggests a heresy; more than that, an object of matter, forcibly striking the senses, tends to draw away and attach to itself the regard that should be given to the spiritual thing it is intended to symbolize. The form becomes something beloved by the senses, and an object sacred in itself and for its own sake. For such reasons, processes of degeneration invariably follow degradation of divinity—it would be easy to quote examples—processes which are foretold in the Second Commandment by the ominous words, "visiting the sins of the fathers upon the children, unto the third and fourth generation"—a long trail of consequences.

I am not making assertions but only asking questions, when I wonder whether the extreme popularity of a picture of Jesus in the arms of his mother has not tended to sentimentalize and weaken Christianity. It appeals strongly, of course, to human feelings—and that is its very danger.

And I wonder whether the crucifix, showing pain so realistically, and hypnotizing men who gazed too long upon it, may not have had something to do with those periods of morbidness and cruelty that have disgraced Christian history. The cross and the manger must not be forgotten, indeed, but their real significance should not be distorted by the trickery of art, and their true place in our belief should not

71

be over-emphasized. Between the manger and the cross stands the Sermon on the Mount.

And over everything, over the entire life of Christ, explaining both the manger and the cross, stand the words of our text: "God is Spirit, and they that worship him must worship him in spirit and in truth." They constitute the very essence of Jesus' teaching.

To worship God in spirit is, of course, to be spiritual; and spirituality needs to be defined. For people are not always very clear about it. I have often heard men and women called spiritual because of their diligence in observing the forms of religion, though they did not seem to my mind to possess much real spirituality. Their interest seemed limited to the outward forms. On the other hand, I have known men and women who were called unspiritual, but whom I thought conspicuous for their essential spirituality. So it is evident that the point at which we differed was in the difference of our ideas of what spirituality really is.

We all live on two levels. The lower level—we may call it the basement of our human house—is the life we live in common with the animals; it is the life of the body with all its strong instincts and desires, very good and very necessary in their place. The upper level, the principal story in our house, belongs to human beings alone. In contrast with the lower level, the physical, the upper level is the spiritual. It is the appreciation and the love of things that do not belong to the animal life. And these things are of three kinds, all spiritual; they are goodness, truth, and beauty. To live a completely spiritual life, then, one must love all three: goodness, truth, and beauty. If a man lives a moral life for the personal good it will do him, for success in business, it is no longer spiritual. If he is a scientist for money or for fame, it is no longer spiritual. And if beauty is made to serve the pleasure of the senses, then it, too, is no longer spiritual. Goodness, truth, and beauty must be for their own sake, or they will be dragged down out of their proper spiritual dwelling-place and made to wear rags begrimed with earth instead of their own shining garments. Spirituality is too often restricted to moral goodness, or even to the mere appearance of it; but it embraces all three departments of the life of the soul, the companionship of goodness, the companionship of truth, and the companionship of beauty.

So, since God is Spirit, we can conceive of him only in the supreme terms of goodness, truth, and beauty. The only image we may make of him is a mental one, composed of all that we can imagine of goodness, truth, and beauty. If we try to create an outline more definite by the use of a sensible figure, we do it at a risk. The old Jews loved the picture of God as a King upon a throne; but from all that we have learned about kings, we are not now so much inclined to think of him thus. Even the endeared expression, God the Father, has its limitations. I remember a boy who translated "Father" into "Grandfather," and saw him therefore as an irascible old gentleman with an antipathy for children.

Since God is Spirit, we shall worship him by pure devotion to goodness, truth, and beauty. We may use symbols to help our realization, if we will use them lightly, remembering always that the idolatry condemned in the Second Commandment is, in essence, to localize God outside of the human soul. There is where God becomes personal to us. No Sabbath day in itself is more holy than any day in which we work as by God's laws; we keep a Sabbath in order to make all days holy. No church in itself is more holy than any home in which love rules the common human living there; we build churches in order to make every house God's house. And no altar in itself is more holy in the eyes of the angels than the common family table at which the Lord Jesus Christ is present as a guest.

CHAPTER 9

What Doest Thou Here, Elijah?

IN OUR FIRST morning lesson, the thirteenth verse of the nineteenth chapter of the First Book of Kings, we have a dramatic incident described: how the Lord of all the universe, the heavens and the earth, addressed a question to an individual man. There, in the awful solitudes of Mount Horeb, after a whirlwind, an earthquake, and a fire, came a still, small voice which said, *"What doest thou here, Elijah?"*

However literal a fact this may be, it has a meaning higher than its literal happening, and is still more true as a symbol than it is as a physical event. For all historical facts are but shadows thrown upon a screen of matter by spiritual realities; and spirit, we know, is the only thing sure and permanent, expressing itself in fleeting forms. The form comes and goes; but that which makes and fills the form, endures. So we will translate this question in the silence of Mount Horeb as the still, small voice of God in the heart of the individual man.

It was born there with the man's birth, this still, small, questioning voice, and grows with his growth, and all the result of his life is but the answer which he makes to it. And this voice of question being thus an element in the nature of man, we may expect its recognition and its manifestation to be subject to the same law of unfolding or evolution, which we see in everything else. And it so happens, that we may perceive this development and orderly sequence of stages of progress, in the very words of our text itself. "What doest thou here, Elijah?" This question, spoken slowly, word by word, may represent the whole history of morality and religion and civilization, as well as the history of the innermost thought and motive in the heart of each individual man.

The first word of the text is "What?"—which, as it is the basis of the whole question, giving the character of interrogation to the entire sentence, so does it lie at the root of man's consciousness, and gives impetus and direction and color to man's whole life. For all life is but an endless question, making ceaseless inquiries of the universe, from its beginning to its end. And man is an incarnate interrogation-point, always asking questions of Nature from the cradle to the grave; from the time when his question is but a gesture as he reaches out for the moon, to that last hour when he steps off from the shores of earth, and launches out upon the dark waters of futurity asking "Whither am I going?" Man has been defined as the animal that walks upright, and as the animal that laughs; and just as pertinently he might be called the animal that asks questions.

A very mysterious universe it is in which we find ourselves, full of wonders on every side, and our souls are big with awe and admiration, until we learn the secret of giving names to things—and names are great dissipators of mystery. What is the earth? what is the sky? what is birth? what is life? what is death? There is a picture of the old stone Sphinx in the desert; a great stone lion-body with a human head; a gray expanse of sand around and a gray expanse of sky, with a mysterious crimson glow along the line of their meeting; and alone in this solitude, with ear held close to the lips of the Sphinx, is a human figure listening. It is human life. It is man asking questions of Nature, and civilization today represents the sum of the answers which man has caught in murmurs from those reluctant stony lips. But only apparently reluctant are the lips of Nature, for God surely means that the answers shall be given, little by little as man's upward progress shall warrant, just as surely as he planted the ever-burning question in man's breast. For there is another great stone statue in the old Egyptian desert—that land which knew so much and lost its knowledge—the huge stone statue of a god, sitting upon a throne and waiting through ages im-

75

memorial, no one knows for what. But the face looks toward the east, and every morning, so they say, as the first ray of the rising sun strikes upon its lips, they emit clear, flute-like notes which are said to be words with a meaning, and blessed are they who can hear them and understand. Every conceivable message is for those only who have the capacity to know what the message means, and Nature is veiled to those who are blind, and dumb to those who are deaf.

The second word in the text is the word "Doest." Man's question, at first so broad and undefined, takes a certain limit and direction. Man begins to perceive that everything is in motion; air, water, fire, stars, seasons, vegetable and animal life, everything is moving incessantly, flowing and changing, rising and settling, living and dying, and he infers that action is the important thing in existence. And as a conception of motion involves a source and an end, the tentacles of his questioning mind immediately begin to grope for a cause and a reason. The phenomena of Nature which he sees, what are they doing, what are they about? He looks around him and asks, Whence come the rain and the wind, and who hurls the lightning? Or, if we find that instead of being the arrows of angry gods, the bright flashes of lightning in the sky are but the fiery mane of a steed which we may name Electricity if we like and harness to our multiform work, still where are its secret stables? What clews guide the wandering stars along their labyrinthine paths? and is there any relation between the map of their roads and the chart of the highways which the wild-birds follow through the air-fields north and south? What heart in the bosom of the ocean is the cause of its mighty pulse-beat? What infestations in the veins of the earth produce its alternate fever and chill? What is the secret of light; of instinct; of gravitation? Out of what egg was the earth hatched? And how sails Life, as master or as freight, in its protoplasmic boats, in the sap of a tree or the blood of a man? And whence cometh man himself? Did he live before he was born? and then from what company of souls did he come? And whither goeth man, and on what ships do the dead sail away, to what islands beyond the horizon-line? Earth and man, in their number-less activities and ceaseless movements and intricate interplay of movements, like the whirling and eddying and on-rushing of a mighty river, whence do they come and whither do they flow? What is Nature doing, and to what does it all tend?

Such questions, in some form or other, men have passion-ately been asking all through the centuries; and as they began adding observed fact to fact, and deducing some sort of con-clusion therefrom, in their effort to read Nature's Sibylline leaves, science was born and philosophy.

The third word in the text is "Thou." What doest *thou?* The question narrows itself. Man soon transfers his keenest inquiry from Nature to himself. If the essential thing in existence is motion, if what Nature is doing is a subject so vital that it includes what Nature is, then the great mat-ter of interest to man is what he himself is doing, and the movements of Nature are important as they relate to him. Observation of natural phenomena has led to comparison, and comparison has led him to a higher opinion of himself. His personality has expanded, and he feels himself more of a king over Nature. "What hast thou for me?" he asks of her, "for *my* pleasure, for *my* use, for *my* power?" And he lays his hearth-stone and fences his field, and comes into relation with his fellow-men. There is many a brute battle among them, until it is learned that, for self-protection, what each one does has to be considered more or less with reference to what another does. So there come about compromises and alliances, and a certain standard of conduct gradually takes shape, to which all members of society are expected to conform. And a sense of obligation arises with the sense of responsibility for one's actions, and the inner voice in the heart of man gains a fuller strength and meaning. The questions which he asks of Nature now take a new coloring from this new emphasis which is laid upon the character of his own action. "What meanest thou to me?" he now be-gins to ask of Nature. "How art thou related to me? What are my obligations to thee?" And with these questions, moral-ity and religion are born.

The next word in the text is "Here." What doest thou *here?* and the question which has gradually been concentrating in the breast of man, is focused into a burning point. What art thou doing here and now, in the hour in which thou art living, in the place in which thou standest here? Man's constant tendency is to shift attention from the present, and to belittle it. The happiest days, they were in the past, or perhaps they are hoped for, yet to come. The golden opportunities, they have been lost, more may yet come, but they are not now. The beautiful city, the city in which we might have prospered more, it is east or west, but it is not this. The proper field for our abilities, it is near or far, but it is not here. We might have done something, we might have seen something—in Carcassonne. And all the while the days are passing by, disguised, offering us presents in their outstretched hands; gold and jewels and magic swords; patents of nobility and deeds of wide estates, together with flowers and candies and trifles. And we snatch at the last, and let the procession of the days go by, carrying the best of their gifts away with them. How we should value Today, if we only knew how we shall look back at it tomorrow! How like misers should we count the minutes of the hours, dropping each one with a sigh, if we only realized how something goes with them which someday we shall long to call back! But illusion is over it all, and we scatter precious opportunities like the petals of torn flowers, knowing not that they are golden coins, and the material of untold wealth. We scorn the spot in which we now are, not knowing that it contains the precious secret for which we look. Like the man in Hawthorne's story, who set forth in his youth to find a treasure, and after he had searched the world around, and come back to his humble home in old age to die, he found the treasure at last at his own door-step. It is a parable. We all are looking afar for things which are at our side. We are searching for things that we have in our hands. We would have looked up when our Lord passed by, but we did not dream that he was here, in the common prose of our twentieth-century life. But he *is* here, he is always here. Not in old Palestine, not in old Jerusalem, but here, as he said. Not in days of a past privilege, and not in a coming Millennium, but now. There is no place but here, there is no time but now, for any man. Time past is gone forever; time future is none of our concern; but Now belongs to us. And the place in which we find ourselves, is place enough to find our duty and a treasure hidden there. Place, after all, is only valuable as a spot in which to stand so as to look up to the sky and to God—and all places are open to the sky.

The last word of the text is "Elijah." "What doest thou here, Elijah?" The question has reached its climax, and is complete. It is addressed to a definite man; and a personal quality, which it had not fully before, now becomes a true part of it. To be called by a name, implies someone else who calls. It implies two personalities, with a more or less intimate relation between them. So that the question has risen out of man's consciousness, and then has transferred itself to One not man. The ever-questioning voice in the breast of man is no longer the spirit of man asking questions of Nature; it is the voice of God asking a question of man. It is Conscience enthroned at last in the seat prepared for it from the foundation of the world. It is God calling man by his name.

But let us look for one moment at the name "Elijah," and see what it is that God calls him. Every Hebrew proper name had a clear and definite meaning, and the name "Elijah" means, "Jehovah is God." So that God, in the symbolical way in which we have looked at the text, gives his own name to man, just as the angel, in Saint John's vision, stamped the Name upon the foreheads of the one hundred and forty-four thousand. We may deem it to be a mark of possession. Man does not belong to Satan; he belongs to God. He does not even belong to himself; he belongs to God. For God's own name is stamped upon him. And this voice of conscience in the very center of his being, this tormenting insistence upon doing right in his very constitution, proves that he is linked to something divine. And as long as that voice shall speak there within him, God is claiming him, calling him by his name. Well may we pray, as old Jeremiah did, "Thou, O

Lord, art in the midst of us, and we are called by thy Name; leave us not."

Again, the name of Elijah has in its meaning an encouragement and a reproof. *Jehovah is God,* and Jehovah stands for eternal righteousness, so that the name is an assertion of the sovereignty of goodness and right. He who is forever righteous is the creator and the supreme ruler of the world; to hear this whispered in the chambers of the heart when sorrow darkens the sky without and misfortune knocks at the door, is to have doubt and despair reproved, and to have courage and hope renewed. To have this truth, "right reigns," so impressed into the substance of our souls that it becomes a part of us, and we no more doubt it than we doubt the words, "the sun shines," this will be truly to be called by his Name.

The old prophet had fled with deadly bitterness of heart into the wilderness. Only a few days before he had won a signal triumph over the priests of Baal, and had slain them all, the six hundred of them, where the little brook Kishon must have run blood to the sea. And yet Israel had not returned to the worship of God, in spite of the overthrow of Baal; Jezebel the queen sent soldiers to get him, and Elijah had had to flee for his life, and out there in the wilderness, mourning over the ruin of his hopes, he had wished that he might die. Then God gave him an object lesson. He made a wind pass by, which broke the forests and left a track of desolation behind, but He was not in the wind; and after the wind an earthquake, which shook the solid earth and split great rocks, but He was not in the earthquake; and after the earthquake a fire, which consumed the wreck that the tempest had made, but He was not in the fire;—but He *was* in the still, small voice.

That same still, small voice is in the heart of each one of us. Hardly may we hear it sometimes for the noise of the whirlwind and earthquake, but in lulls and hushes it will not fail to raise its question, "What doest thou here, O child of God?" What art thou doing, it asks, at the desk, at the counter, in the shop, in the street, in the home? Art thou doing the work and will of the Lord?

We, waxing impatient over the strength of sin, and the dishonesty and selfishness of men, and the wrongs and mal-adjustments of our social system, often may ask, as the Sons of Thunder did, for a fall of fire from heaven to burn up the mischief-makers, grafters, and profiteers. And we may learn, as did Elijah, not to go faster than the still, small voice in in-dividual hearts. There are reforms enough brewing, one might think, to blow away all the abuses out of one such small planet as this, to say nothing of the earthquakes which have been planned to upturn a sudden Millennium upon the ruins of the old order. But men are not made good by legis-lative enactments, and it was long ago observed that the mills of the gods grind slowly, so that we may question the presence of God in some of our modern winds, our modern earthquakes, and our modern fires.

But we may not doubt the responsibility and obligation resting upon each one of us to do his own duty in his own place. We may not stop our ears to the still, small voice, which calls us away from living on any plane but our high-est, and from pursuing any ideal but our best. We may not forget that right reigns, in the counsels of Nature and of God.

"A new covenant will I make with men," said God to old Jeremiah: "not on tablets of stone will I write my law, but upon his heart will I write it. Not from Mount Sinai will I speak to him, but with a still, small voice in the center of his soul."

"Thou, O Lord, art in the midst of us, and we are called by thy Name; leave us not."

CHAPTER 10

The First and Great Commandment

"Thou shalt love the Lord thy God with all thy heart, and with all thy soul, and with all thy mind. This is the first and great commandment."

Matt. xxii:37-38.

THIS COMMANDMENT STOOD first in the old Jewish Law, as it still stands first in ours. Mount Sinai once thundered behind it, before our old theology took it up, making God stand over men with a whip in his hand: "Love me," he said. "I am a jealous God."

But love is a hard thing to force. Indeed, we feel that love can never be forced at all. It comes of itself, or it never comes. It may be rooted in natural instincts, or in common tastes and interests, or in gratitude for benefits bestowed, or in magic appeals which we do not understand; but however it arrives, we deem it due to something beyond our own will. We simply respond with love to objects that appear to us to be lovable. It is a matter of attractions, like chemical combinations. Certain elements rush to meet other elements, often with violence and explosion. No one can tell why, any more than the elements themselves. It is simply the fact. And other elements are absolutely inert toward one another. They may hang together in solution for a thousand years, and be no nearer a chemical compound at the end of that time than they were at the first. No one can tell why; it is the law of their being. And so, to the natural feeling, is the matter of love. It may be won, oftentimes, by great love itself, through the inductive transformations of love, but it never can be made to order.

And yet—here is the first and great commandment of the Law: *"Thou shalt love the Lord thy God."*

The sense of obligation laid upon humanity by this first and great commandment, combined with man's instinctive feeling that love cannot be summoned at will, has cast at certain times in history a gloomy shadow upon human happiness. Men and women, very conscientious, often have suspected that they loved father or mother, brother or sister, husband or wife or child or friend, first of all and more than God. And they felt, therefore, the guilt of living in constant disobedience to the first and great command. What bitter struggles have filled with tears and sighings many a midnight hour, in fruitless efforts to love some loved one less, as human beings strove to tear away some fond affection from their hearts through fear of God's dread jealousy, only the Judgment Day can reveal to the pitying eyes of heaven and earth! And how often, when one on whom great love was centered, has been stricken down by death, how often has this sharp vinegar been poured into the deep wound of the heart, that God took away that loved one just because he, or because she, had been loved more than God himself! the punishment that God inflicted for violation of his first and great command. Did you never overhear the neighbors say, with emphasis sinister and drear, "They loved their child—too much"?

This was a hard thing in that old grim-visaged Puritan religion, to make God stand beside every cradle as a rival to the sleeping child in it, the parents believing that their very love might draw God's wrath and destroy their child; to make God sit at every fireside as the invisible rival of husband or wife, ready to stab the object of love if that love ever threatened to outweigh the love given Him.

We might smile, if it had not produced so piteous a harvest of tragedy, we might smile at such a conception of a God defined as a God of love. But whether with smiles or sneers or desperate revolt, the sons of men would not always submit to worship such a caricature of God. They could not, and they did not. And yet, in spite of all rebellion, the words of the first and great commandment unchangeably remain, being read in our synagogues, like the Law of Moses, every Sabbath day. So let us try to see, if we can, on what, in reason, such a command may stand.

In the first place, is it true that love has nothing to do with the will? Is it true that the will has no control over love's coming or love's going? Is it simply a thing of certain conditions and natural laws, a flaming up of nerve-cells under appropriate stimulus, as purely an irresponsible thing as a spark of fire in the dry grass?

The nearer we look at man in his primitive savage state, the nearer to truth this representation of love seems to be. Love on that low level is very much a matter, indeed, of instinct and caprice. But the higher up the road of development and culture we travel, the more we find that control of love has followed the education of the will, and that the will has more and more to do with widening the field in which love acts, and in choosing the objects towards which it exerts its desires.

Man is an animal with a will. It is one of those endowments which allow it to be said of man that he was made in the image of God. The most striking operation of the will appears as soon as man becomes religious. Religion of any sort involves the exercise of the will upon the conduct of life. The very word "religion" is said to be derived from a word meaning "to bind." So when a man assumes loyalty to a religion, he undertakes to bind his actions in a certain prescribed fashion: to perform certain things, and certain things to hold forbidden.

Now the Christian religion differs from all other religions in being a religion of love. Other religions ask the will to do something; Christianity asks the will to love something. And the first and great command it lays upon the will is this: "Thou shalt love the Lord thy God." If we do not now love God, we must will to love him. So this commandment rests upon the assumption that love is a matter of will, and that we can learn to love what we choose to love.

In the second place, then, why should God command the

love of himself? In asking this question we are, indeed, trying to see into the unknown; but we do, at least, touch one pertinent fact. It is that the things we love and the persons we love have a miraculously transforming effect upon ourselves. It is as if in loving a thing we appropriate the qualities we love and make them a part of our very souls. For love in its essence means desire, and desire may be described as the reaching forth of the mind, as it were sending out feelers and tentacula, in order to get the beloved object somehow within the horizon of its own life. There are different planes of desire: physical planes, intellectual planes, and spiritual ones. In all of them one's self is the central point. In spite of any device of altruism, this is the truth. No matter what form that desire may take, our will is to have those objects which we deem lovable, abiding with us at our fireside, or standing as the landscape around our lives. They may be far off, too far for us to touch them, too high for us to reach; but we still would have them like mountain peaks of strength rising above our valleys, or like stars of reassurance shining in our night. We want them to environ us, however unattainable they may otherwise seem to be. They still will belong to us, because we love them. We have their presence in our lives, throwing their shadows and their lights across our daily paths.

So it is an invariable and inevitable law of love and result of love, that the persons we love and the things we love become a part of our inner world. We grapple them with the hooks of desire and draw them to us, and we make them bone of our bone and flesh of our flesh. If we love noble characters of men and women, then noble qualities will begin to take root in us. If we love beauty in the things we see and hear, then beautiful ideals will begin to realize themselves in what we think and say and do. But if we love wrong things, then most surely our souls will acquire a warped and twisted growth, making us more and more incapable of loving right things, until at last we find ourselves regarding beauty in ugliness, and pleasure in soul-sickness, and darkness in light, and good in sin.

Therefore, if we conceive of God as issuing commands at all, is it so strange a thing that he should lay a command upon us as to what we shall love? More, should we not expect him to point out to us what to love? Should we not expect him to urge us to love the very best things? Should we not expect him to require us to love the truest things, the purest things, the loveliest and the highest things? Should we not expect him to command us to love that which, by the very act of loving, will be for the health and salvation of our souls?

But what are all these things summed up into but God himself? All good things, true things, beautiful things, are but manifestations of God, things that we may know him by. He combines them all in himself, and yet is as much more as he is like the sky; which we see, indeed, as a blue dome full of sunshine or of stars, and yet we know that it is infinite space.

So this we may conceive to be a sufficient reason for the first and great commandment: "Thou shalt love the Lord thy God with all thy heart and with all thy soul and with all thy mind." It is a sufficient reason from our standpoint: to constrain us to love that which will make us more and more like God himself, and more and more worthy of being loved by him.

Now the first and great commandment standing where it does, in the very fore-front of our religion, we, if we take our religion seriously, must often pause to put this question to ourselves: "Do I love God with all my heart and soul and mind?" And it would be little wonder if we should find this question difficult to answer, and beset with doubts and fears.

For it is not easy to feel what we call love for a Being invisible and infinite, defined as having neither body, parts, nor passions, a Being who often seems so far away from the world he has made, a Being who seems so utterly a Being we cannot know.

But perhaps we love him more than we realize. So let us ask ourselves just what the love of God may mean.

The first question that we derive from the great commandment is this: "Do I love God with all my heart?" What is

86

it, then, to love God with the heart? We employ the term "heart" to indicate that precious, dearly-guarded, inmost chamber of our being where the mysterious sense of comradeship enters and dwells. It is the most sacred place on earth we know, if we can call it a place, that place within where a consciousness arises to welcome the presence of something which it recognizes as kin to itself. And the joy of that meeting is the sweetest joy on earth we know—so sweet that we have planted Paradise, the Garden of Heaven, with it.

But now what is it we say we love in the man or the woman or the child whom we love, we declare, with all our heart? Is it not some quality which we feel responsive to something in our own truest inmost self, and which is, therefore, attractive to us? We love it because it really is a part of ourselves. We demand its companionship in our life, and without it we feel our life to be bereft and despoiled. But these things which seem so rooted in our own heart, are they good? Then they are manifestations of the presence of the Supreme Good, that is, of God, and in loving them we are loving qualities that belong to God. Although not knowing it, perhaps, we are loving God.

But this power of perceiving lovable qualities in our fellow-men is something that quickens and expands at the bidding of the will, and it is something that strengthens and grows by deliberate practice. And as more and more we allow ourselves to become acquainted with what is the best in every human being whom we meet here in our pilgrimage—going aside to pick him up on any Jericho road; as more and more we learn to discern the scattered gold in the mud of humanity, seeing in it the broken image of God, the more shall we be learning to love God with the heart, and the more shall we be finding an indescribable sense of divine comradeship taking shape within our inmost life. As humanity grows more personal to us, God shall grow more personal. As we grow to be more the friend to man, God shall the more reveal himself as Friend to us. To this all the wise books testify, and all the saints declare it: the door into the Divine is through the human—or our Lord Jesus Christ need not have been born in Bethlehem. It is he who teaches us how to love God with all the heart.

The second question that we ask ourselves is this: "Do I love God with all my soul?" What is it to love God with the soul? We have said that to love the divine in humanity is to give Personality to the Divine. But when we conceive of God as personal, then relationships spring up immediately between ourselves and him. And that within us which we conceive of as coming into touch with him we call the soul. Something within that soul suggests to us that we may advance or retard our intimate relationships with God by the quality of our actions on earth, and we call that faculty conscience. Something else in the soul asserts a certain control over our conduct in the world, and we call this faculty the will. We decide then to choose true and noble purposes, as being things of soul and making for unity between our soul and what we feel as the Divine Soul or "Over-Soul." To love the highest things, the things of soul, will be to start corresponding aspects in our outward lives; and these aspects will be visible in our daily conduct in the world. And this nobler quality which shows in such conduct, we know by the name of righteousness. To love God, then, with the soul, is to love righteousness. Do we love courage? Do we love truth? Do we love generosity and justice and pity and patience and self-sacrifice and self-control and honor and hope? Then we love God whether we call him by his name or not. So far, we love God. To love God with all the soul is to love righteousness above all things else; it is to feel such loyalty to the right, that no earthly relation can tempt us to swerve aside from it. And such loyalty is within the power of the will. And to resolve to do the right is presently to learn to love the right.

So the only love that God could be jealous of, would be a love that hinders righteousness. We may love father or mother, husband or wife, brother or sister, child or friend, with all the intensity of our nature and with all the fulness of our heart; we may toil for them, live for them, and die for them, and let us never believe that God is jealous of that love.

Nay, he may even see in it but the greater love poured out at his feet. But if such love ever stands as a hindrance to righteousness; if human affection ever takes such a shape that it calls on us to sin for the sake of it; if it blurs our sense of allegiance to God and separates us from him, then God must be jealous of that love, because it is a love which is ruining ourselves with a ruin which may involve also the very objects of our love. The fire of any love in our lives must be a consecrated fire, consecrated to good ends, and fed with pure oils and pure service, or else an evil smoke will blow from it into our eyes, to blind us at last to great Love himself. So sacred is love, that God will have all serving of it done in his own name.

And now the third question will be: "Do I love God with all my mind?" What is it to love God with the mind? It is to lead our thought to dwell upon him as Creator and Worker and Artist, and it is to make our reason take account of his ways in the world. All men everywhere, who are searching for truth, are loving God with the mind—however they label themselves. Scientists and philosophers and inventors and poets and musicians—they all love God with the mind, to the degree of their love for beauty and truth. There is no course of study in a college that does not open windows into regions of infinite wonder; and no student will ever look through them, no matter how carelessly, and come away the same that he was before. He gets a glimpse of the fact that the story of man on the earth is not a mere catalogue of dates and kings and wars. He gets a glimpse of the fact that the story of nature is not a mere system of tables, reactions, resultants, and formulae. Something is going on behind all that.

The presence of God is visible everywhere, to the extent to which we open our eyes to him; and the search for him in the beauty and mystery of trees and flowers and river and sky, is an adventure whose eternal romance was the inspiration of the lovely god-stories of old, as it will be the inspiration of mythologies and songs a thousand years from now. More and more as we spread the sails of our venturous thought to this enterprise, shall the Mind of God reveal itself to us in ways more and more wonderful, appearing as something everywhere working and made visible in its works, and as always planning we know not what; but we believe that it is always beneficent, and we know that it is always beautiful. And so shall the love of God follow the illuminating discoveries of our observation and our reason until it fills all our mind.

We may never forget that all this is a process and a growth. We cannot accomplish a premeditated love all at once, especially in such high regions. But if we feel that the love of God is only a groping effort within us, not possessing us entirely as our first great commandment enjoins, we still can will to begin to love him as we ought. We still can will to love, because we can direct our desires as we choose. This is the beginning of the love that we seek, to direct our desires in certain ways, the ways our conscience and our judgment lay down for our will to work within; definite desires leading toward God and firmly held until they fuse together into one burning and permanent passion of love for him.

Here, then, are the three ways in which we obey the first and great commandment:

The first is to love humanity, from the wounded man by the road-side to our Lord Jesus Christ on his throne. To love humanity is to love God.

The second is to love the right, like a pillar of fire for us to follow through earth's wilderness. To love that which is right is to love God.

And the third is to love all Nature as God's Book of Miracles, knowing that it is his laboratory fires flaming every morn and eve, and that we walk in the hush of his Thought every moonlight night. To love Nature is to love God.

CHAPTER 11

Baptism

"Jesus answered, 'Verily, verily, I say unto thee, except one be born of water and the Spirit, he cannot enter into the Kingdom of God.'"

John iii:5.

WE HAVE JUST taken part in an event which ought to have great interest and meaning for us; we have seen a child born again, born of water and of the Spirit, and entering so into the Kingdom of God. For that is what baptism means.

The early Church tried to express the importance of this event by surrounding it with every possible detail of solemnity. Magnificent buildings, octagonal in shape, were erected, exclusively for the rite of Baptism. There was a long preparation of the candidates, during the period we call Lent. The water was consecrated with elaborate ceremonial, with chanted psalms and blessings, with holy oil poured into it, and with a burning torch thrust into it to indicate the coming of the Holy Spirit. The baptism itself took place, normally, early on Easter morning, followed by the bishop's laying on of his hands, and by the Easter Communion immediately after. The bishop himself performed the significant acts of the service.

In the course of time, the number of candidates for baptism becoming very large, the baptismal season was extended to the Feast of Pentecost, seven weeks ahead, which after a while was known as White-Sunday, Whitsunday, on account of the white garments that were worn by the newly baptized.

In such ways the early Church endeavored to show the real significance of Baptism, the greatest event in the life of a human soul, its second birth, its entrance into the Kingdom of Heaven. It was not long, however, before the symbolic be-

91

came the essential. It was the actual application of the baptismal water that was necessary for any soul's salvation. All souls unbaptized were lost. The water was indispensable. But suppose you were in a desert. Then the Church in its mercy made provision for situations in which no water was to be had; if there was no water, wine would do; if no wine, sand would do; if there was no water nor wine nor sand, then the words alone might avail. But baptism there must be.

We read how the Jesuit missionaries among the Indians of Canada, when the warriors were preparing for battle, used to run out and throw the consecrated water over them like rain, knowing that many of them would be killed in the war, but hoping that drops of the water falling on them might save their souls—even against their will.

And I recall a good old lady who told me that now she felt quite easy in her mind, because she had had all her children vaccinated and baptized. But she was expressing frankly what was for many centuries the common belief of Christendom: that Baptism is a kind of magic.

Great controversies on questions connected with baptism have divided Christendom. One of particular prominence has been the amount of water to be used. A very large society of Christians today still maintain that actual immersion is necessary; the entire body of the candidate must be submerged in order to make the baptism valid. There is a version of the Bible in which the word "baptize" has been carefully changed into "immerse," and in which John the Baptist becomes "John the Immerser."

On the other hand there are Christians who repudiate the use of water altogether, laying every stress upon baptism in the Spirit. And there also are those who, forgetting or ignoring the meaning of the water, substitute for it a pretty sentiment, and baptize a child with flowers.

The old theology that condemned the unbaptized to the regions of the lost has pretty thoroughly faded out—although I heard, not many years ago, a well-known preacher (and a good man, too) declare in the pulpit that no child is able to love God, and God is able to love no child, until it has been baptized. Which shows how an intelligent man can be caught and tied up in a spider's web of logic when his premises are false.

Along with the old theology have gone the old superstitions mostly. Perhaps they have carried something valuable along with them. No more do we place the font beneath a soaring dome of its own, with beautiful doors to enter through to it, doors once called fit to be the doors of Paradise. This is only one of many signs that the old emphasis upon baptism has disappeared, until now there is not emphasis enough. The splendid ritual with which its supreme place in a Christian's life was indicated has passed away, until now it is usually a mere formality, performed in an obscure corner of the church, perhaps, when nothing else is going on; sometimes it is made a kind of social function in the home, a kind of fashionable party, with a salad-bowl or a silver punch-bowl brought into service as an appropriate baptismal font. Baptism is still considered desirable, for different reasons in different circles, but its original sharpness of meaning as a crisis has been dulled by time and custom.

Let us return to the words of our Lord, upon which, more than anything else, the idea of the absolute necessity of baptism was based. No doubt from the very first the application of water in some form was an outward public sign of a convert's entrance into the brotherhood of Christians, his passing from an old life into a new one. It was the accepted initiation symbolism, approved, we believe, by Christ himself. But the words of our Lord, when disseminated through Saint John's Gospel, and interpreted literally, gave it an importance much greater than a mere initiation ceremony. The sacrament itself was indispensable to any soul's salvation. "Except a man be born of water and the Spirit, he cannot enter into the Kingdom of God." This seemed very definite; the water was the water of baptism, and the Spirit of God was given by means of it.

But our Lord's favorite method of teaching was in pictures —symbols—and the outward element of water was a symbol of something interior and spiritual; it was a symbol of repentance, by which the old life with its guilt was washed away, so that the new life of the Spirit could begin. Hence the words of our Lord may be expanded thus: that the passing of a soul from a lower material life into a higher spiritual life—that is, into the Kingdom of God—is like another birth. But it depends upon a recognition of sin and a decisive abandonment of it—repentance—along with a definite act of will to follow the leadings of the Spirit. And this, indeed, is necessary, and it is like a birth into a new kind of world.

There are some, consequently, who refuse baptism to children. It is impossible, so they contend, that a child can have this experience and can make this choice, so that the pronouncement that he is "now regenerate" after receiving the rite of baptism has no reality and is a misstatement. The New Testament contains no precedents, no instances, of the baptism of children, and no passage authorizing it. But our Church, conceding the point, of course, that a child cannot yet have had the necessary experience, explains our action on the ground that we look forward to the accomplishment of a lengthened process, in which baptism is but the beginning. Regeneration, what we call the "new birth," is usually and normally, in Christian surroundings, a gradual growth along with the physical and mental growth of a child. It is like the dawn, which begins with an almost imperceptible light, and increases until the world is filled with the new day. And in the rite of baptism we take a swift glance into the future, and we concentrate, in a dramatic manner, the child's coming development into the present moment, a development of which baptism is but the beginning. For it actually is the beginning. The child is "regenerate," it is born again, because now it is grafted into the body of Christ's Church; and henceforth it is, or it ought to be, surrounded by all the gracious influences that such an environment implies. The child is potentially regenerate, we may say, because it is grafted into the body of Christ's Church. Sponsors take the necessary vows in place of the child, vows which the child will acknowledge and confirm later, in Confirmation. Confirmation is the completion of Baptism.

94

What a guaranty of safety it ought to be, what a promise of a new birth brought blessedly to pass, when a child is grafted into the body of Christ's Church! A whole community of established Christian men and women back of him, responsible for him, caring very much that he shall grow up good. And if, after all, he should go astray, no member of that congregation but may whisper to himself, "A part of that failure is mine!"

CHAPTER 12

The Holiness of Beauty

IT IS A picturesque device, when we wish to get a fresh and vivid view of a subject, to take a new standpoint from which to consider it and attempt to look upon it through the eyes of a fancied traveler from the planet Mars. We assume that in his red world the object of our interest is unknown, and we picture to ourselves the thoughts of wonder with which he examines the matter so strange to him, and in this way, through his unaccustomed vision, we contrive to stimulate the sharpness of our own.

Let us take advantage of this Martian tourist's peculiar adaptability for a little while this afternoon, and let us conceive of his native environment as a region where there is no sense and no knowledge of beauty. There might be strange appreciations of which we could have no understanding, but to beauty, as we recognize it, there is utter insensibility. Now with this inhabitant of Mars so mentally constructed, let us start him on his travels, and let us fancy that it was his privilege to be one of the company who gathered a few evenings ago to listen to the music which was then let free from piano and violin, Afrit-like to fill the air with wonders from their unsealed, brazen jars, and then to vanish away. How strange must all have seemed to the man from Mars! Were there not sounds enough in nature,—so he might have asked; were there not sounds enough in the habitations of men, and on their roads of travel, that a hall full of people should sit for two hours simply to hearken to sounds deliberately made for the mere sounds' sake? And how much more puzzled he must have been when we told him that we have a system of symbols by which these sound-arrangements are preserved for reproduction at any time, and that some of them represent the best efforts of some of earth's most divinely inspired men, and that she treasures them in her jewel-box of most precious things. And more, that men and women, beginning from childhood, spend long years of study and toil in order to acquire the ability of presenting these sound-arrangements to the ears of other women and men, taking them out of the casket of silence, as it were, and holding them sparkling for a short space before the delighted perceptions of an audience. Sounds, nothing but sounds, and yet, what magic was wrought through them upon the minds of all the people there! So that they *heard*, instead of seeing, bright colors woven in intricate arabesques, and felt through the ears instead of the eyes the satisfaction of proportion and order and law. And more, gates were flung open as they listened, into the future and the past, so that the cadences of long silent voices mingled with the hopes of prophecy, and bells swung again in the towers of old romance to answer all we dream of to make the perfect life.

But nothing of all this was heard by the man from Mars: it was to him only a meaningless welter of noise—because he did not know what beauty is.

Then, another day, we took the man from Mars into a room in an art-school where we showed him the walls covered with pictures and sketches in charcoal and color, and we explained to him with pride that it represented the work of the students of the school.

"Do you mean that they *study* to do these things," he inquired.

"Yes," we told him, "long years."

Then the man from Mars was still more mystified. "Why?" he asked.

And we tried to show him why, beginning with the drawings from the cast. "Note," we said, "those subtle curves, how they express strength and movement happily conjoined, and calmness and poise presiding over eager life. How they suggest to us as we look upon them that fuller life which the gods once lived before they were driven away by the uglier living

97

of men, when muscle and mind and heart danced hand in hand by the water, the field, and the wood."

"I do not understand," said the man from Mars. "But maybe you could make clear to me these curious splotches of color. What are they?"

"They are hints of the meaning of nature," we explained to him; "notes we take to keep, of the answers we believe we have from nature when we ask her what she means. The color and the form are an alphabet which spells something more than the color and the form. This little picture tells how a flower felt when it bloomed; and this how a face is the prison-wall of a soul; and this describes the mood of a moment in spring. Here a summer-day dreams, and here an autumn evening sighs; and here clouds build a mountain for the fancy to climb, or a Babel-tower to reach the sky. And here are human attitudes, simple and eloquent, and here a group of trees 'commune and have deep thoughts.'"

"How strange!" murmured the man from Mars; and we could not make him understand a meaning which had no meaning to him.

Finally we saw our visitor off, going to the dock with him as he took ship for Mars. He noted with great interest the numbers of passengers who were embarking on various boats for various shores.

"Whither are they all going?" he enquired; "and I should like to know for what."

"Many go on matters of business," we told him; "and many go out of curiosity and many go out of restlessness. But perhaps the largest number go to behold beautiful things of nature or of art: the Alps, the Trossachs, or Lake Como; the arches of Westminster Abbey or the dome of St. Paul's; the Sistine Madonna or the Parthenon; the treasures of the National Gallery, the Louvre, or the Vatican. In other words, they are traveling in pursuit of beauty. It is at least to see, perhaps it is to spend long years of study upon, those things which are counted earth's crown-jewels. It is for this that they make these journeys over land and sea, at the cost of labor and money and time and long separation from home."

"How strange!" exclaimed the man from Mars; "and how glad I am that I am going back to a world of practical things!"

So farewell to the man from Mars. He has no place in this world of ours, for this is a world in eager pursuit of beauty. Call it by other names, smother it in the mud of lower motives, yet this is always what emerges as the moving-impulse of civilization and the measure of progress: the love of beauty. Inevitably whatever is best and dearest to us in life takes for us the shape of beauty. It is the light of our earthly life, and it is only when this lamp shines clear in our dwelling that the world to us is full of light. The operations of the religious principle itself we know as the beauty of holiness.

Therefore, since it is in the nature of man to respond to some appeal of beauty as naturally as he breathes, it is the supreme effort of any life which endeavors nobly at all, to get some satisfying order and comeliness and grace into its material environment. We respect our lives so much that we would have them set, like diamonds and rubies and sapphires, in a fitting background. And so, whether we are building a house, or furnishing a room, or buying clothes, a question quite as important as any other is, how it will look. For consider only a moment the vast amount of attention given, of money spent, and of work expended, upon things which are not necessary at all, but which are merely the ornaments of necessary things, or are even without the most distant relation to practical use. Humble is the house whose exterior has not mouldings and beadings and cornices and projections for mere appearance's sake; while inside, where individual taste has wider scope, walls and floors and furniture seem to be considered as first of all simply opportunities for decoration. If they can be useful after being decorated, so much the better; but decorated they must be, cheaply or expensively, in good taste or in bad. The poorest wall-paper must have its trellis of flowers.

But this is only the beginning, the rudiments, of beauty's requirements and operations; they extend in widening circles. Men demand beautiful thoughts, worthily expressed, to read; they demand beautiful music to hear and beautiful pictures to see. They demand the institutions of which they are a part to be appropriately set; they want their business-blocks to be palaces, their senate-houses to be temples, their places of worship to suggest some beauty of holiness. It is the soul's unconquerable impulse to build itself ever "more stately mansions, as the swift seasons roll."

So the appreciation of beauty runs through life from top to bottom, and the range of life's excellency depends upon the limits of that life's appreciation of beauty, and the kinds of beauty which it is capable of apprehending. For beauty be-longs to every department of existence, from the lowest and most material up to the highest and most spiritual. It is like a great scale of music running throughout human life, from the lowest bass to the highest treble; and no one man is able to hear all of the scale. Some men have ears such that they can hear only the bass tones; these are they who can perceive beauty only in physical things. Other men have ears such that they can hear the treble tones best, and these are they who see most beauty in things of mind and soul. The perfect man will be responsive to the harmonies of the whole great scale, from the lowest tones to the highest ones. And toward this capacity the course of our evolution draws us; so that, if we develop at all, the range of the scale of beauty is continual-ly widening to us as we progress, lower tones in the bass and higher tones in the treble gradually being added as we see deeper into the mysteries of nature and higher into the mysteries of grace.

Now in all this pursuit of beauty a noteworthy fact is this, that everybody considers his own opinion of value in a ques-tion of what is beautiful. We might shrink from giving a decision in a matter of science or philosophy or even religion; but in the realm of esthetics one is not apt to hesitate. Before a work of architecture or painting or music or literature, everyone feels called upon for a judgment. We cannot here say, "I do not know whether that is beautiful or not." Some-thing within us arises and weighs and declares, "That is beautiful," or "That is ugly." The opinion may be exactly the reverse of the opinion of people better educated than we in the principles of beauty, but the quality of the opinion is an accident, dependent upon many things. The important fact is that the observer feels within himself an inalienable right to an opinion, and that to him his opinion is necessarily a true one.

Indeed, so much a part of one's inmost self is this response to beauty, this sense that the recognition of beauty is one of the soul's highest endowments, that to cast an aspersion upon a person's taste is to throw an insult at him. You may call a man desperately wicked, and he may even take it as a kind of compliment; but beware of telling him that his taste is poor. You have touched the quick then and the man winces, and it will go hard if he ever forgives you. To be sure this seems a strange thing, at first thought, that any person's instinct should rate his taste above his morality; but it is true, and very often the best argument which you can use against a sin is to show that it is in poor taste. To say that a certain action is ugly often has more effect than to declare that it is wrong.

Let us ask ourselves why this is so, and the answer is soon apparent. It is because the soul recognizes that a decision of taste is an expression of its real nature, is a betrayal of its true preferences, is a revelation of its inmost quality. But the case is different in the sphere of morals. Here the soul will never admit that a lapse into sin is an indication of its real character. In fact, the soul always insists that it is better than anything it does. No matter what the wrongdoing is, the soul has its explanation and excuse. It has been beguiled and deceived into its evil choices, and they do not represent the best part of itself. That best part of itself, it knows, is its sense of beauty. There is nothing but its own inherent character to limit it in the apprehension of beauty; and hence it knows that to express a taste is to reveal something ultimate in its actual state, behind which it cannot go. It cannot here say that it is better than the things which it admires. Its sensitiveness to beauty is the measure of itself.

Love of beauty is as omnipresent as the Holy Spirit himself; indeed, it is the operation of the Holy Spirit as truly as con-

101

science is. Conscience may declare to us the existence of the right, and spur us into seeking it; but it is the sense of beauty which makes us love it. When we love the good, it is because the good appears beautiful to us; and when we hate the wrong, it is because we see how ugly the wrong really is. Conscience is the effort of the Holy Spirit to make us do the right; the sense of beauty is the effort of the Holy Spirit to make us love that which is good and true.

CHAPTER 13

Sir, We Would See Jesus

ORDINATION SERMON

"Now there were certain Greeks among those that went up to worship at the Feast; these therefore came to Philip and asked him, saying, 'Sir, we would see Jesus.'"

John xx:20-21.

DEARLY BELOVED, WE are gathered together here today to behold, and to take part in, one of those events which can occur only once in the life-time of a man, and which are always of transcendent interest to those who look on, because the door of a wide and unknown future swings slowly open upon this event as upon a hinge. Birth, baptism, confirmation, marriage, ordination, death—each one is the door into wonderful new realms, and no one of them can take place before us without our catching, prophetically, as the elect one enters in, echoes of voices yet to speak, and reverberations of footsteps yet to come. And today, as each of these our brothers approaches to receive the Bishop's hands upon his head, and to be set apart for a special holy work, we hear the murmur of future voices asking him, "Sir, we would see Jesus," and we know that his life-task henceforth will be to endeavor to answer this world-question, and to make men see Jesus and God. From this day onward, to the end of his life, his finger must point, with a special certainty, to Jesus and to God.

For the two are one, as Christianity has held ever since the Resurrection: to see Jesus is to see God; to know God is also to know Jesus. From the dawn of time, when man began

103

to be man, he has always had two desires playing above the desires of his physical life; one was the desire to see God, and the other was the desire to see a perfect man. One hand groped about in the skies, and the other groped about on earth. So all through history man's life has always shown a double loyalty: the worship of something above to which he made sacrifice, and the obedience to something below which he saw in heroes and kings. And at length in the fulness of time, that something above came down so close that it became man himself, and that something below was lifted up so high that it was now seen to be very God. And lo! the Word was made flesh, and Christ was born in Bethlehem. And ever since, to know God is to know him in Jesus; to see Jesus is to see God. Jesus, then, is the conjunction of heaven and earth, and of their age-long struggles to reach each other. Man has climbed Asgard and Olympus and Sinai, and has found his one God to worship; he has followed every mark of a hero till he has found the one hero of his search. And behold, his hero and his God are one. To see Jesus is to see God.

Now this identity is something which in many places has become obscured in our day. It is maintained by a certain school of thought—and its influence penetrates and chills many a Christian faith—that in this high region where some certainty is so necessary to man's welfare and happiness, there is no certainty to be attained. There may be a God, such as we desire him to be, but man can never be sure of it. It would be man's deepest joy to know, but man never can know, for God is simply outside of the region of man's knowledge. There is no bridge between God and man.

The fundamental reason for this uncertainty—is it not the failure to keep in mind the fundamental position of Christianity? the failure to keep the eye fixed on Jesus, and so to keep a hold on God through him? When the scientific spirit attempts to know God through its own processes, it can reach only uncertainty. It discovers magnificent Force, but it hears no heart beat. It must approach God through Jesus, and not through logic. Then, on the other hand, when

104

it studies the life of Jesus as a phenomenon, to be classified and given a place on a museum shelf of anthropology, it no longer truly sees him, and no longer knows God through him. Jesus lived once, he does not now live, and God recedes into the region of the Unknowable.

This trouble of the Agnostics is our own practical trouble, too—only we will not follow them to their despairing conclusion. We may not know, but we will not admit that we never shall know. We believe that we hold in our Creed the means of knowing. We insist that the most important thing of all things in our life—is it not that God shall be real to us? more real than city streets and country fields, than business and society, than family and friends? We shall never love with all our heart and with all our mind and with all our soul something which is not real to us. And yet we all know how difficult it is to come near to God in consciousness; how seldom we feel that inexpressible sense of soul companionship which we long to make constant. All the hardness of our lot lies in this insensibility of ours, in this incapacity of ours, in this failure to recognize God as forever at our side in a presence of love. What temptation would be strong if we thought of God as holding us back; what sin would make us despair if we believed that God forgives; what grief would paralyze our energy if we felt God's sympathy? No, we yield to sin, despair, and grief, simply because we conceive of God as indifferent or far away. To feel him near would be the cure of all our woe.

Let us go out into the open and try to find God. How beautiful it is, and how wonderful it is! "Nature," we cry, "we would see God." And as we stand, awe-stricken, we see him, surely. His robe trails over the valley, his smile shines down the blue. From the beginning men have found God here, just as we; from the beginning, until modern wise men told us different, the movements of nature have all been held divine. Every oak-tree was the home of a dryad, and every fountain had its nymph, while down by the river it was the great god Pan who sat playing flutes. And the dawn was Apollo, and the moon Diana, and the lightnings were arrows

105

shot by some supernal wrath. And the seasons as they rolled were the celestial chariot-wheels of divinity, and merry dieties presided over the vintage and the wheat. All nature was a tapestry moved and tossed by a half-hidden tumult of life behind, from which came forth now and then a peal of laughter, and now and then there dropped a tear. Surely we, too, must find nature divine. This intricate web of life, so full of relationship and design, cannot appear to mind as anything else than the work of Mind, and Mind with marvelous force at its command to carry out its will. Nature is divine, but the over-powering question which arises in us men is, what do we ourselves mean to the God of nature? How does the God of nature regard us?

And then, as we stand gazing—perhaps trying to worship —our heart is pierced by a piteous fact. Nature is full of triumphant joy, indeed, but it is her own joy she is intent upon as far as we can see, and she is in no way concerned with that of any of her creatures. She creates them prodigally, but is utterly careless of them, nevertheless; her lavish production of them permitting a system of cruel war forever to be maintained among beasts and birds and even the very trees and flowers. She herself has decreed that war, and she sits as over an immense arena, watching interminable gladiatorial combats, with her savage thumb forever turned down. Nor does she seem to love men more than her other beasts. If man is her favorite, as he fondly dreams, she allows no sign of her partiality to appear in her treatment of him. She takes as much pains with the ingenious poison-sac of the rattlesnake as with the convolutions of man's brain. Man's ironical fate, between his dreams and his environment, has long been his puzzle and his despair, and whatever we see of divine in nature, it surely is not divine love, and well has the God of nature been named, at least from man's narrow, self-centered standpoint, the Supreme Indifference. It is not from nature that man receives the revelation of God's love.

But let us not yet turn away in despair, with no other answer to our question than God's pleasure in a cruel sport.

"Nature," we besought, "we would see God." Our first glance filled us with wonder; our second glance filled us with fear; let us look again with more self-forgetfulness, and now we see something to fill us with hope. A secret stands revealed which we will bear away with us to meditate over alone. It is this: God loves beauty. Can any deduction from nature as to the character of God be more positively laid down for a fact than this, that God loves beauty? Whether he loves man or not, is it not reasonably certain that he loves beauty? For it is universal, as far as we can see, in God's creation. Everything that he has made is contrived to bear some peculiar aspect of beauty. Every blade of grass, every attitude of every animal is beautiful. For look around; trees, flowers, rock-crystals, moth-wings and bird-wings, hill-slopes and water-stretches, noon-clouds and sunsets, sun, moon, and stars— all are full of the color and curve and form and mystic meaning which make up beauty. And those who look through the microscope and telescope tell us that the world of beauty visible to us is as nothing compared with the universe of beauty we cannot see. The whole vast current of life is one vast current of beauty.

This is a fundamental fact which we can build upon, then, that God loves beauty. However far beyond the facts of his power and his love of beauty God may be unknown and unknowable, yet the creator of a universe of beauty must love beauty. And so upon this fundamental fact we may lay down two inferences to give us hope.

The first is this: so overwhelming is the beauty of nature over what we called the cruelty of nature, that the second can only be regarded as subservient to the first. What we called cruelty must be something instrumental in the production of beauty. How, we know not; but if we did know, in nature's large result we should surely acknowledge a compensation for every pain. If the sentinel-instincts and the killing-instincts, if the wrestle and the overthrow and the death, all contribute to the extirpation of ugliness and the development of loveliness and perfection, we may grieve at the cost, but what we blindly called cruelty is no longer cruelty. It is a method working toward an end. If blood poured out at the root of the plant glows again in the crimson of the flower, we shall see here simply another aspect of the great world-mystery of sacrifice which we have learned to accept in the mystery of the Cross. The birth of beauty, like the birth of man, is brought about in agony.

So much for the first inference; the second one has regard to our own relation with this God who loves beauty, and is this: as far as we ourselves recognize beauty anywhere, and rejoice in it and strive to add to it—by art or any other way—we are to that extent in harmony with something in God's own mind and heart. He sees something of himself reflected in us, and must embrace this our appreciation of beauty in his own love of beauty. Is not this something, at least beginning, to establish a sense of communion between ourselves and the divine? This communion is what we long for, with longings unutterable, and it is what they tell us can never be attained. But here it is. I beg of everyone who loves a sunset or flower or star to try it. Only, remember this: the emotion of beauty springing up in you must be made a kind of worship, a flame upon an altar, as it were. To maintain and develop a communion with God on the basis of beauty, requires that we keep inviolate our sense of the relation between beauty and God. We must always look on nature as the Burning Bush, forever consuming and never consumed, with a mysterious Voice coming forth out of it, and the ground whereon we stand holy ground. Then we shall never wander far from true standards of beauty; we shall never for long mistake ugliness for beauty; and we shall walk in the garden with God in the cool of every day.

But—it is this very nearness which is our undoing. We are emboldened to reach for a Hand which we do not find; we are tempted to appeal to a Heart which does not respond. Our very sense of communion with the God of nature only makes us conscious of a wider vacancy. For man is not only brother to the trees; he is also brother to other men. His environment is not only nature, it is also humanity. And this is a matter of such tremendous import to him, that any god whom he can conceive of, any god who will be real to him, must also be human. And so the same cry which he has ever been raising to nature, "Nature, we would see God," he has also been asking of humanity: "Men, we would see the Supreme Man." For the communion he longed for could be only with a Being, or with Beings, having qualities, however magnified, like his own. And so he peopled the skies with guesses and imaginings, a race of gods and goddesses for whom he built palaces on mountain-tops, and devised for them loves and comradeships and feastings and journeyings and wars—a kind of glorified mirage, in the heavens, of the manifold doings of men. These noble inhabiters of the world above were patterned after the best hero-life that earth had produced; but still the agonized question among men always was:

"How much regard have the gods for men? Beat the cymbals and kill the sacrifice; perhaps they will hear, perhaps they will see, and perhaps they will come down."

For, bitter as is the warfare which we see in nature, the warfare among men, and in men, is more bitter still. Man has always had to fight for his hearth-stone and for his liberty and for his life. Other men have always been trying to surprise him and betray him and climb up over him,—just as he, driven by some madness within, has also sought to surprise and betray and climb. History is but a record of war. And if the noble qualities which men are always enraptured with have been conjoined always with some fatal defect: if courage were likely to be crowning a hard heart, and kingly power to possess a tyrannous hand; if generosity often raveled into vice, and friendship could never be guarded against forgetting; if humanity could never be relied upon— then the divinity which was fashioned out of this humanity bore in itself the same ground of doubt. And man, harassed and torn without and within, never could address the god he had made, without suspicion that he still was addressing the Supreme Indifference; that he still was the object of the "great gods' laughter on their unscaled slope." It is not even from humanity that man receives the revelation of God's love.

But let us not yet turn away in despair, with no other answer to our question than an echo of mockery from the skies. "Men," we cried, "we would see the Supreme Man." Our first glance kindled our fancy; and our second glance quenched it in disgust; let us look again with more of faith, and now we see something to fill us with hope. A fact rises into view which we will bear away with us to meditate over alone. It is this: God not only loves beauty; God loves goodness. For in every human creature that he has made, as far as we know, he has planted in the soul of him or her the sense of the distinction between good and bad, and a sense of obligation to choose the good. We have named this sense "Conscience," but it stands for the innate longing of the soul to flower into some form of admirable and noble life. And this every soul possesses. Every soul which God has made is contrived to hold some peculiar possibility of goodness. Hence can we not declare, as a certainty, that the God of nature who loves beauty is also the God of men who loves goodness? And is not the love of goodness the same thing as the love of beauty, only in a higher sphere, the sphere of soul? Whether God loves men or not, he surely values something which he has planted in men and which keeps struggling painfully to reach the light. And so filled is all history with this struggle for goodness, that it is not too much to say that the whole vast current of human life is setting—though with many an eddy, swirl, and cataract— towards the good.

This is a fundamental fact that we can build upon, then, that God loves beauty of soul, that is, character. However far beyond these facts of his power and of the value he seems to place upon character—however far beyond these facts God may be unknown and unknowable, yet the creator of a stream of life, through age-long processes making persistently towards the good, must love the good, or beauty of soul, or character. And upon this fundamental fact we may lay down two inferences of hope. The first is this: so invariable, in the very midst of evil fate, is the sting of soul demanding growth that the evil fate itself, if God loves the good, must be regarded as in some way conducive to that growth. How, we know not; but if we did know, in God's large plan for the good we should surely acknowledge a justification for all harsh heredity and environment. It is a method working towards an end, and here again we see in humanity's pain the great world-mystery of the Cross. The formation of character, like the development of the physical man, is achieved through cost and stress. It is hammered out upon an anvil.

And the second inference of hope is this, and it has regard to our relation with that God who loves beauty of soul. As far as we ourselves recognize the value of character, and rejoice in it, and strive to enact it in our own soul, to that extent we are in harmony with something in the heart and mind of God. He sees something of himself reflected in us, and so must embrace this much of us within that which he loves. Here, then, is ground for yet closer sense of communion with him, though still our hand gropes for his Hand, and our heart yearns to feel the throb of his.

But if character in us is the reflection of something in the heart and mind of God, we shall advance a step. For character is something personal, and so we shall be able to make, from that dim reflection within ourselves, some kind of an image of God. Painfully we shall follow the wavering lines of our ideals, tracing out those qualities which we have learned to worship as hero-qualities, and striving to stretch them out into measurements divine. And then, to meet our high and heartbreaking endeavor, a miracle occurs: out into history steps the figure of a man, and if a Voice from heaven declares Jesus to be the Beloved Son, a voice within us declares him to be the hero whom we sought; those bright hero-qualities out of which we have been endeavoring to construct a conception of God, we find here in highest human terms, patience and courage and energy and hope and loyalty and love. Here at last is something to measure God by—and yet producing a quotient which we shall understand, a Supreme Man. And because our hero is now also our God, he ascends up out of history into the present and the everywhere. And now, not only do we walk with him in the garden in the cool of the day, but he cometh in and suppeth with us, and we know him in the breaking of bread.

And yet, this divine communion is only just begun. Even the instant that we recognize him—such are the conditions of our earthly life—even the instant that we recognize him, he vanishes from our sight, now as in old Emmaus. He leaves us with a vaster longing, but strengthened with hope.

All men ask to see Jesus. And the only way we can see him now, since he walks Galilee no more, is his Presence in human life. And all men's doubts arise because he is so dimly discerned there. Sometimes we talk of the Higher Criticism as undermining faith, but we talk unintelligently. Nothing can undermine faith but doubt in the power of faith—and we look into human life to find it, and not into books.

So what will *you* have to say when we shall come to you and ask, "Sirs, we would see Jesus"? You may open your books and read us the story of him, and we shall but envy the eyes that saw and the ears that heard—two thousand years ago. You may tell us the old saints' testimony, of rapturous glimpses of the Holy Child, and we suspect, these days, that we are in regions of psychology. What we want to know is whether you yourself have seen the Lord. We beg of you to tell us that, and it is all we want to know. We beg of you—and it is the one thought I leave with you—be true, be true to your own experience. What Jesus means to you, though it be no more than the stammering fraction of a revelation, what Jesus means to you, *that* is your message to other men.

CHAPTER 14

The Secret Garden

*"Awake, O North Wind, and come, thou South
Wind, and blow upon my garden."*
Song of Solomon iv:16.

IN ONE OF the popular magazines of the day, there was
running last year a serial story entitled, "The Secret Garden."
I did not read the story, and the garden and all that happened
therein to make a story are still a deep secret hid from
me. But a haunting curiosity exhales from the charming
title, as if a fragrance blew over the wall of the Secret Garden,
and one finds one's self pondering the fascinating question
again and again: "Where is the Secret Garden, and what
mysterious beings plucked mysterious flowers therein?"

The Secret Garden! It is a thing to dream about! Where
is the Secret Garden? It is a thing to send the errant Fancy
forth upon adventure to find and to explore. So westward ho!
or eastward ho! let us set forth for the Secret Garden.

We turn aside from that beaten path which is free to the
feet of all who may come, and open to the sight of all who may
see. The familiar buildings, the slim church spire, the college
tower, all disappear, with all the happy people passing to
and fro. All the noises of the world, the talk and the laughter
and the chiming of the bells, sink away after them, as silver
coins slide softly away in a well of deep green water. For we
are entering a profound forest; and as the stage scenery
glides away to transfer us in the play to the Forest of Arden,
so glides away the scenery now toward the heart of an Enchanted Wood. Single trees become groups, and groups of
trees become battalions, close-ranked and dense. Dimmer

grows the filtered light. Instead of open glades now and then in a golden glow, appears now and then a blacker shade, suggestive of a cavern's mouth. Closer and closer stand the trees. On we push through the tangled foliage; low we stoop under bending boughs; with care we follow certain signs known only to us; and here, at last, deep among the vines, is a small low door with a lock. But we have the key. So easily we turn the bolt of the lock, and easily we pass in through the narrow door, which we carefully close behind us. We are in the Secret Garden.

But do you not remember that we set out to find the Secret Garden in an Enchanted Wood? We did not guess, perhaps, what that fact implies, if we did not bear in mind the possibility of strange happenings here. We saw the wood that it was deep; we saw the way that it was intricate; but nothing more. Whatever magic spells are latent or are potent in that wood, they did not manifest themselves to us—until now. For we came to the Secret Garden in a merry company; but the moment we passed within through the low dark door, enchantment fell on us. And behold, each one of us is alone! Look here, look there, before, behind, and all around, no other one is in the Secret Garden but you!

If there are walks winding away into the intricacy of the place, they are walks for you to tread alone. If there are seats in shaded arbors, they are designed for no one's rest but yours. If there are dusky pools of water with lilies afloat, or a playing fountain, or a jet from a mossy lion's mouth, for you the liquid coolness flows. If there are flowers in close companies, or in solitary loveliness, it is to you they offer their cups of intoxicating bloom, it is for you their red hearts beat. If there are pergolas roofed with grape, wistaria, honeysuckle, and clematis, and leading away to white entablatures beyond, for you that garden-palace waits. And if, in the midst of all, a marble sun-dial stands like a lily on its slender stem, the center of a circle of golden lights and poppy-bloom, it is for you the delicate shadow slowly swerves from west to east. Here time exists only for you. If the north wind wakes, or the south wind comes, it is only at your bidding. You are in the Secret Garden, and it is all yours.

For the Secret Garden is the human mind. Deep within the human breast the Secret Garden lies. Small wonder it is hidden; small wonder we have sought for it so long. And the plants that grow there, and the flowers that bloom, are the thoughts of the mind—where the feelings and emotions, love, joy, and peace, anger, grief, and despondency, are the weather of the soul, the sunshine and the clouds, the wind and the rain.

And this mysterious place where our thoughts start and grow and blossom, if it is not wonderful to us, that is simply because we live in it; just as the dwellers in the Alps are seldom inspired to write poetry on the grandeur and the beauty of the mountains round about them. We require a little distance in order to appreciate anything aright.

Now when we pause and turn our attention inward to contemplate and study the place of the mind, the first aspect of it, probably, which will strike us, will be the tropic luxuriance of the life going on there. Thoughts, what a wilderness of thoughts! Tangled thickets of insistent thoughts; intimate bowers of thoughts; overhanging branches of shadowy thoughts; thoughts riotously budding, leafing, flowering, and withering, all the day. Every moment new blades shoot from seeds which our senses sow, or spring from germs which come we know not whence. How they crowd one another, and struggle together up into the consciousness! Give one a momentary advantage, and how it bursts forthwith into its own proper vigor and bloom and scatters its seeds all around to propagate other thoughts!

And the second aspect of the place of thoughts which will meet us, must be its mystery. Although you live in it, it is beyond your understanding or control. As you sit thinking of today's work, or tomorrow's pleasure, why does an unrelated thought suddenly leap into your mind of a word spoken yesterday, or of a face to which you bade farewell last year; the hint of some undreamed-of pain, the reminiscence of some forgotten grief, an unexplainable hope or fear? You do not know.

And if to you it is a mystery, who live within the Secret Garden, what is it to those who live outside? Well do we name it the Secret Garden. And yet, do we not ofttimes hear someone say of another, "I know him, or I know her, like a book"? Yes, like a book in a language we cannot read, high on a shelf which we cannot reach. Only so do we know anyone, though our nearest and dearest, "like a book."

In spite of all our close-knit social and family relationships; in spite of the necessity which compels us to find our happiness in proximity with our human kind; every man and every woman is a sphinx-like mystery to every other, dwelling in a solitude impenetrable and complete. Each man and woman lives his or her real life in a Secret Garden, into which no other soul, as far as we know, can ever come. Over the wall may blow the fragrance of invisible flowers, and out of the gate may be swept garlands of gathered blossoms, fallen leaves, and all the rubbish of a garden, but inside the wall and inside that gate, no other soul may ever enter in. From the time the south wind begins to blow over the buds of a child's life, until the north wind scatters its ripe petals on the grass, all its growth is a mystery. Small wonder we call it the Secret Garden!

Now, although we cannot know another human being's inmost thoughts, except as we guess at them from external signs and ingenious inferences, yet that inner world of thought has an absolutely determinate decision upon every man's rank and every woman's rank in the scale of humanity. The difference between men is altogether and distinctly the difference between the thoughts they think. A man is worth just the thoughts he thinks, no more, no less; every other item of difference between people is delusive or evanescent. By some fortune they may be set in circumstances very contrasting, as we judge circumstances; one man's lot in life may be easy and another man's may be hard; one man may live in luxury and another be poverty-stricken; one man may know little but pleasure and another little but pain;—and yet the real difference between the men who occupy these differing places will be strictly the difference between the thoughts they think.

One man may be so brutish in his conduct, so narrow in his outlook, so bent with despondency, so cloddish in aim, that he is the Man with the Hoe, although he should sit on the throne of the Czar—and it is his thoughts that make him so. And another man may be so free from ignoble slavery of soul, so tolerant and charitable in his views of humanity, so radiant with hope, so loyal to his endeavor after a perfect life, that he has a patent of nobility and belongs to the aristocracy although he digs in a ditch—and it is only his thoughts that make him so.

One day last summer I came upon an ancient negro working in his garden—an open garden beside the road which passers-by might see. And patiently was he laboring among his vegetables, which grew luxuriantly in a soft soil clear of weeds, all as proud of care as if they had been exotic flowers. "You see, sir," he explained, half apologizing for his pains, "you see a man must have something to express himself in."

Quite so! and this old negro's thoughts of perfection were making an artist out of him. We lift our hat to a man like that, perhaps with a silent prayer to God that we may take care of our own garden as he takes care of his.

And so, although a man's thoughts make his real measure, whatever his station in life may be, this is not all of it. Thought has a creative power, perhaps far more than we now dream. It tends inevitably to change outside conditions into harmony with its own quality within. Thought sets a man at work to realize his thought—and so "a man must have something to express himself in." A thought demands something outward, an act or an object, to mould into likeness to itself. Consequently to an eminent degree a man's career is determined and built up by his thoughts. In pre-eminent degree it is colored by them, made beautiful or ugly thereby. Large results are produced only by large and royal

117

thoughts; while low, slavish thoughts put hand-cuffs on a man's wrists and lock him in a chain-gang.

This being true, is there any question in our life anywhere comparable in importance with this: Are we able to think what we desire to think? Are we able to determine the nature and the quality of our thoughts? Our inward value and our outward state both depend upon the kind of thoughts we think; are we able to choose the right sort of thoughts, and then to think these definite thoughts persistently to the exclusion of all harmful, deteriorating, antagonistic thoughts, and so to build character and life into something worth their existence in God's world?

The soul of us, in spite of all experience, makes haste to declare: "Yes, I can think what I please to think." So replies the soul of us, in the manner of a king who is certain of his divine right. The kingdom of thought is, indeed, a territory over which we may claim an absolute control— and it is the only one. In the material world, what with other human claimants, and what with the mischief of chance and the vetoes of fate, we can at best subdue but a very partial dominion over a very small domain. But the region of the mind is all our own; we can think what we please. Here we are Caesar and Pope, pyramid-builders and circumnavigating mariners, with nothing but our own will to limit our ambitions and desires. The outside world is ruled by other lords, with little regard for us; but the inside world must take exactly the shape which we compel it—or allow it—to take.

This is a proud boast of ours—and yet, perhaps, even while we assert it, our thought has shot off like a rocket and scattered itself in a shower of wayward sparks. Did you ever sit down and try to hold your mind upon one fixed point for five minutes? Then you will appreciate better a comparison made by some old Hindoo philosopher. He compared the human mind to a monkey, which is the most restless of all living things. And, as if that were not enough, he compared it to a restless monkey intoxicated with wine. Then, as if that were not enough, he compared it to a

118

restless, intoxicated monkey which has been bitten by a tarantula, whose bite causes its victim to dance himself to death. Such, said the Hindoo sage, is the human mind.

Notwithstanding this, we will never relinquish one iota of our proud claim, even though we know that to accomplish that lordship is the most difficult task in all the world. It is the most difficult; but at the same time it is the enterprise most worthy of our enthusiasm and our arduous toil. We are eager to take lessons in business efficiency, in art, in physical culture, or in craftsmanship. We deem it nothing too laborious to practise scales and gymnastics every day, in order to train our muscles to be obedient and alert. We spend long years in learning a language or a science, in building a home or inventing an airship. Shall we devote less time, less energy, less pains and perseverance, in taming the jungle of our thoughts, wild with weeds and poison-ivy, into the fair garden of our dreams, as if ready for eternity?

Eternity! And the moment we speak this word "eternity," we perceive another light shining upon our Secret Garden —the light of religion. So far we have looked upon it as belonging to this world; we have touched upon the training and cultivation of thought as a means of attaining a certain worthy status in this life below. But religion regards this world as merely a bridge over a mysterious river into another Life beyond. And across this bridge we go, carrying with us for baggage just what we are, nothing more. And we are what we think, nothing more. In other words, to revert to our parable, we carry with us our Secret Garden—that is the one thing we shall not lose, just because it is ourselves. We carry it with us and it also waits for us. And suppose that the Judgment Day shall hold no other doom for us than just these words pronounced from the great white throne: "Go, thou, go and live forever in thy Secret Garden!" Would that be heaven? Or would that be hell? No one on earth can answer—except ourselves.

With such a possibility ahead of us, it would be a practical thing, would it not, to look into our Secret Garden, and gird ourselves to better, to more definite and energetic work there? It surely would.

What we need first in such an endeavor is system. In old times, men and women who made a life-work of religion, had a daily exercise in which they withdrew regularly from all disturbance, and spent a set time in definite directed thought on the highest things. They called this exercise "meditation." And because it grew too artificial, it dropped out of later religious methods, and, to our great loss, has small place now in our busy modern days. But some such method is indispensable to one who is seeking efficiency in thought, just as routine is indispensable in any effective work. Not only religion but business also is a thing of thought. So there are active business-men whom I know who spend the first waking hour of every morning in going over the coming day in thought, preparing themselves to meet its emergencies and to deal with them in a way to make them fit into a perfect life. And they who are acquainted with these men have testified that this morning hour of calm and concentrated thought, seems to clarify and vivify them for the whole working day.

Our first need, then, is systematic determination of the will to control our thoughts. Our second need is to maintain our thoughts upon a high level. Let us keep our thoughts all "purple-clad." Let them become thoughts worthy of having place, as it were, in a palace or in a temple-court.

And this is not impossible, for our religion demands this very thing of us. We are to bring every thought into captivity to the obedience of Christ, declares Saint Paul. And Saint Paul's mystical method of bringing our thoughts into captivity and obedience to Christ, is to invite our Lord himself into our souls to think them. There he becomes the substance of our thought, the very blood of our heart and the Dweller in our soul. It is not in external rules of obedience and in tables of stone that men find life. That was proved in painful experiment long ages ago. But it comes about through a sublime and miraculous thing: it comes about through the establishment of a new spirit of obedience

120

in the center of the forces that obey, and in thinking new thoughts because it is the Spirit of our Lord himself within us who thinks them—the Spirit of our Lord, the Spirit that is the Wind that bloweth where it listeth, and ye hear the sound thereof but cannot tell whence it cometh or whither it goeth.

"So come, thou South Wind, and blow upon my garden!"

But our third need in the development of thought is to detach it from its strong and obstinate adherence to things of earth. It is a human instinct to strike root in the spot of ground on which we happen to dwell, as if to stay forever. And when we dig a grave we often act as if we buried our hearts there. This disposition of ours would be fatal to our soul's welfare if it were allowed;—and so the inspired singer sets these words also into his garden-song:

"Awake, O North Wind, and blow upon my garden!"

But the North Wind! Why the North Wind? The Wind that brings the winter, blowing from the regions of cold and snow and night! Why should we call upon the North Wind, the Wind of pain and death, to blow upon our garden?

It is because, if we would be happy in a world woven of light and shadow, we must never forget the meaning of pain and sorrow. This meaning lies in the fact that life means education and discipline, and it means unceasing movement. All pain can be justified by its effects upon human character, and all death can be justified as being but one step in life's processes. If we shrink from them, it is because we have the wrong thought of pain, and the wrong thought of death. God created this world with pain in it as a constant factor—so can pain be anything else but right? God made death as the close companion of life, hand in hand with it —so can death be anything but beautiful and good? The fault is with our thought of it. We keep looking upon death as the enemy of life, whereas it is Life's own firm but gentle hand.

How dreadful would be a deathless world—a place where no change comes! That would be death indeed—a world which would be a beautiful crystal, a world embalmed in amber, a garden of wax flowers and mournful immortelles! A world without death would be a dead world; a world full of death is a living world—where the Angel of the Tomb is the great white Angel of our desire, to whom we have given two names, calling him Life in the morning sun, and Death at even-tide.

So all our thought should be so much detached from earthly things that we never quite forget how the time shall come when we shall arise and drop them all, and bind our sandals on for travel in a country very far away. And yet it is not so far—less than a single day's journey. "This day," said our Lord, "this day thou shalt be with me in Paradise!"

Now Paradise is a Garden! And oh, that it is a Secret Garden we all know very well who have seen our loved ones disappear within its shade! But it is also a place where God walked in the cool of the day. And if we may but walk there with God, we shall surely there be nearest to all that we have loved and lost.

It was in a Garden, in the old, old story, where God walked in the cool of the day. But in God's life there are no tenses, so that it still is in a Garden where God walks in the cool of the day. A Garden, in our parable, is the place in which thoughts grow and bloom. And the cool of the day is that sweet hour of calm meditation over a measure of work accomplished, when all nature seems to pause beneath the eyes of its Creator. All the world is his Garden, and all the civilizations of all the people in it—their social institutions, their philosophy, their science, their art—all these things are but thought-systems, each one of which gives its recognition of the Presence of God, as God, the Supreme Thinker, passes by to overlook the products of thought.

It is in the sphere of thought where God walks, and it is there that we shall meet him, if we meet him at all. Look not for him in the whirlwind and the fire, miraculous outward signs! His still, small voice is only heard within, in the shaded alleys of the heart. Let us learn to listen; let us learn to answer; let us learn to meet him there. What romance of earth can match this romance of the soul, as it keeps a tryst with God!

The leaves of the Garden all hang motionless, the flowers all wait expectant. The thin shadow of the sun-dail points to the east, and marks the cool of the day. A Guest is coming to sup with us—so wondrously intimate is God with the human soul! A Guest is coming to sup with us. And as we stand waiting at the arbor door, we see all the vicissitudes of earth—all its joy and pain, all its beauty and its woe—bearing upon this ultimate hour. And so, looking before and after, we may lift a humble, happy voice and sing our garden-song in its entirety:

"Awake, O North Wind, and come, thou South Wind,
    and blow upon my garden,
    that the spices thereof may flow out;

    that my Beloved may come into his garden,
    and eat his precious fruits!"

(1912.)

CHAPTER 15

The Burning Bush

"And the Angel of Jehovah appeared unto Moses in a flame of fire out of the midst of a bush; and he looked and behold, the bush burned with fire and the bush was not consumed. And God called unto him out of the midst of the bush and said, 'The place whereon thou standest is holy ground.'"

Exodus iii:2-5.

IT IS TOLD OF William Blake, the poet called insane because all things to him made poetry; it is told of him that he once went out into the morning with a scientific friend to watch the sun rise. "Tell me," said William Blake to his friend, "what is it that you see?"

"I see," was the reply, "I see a red, flat, circular disc, perhaps half a degree in diameter, which appears to be rising very slowly above the horizon."

"Is that all?" asked William Blake.

"That is all," replied his friend; "and now, in your turn, tell me what *you* see."

"I see," said William Blake, "I see the whole sky filled with angels and archangels, and they all are singing 'Glory to God in the highest.'"

And beyond all question, William Blake's account of this sunrise, or of any sunrise, was far the more true. Everything depends upon the sight of the one who looks at it. When Moses stood before the burning bush, the other shepherds, we have no reason to believe, saw anything more than a common bush; they perceived no fire, they heard no voice.

124

But Moses saw that bush, that it was full of living fire, and out of it he heard a Voice declaring the presence of God.

Indeed, a burning bush is not so rare a thing. Take any bush whatever, a barberry bush for example, and go out to watch it every day from spring to fall. It is only a tangle of dry and apparently dead branches at first. But presently green tips begin to appear all through it, like green star-dust. Then little tassels of pale yellow flowers burst forth all over the bush, filling it with pale yellow flame. These fade away, and leave the bush a mass of green foliage, or green fire, throughout the summer-time. At length the green leafage burns itself out and turns to dull red, like a heap of smoldering coals which drop away presently in dull ashes—and behold, the bush is now full of clusters of crimson berries, to burn all the winter through in the midst of the snow, and to it through all the wintry weather the birds will come for food and for cheer.

Is not that a burning bush? Is it not full of mysterious fire? No, it is only alive, we say. Only alive! And not only the barberry bush, but countless bushes everywhere, and countless plants great and small, and countless trees throughout the world, they all are only alive! As if life itself were not a fire, most beautiful and wonderful, declaring the Presence of God! For all nature exhibits the astonishing spectacle of things consuming and yet never consumed, forever dying and yet forever born again, through the circles of the years. So that it is not so far for us to go to see in all nature one magnificent, wide-spreading bush, around which all men, shepherds, tend their sheep, while it burns with fire and is not consumed, and utters a voice which declares that all the earth around is holy ground because of the Presence of God.

But the burning bush of nature is not the only thing that presents visibly the progressive changes of an invisible force. Take the career of a man, every man, which is altogether analogous to that of a bush. He appears as a child at first, a bud as it were, springing out of mystery, with all sorts of activities and possibilities folded up in him. Of all interesting things, what is more absorbing than to watch that child's life unfold from its spring to its autumn! The quick development of physical instincts and maneuvers; the eager curiosity to know about everything; the active imitation of all human doings that he sees; the curious appearance of shreds of old heredities; the expansion of mental qualities; the passionate ferments and ecstasies and aspirations of youth; the outreach upon the world, to build a hearth-fire and a roof-tree, and to make a place of value among other men; the up-reach, too, towards that invisible sky which is above our blue sky, manifesting this up-reach in a religion of some kind; then the gradual ripening of action into reflection and thought, and the final resignation of life into the place of mystery whence it came—is not a man's life a burning bush, full of mysterious fire?

And all this may be seen in any man's life, in countless men's lives throughout countless ages. So humanity itself is one vast burning bush, always burning and never consumed, revealing the Presence of God.

But man's individual life is not the only human thing that shows development of tendencies and qualities in a series of change. A society of men does the same. The history of a race of men seems to exhibit a cycle of changes analogous to those of a bush or a man: a start, a growth, a climax, a decline. It has to fight incessantly for its place in the world. It slowly unfolds a government; it slowly evolves a religion; and it blossoms at length into creations of art, sculpture or painting or music or literature, creations of beauty which are the product of men's living together, the consummate flower of human feeling and thought. And then, in due time, it slides down the arc of its destiny, and whatever it has of civilization colors like the autumn leaves and drops—to be kept pressed in museum books by other civilizations to follow. This sequence seems inevitable; and Macaulay's New Zealander, who shall stand on London Bridge to gaze on the ruins of St. Paul's, may perhaps sail still farther west to dig up antiquities in New York.

Is not all this complex display, rooted in darkness and in tragedy and culminating in beauty, is it not a burning bush, full of mysterious fire? All history, testing on a grand scale the worthiness and unworthiness of all systems and creeds, is but a splendid burning bush, revealing the Presence of God.

This, then, seems to be the meaning of the burning bush: wherever life is, God is; and, as far as we know, life is everywhere. We see its marvelous operations, never ceasing on every side of us, without stopping to think that it is marvelous. Wherever we discern change and motion, there we see life in action: in nature, in man, in all the intricate results of human thought and genius. But it is the products of life, only, that are in sight; we never see the base out of which they spring. We cannot see the Hands that weave the gorgeous tapestry which keeps sliding, inch by inch, out of the sounding looms of life. We cannot see the Pen which keeps writing leaf after leaf of the manuscript which is our world—a manuscript illuminated, as the old monks' work was, in cunning devices of rich color and gold.

Did you ever hold a match over a lamp and see a flame leap down presently out of the air upon the wood? Even so life slips out of nothingness, and sets the world aflame, bush and bird and the heart of man.

We call this mystery *Life,* to give it a name; but why not call it God? We grope after God, we plead with him to reveal himself to us—and all the while the barberry bushes bloom, and the cry of brothers down in Egypt afflicts our ears, and it is only Moses, the earnest-hearted shepherd, who sees that the bush is all aflame with the Presence of God, and that humanity's call is his Voice.

This being so, all life revealing the Presence of God, and life being everywhere, then all ground is holy ground. We have got into the habit of thinking that the church is more holy than other buildings, that one day out of the seven is more holy than all other days; the Christian cemetery was named "God's acre," as if all acres did not belong to God. And in old times when men were said to enter the "religious" life, what do you suppose was meant? Why, of all things, that they separated themselves from other men and went apart into a monastery!

Are such distinctions true? No; if God is present everywhere, that spot is always most holy to us where, at any given time, our duty lies. Our duty is the burning bush, and God is there. The religious life is the every-day life. So, the kitchen floor is holy ground, and the garden-patch, and the yard where children play, and the factory where men work, and the city streets and the country roads on which we walk; the office, the shop, the harvest-field—where shall we look for a place which is not holy ground? Where shall we look for a place which is common or unclean?

We begin by calling one day holy, in order that by and by all days may be holy days. We begin by calling a church holy, in order that after a while we may make every house God's house. Unholy things may be done in holy places; we may be blind to the fire in the bush. But that does not alter facts: God is everywhere, and all we need is the power to see him where he is.

This modern age of ours is perhaps the only age in which a sense of divinity of some sort has not been mixed with a sense of the world. Every nation and every tribe, every little town on mountain or sea-shore, had its god or its gods. Men often worshiped the sun, moon, and stars, and no wonder. They often worshiped fire, and no wonder. They worshiped trees, or divinities that dwelt in them, waters, and rocks, representing mysterious powers. Nature was full of personality, with ears that could hear and eyes that could see and a will that could act, somehow incorporated within it. You could pray to the winds, and pour libations of wine into the waves, and when you walked in the woods there was quite a fair chance that you might catch a glimpse of a nymph flying into a brook, or a dryad melting into the trees, or hear the great god Pan playing on his sweet reed-pipe.

And even after Christianity came, nature was no less

alive. Down to the birth of science, two centuries ago, thereabout, people thought of the world as still full of nature-spirits, mostly devils, no doubt, making of nature a thing of dread and fear, but still alive.

But we have lost their sense of a living nature. Perhaps for one reason, because we have such a new sense of machinery. We have learned how to harness the old god of Fire, and how to steal and utilize the thunderbolts of Jupiter, and how to set the water-nymphs to tending spindles, and Pan to running a lumber-mill, and the Muses to editing illus-trated magazines, and the Titans to digging canals, and the great god Thor to forging shafts for battleships. And we have learned how to combine wheels and pulleys and levers and a million quick steel fingers in such a marvelous way that more cloth is woven, and more metal wrought, and more stone quarried and cut, and more merchandise carried to the ends of the earth in one of our days than all the men and all the canals and all the ships of ancient time could have woven and wrought and quarried and carried in a cycle of years.

So it is small wonder if we have come to think of nature itself, so contrived in regular courses and intricate play and interplay, as a kind of vast machine; the circling seasons revolving wheels, and the rolling stars a great celestial clock-work, and the growth of things—barberry bushes, trees, ani-mals, and men, with all the doings of them—as simply products of machinery, running out of spouts into appropriate bins. And nature is dead.

But more important still in our changed way of regarding nature is our widened conception of law. Science has taught us to expect unvarying results from unvarying causes, and has named their connection "Law." The old idea of nature allowed constantly the interruptions of changing purposes in the divine Mind which somehow was hidden in the forces of nature. By prayer and sacrifice to the proper deities, you could ward off storm and disease, and invoke health and fair weather. Anything unusual in the course of things was always to be explained by some secret change in the counsels

129

of the gods—which might be discovered, perchance, from the voice of the wind in the oak-trees or from the flight of birds.

But science has blown all such fancies far enough away. Law reigns, silent, inevitable, and unchanging; and whatever occurs that seems exceptional is ever to be ascribed to the restoration of an equilibrium in the steady processes of Law. So absolute is this sphere held to be, that man, especially the scientific man, is often found declaring that human life, in all its acts, is simply the result of forces that play upon it, and therefore is never to be praised or blamed.

Now, true as this new conception of nature may be, and it is so true that we are staking more and more upon it, yet a system of balanced laws is not all we want of nature. Something is missing out of it. It may arouse our wonder, or our prudence, or our terror, but it is no longer personal to us; it is no longer company for us. We may admire it as a machine; we may enjoy it as a moving-picture show; but we have a sense of loss. For a system of laws is inanimate. And nature is dead.

And so the different parts of our world do not fit together; we live in fragments. We are restless and dissatisfied. We seek in excitement the consciousness of life which we crave. We can never go fast enough, nor travel far enough, in our hunt for something to fill the sense of lack within. We may not realize it, but that lack is a sense of comradeship with the universe—with God.

What we need is a theory of life which will unify all sides of it; which will embrace at once the conception of law and the conception of a living universe whose thoughts are laws. We need to feel ourselves a part of the universe, closely akin to it; so that our heart beats in its heart, and our nerves thrill in its nerves; so that it suffers when we suffer, and it is glad when we are glad. We need to realize that we are not isolated human beings impotently struggling against Fate, but that Fate is working in us and for us; we are a very part of Fate. The greatest misfortune that can befall a man is to come to feel that he is an orphan in the universe—it is the source of all degradation and despair. We need to realize that we are a part of the history of all men, and that that history is not a confusion of aimless and unrelated conflicts, but one long campaign for one final victory.

September, 1914.

CHAPTER 16

Faith

ONE DAY, ON Gambier Hill, a young man who had grown up carefully protected from modern thought made a momentous discovery. It suddenly was revealed to him that certain materials built into the structure of our sacred book, the Bible, are no longer taken to be historical events, no longer conceived of as crude history. That they stand, immutably, for spiritual events, and explorations of the soul, the young man was not yet able to grasp, and his first exclamation of astonishment and dismay was a pathetic one:

"Alas!" he declared, "you are taking away my faith!"

One can have nothing but sympathy with an expostulation like that, although it betrays a misconception as to what faith really is, and the foundations upon which it rests. It is as if a man had lived only in the night, and had moved about always in the pale light of stars, with their rising and setting, as seen from his threshold, essential epochs in his universe. At last a dawn approaches, spreads up over the sky, and absorbs the constellations, one by one, into its deeper and wider effulgence.

"Alas!" the man cries out at the dawn, "you are taking away my light!"

That young man on Gambier Hill represented far more than he knew. He represented ten thousand years of history. He was a young man ten thousand years old. It was he whose mournful cry was heard by the sailors, ages ago, upon the Aegean Sea, "Great Pan is dead!" His voice is always the voice of that which is in the pain of passing, giving place to something changed. His voice is the voice of every human heart, at some stage of its career. "Alas!" we all of us exclaim, as we see things which we have held fundamental and sacred, melting into new forms under the processes of time:

"Alas!" we cry, "you are taking away our earth!"

But our consolation is always at our hand. It is to face bravely the change, and analyze what is changing. And then we discover that the essential things are not changing, but only the forms in which we saw them.

And when we have a sudden fear that our faith is shaken toward ruin, it is a good thing to examine that which we call our faith, and define it to ourselves, and try to find out what there is in it which makes it vulnerable. Does it really lie at the mercy of historians and scientists? If it is weak, is there any method within our own power by which to make it strong?

What *is* faith, anyway?

Faith is always fundamental in any thought about religion; so that it is important to have a clear idea of its meaning. Now, although it is not used to denote one clear thing always, yet there are three points always more or less assumed in connection with it.

First: Faith lies at the foundation of any religious life. Second: Faith is something which every human being may have. Third: It discredits any human being not to have faith.

But it is not used to mean one clear thing always; usually three very different aspects of the word are entangled in our thought, and blended in our speech.

First, Faith may mean simple trust in God—the realization of a personal relationship. This does lie at the roots of an established religious life, but it is not energetic enough to represent the faith which moves mountains; and, again, there is a question whether every human being is able to attain it all at once. The man who is caught in a spider's web of doubts is not much helped by being told simply to have trust in God.

Again the word *faith* stands, and has long stood, for a creed, a theological scheme, a numbered and lettered system

133

of doctrines. This is something which belongs to the trained intellect, to the reason; and a man, in his intellect, may hold it in its entirety, and still be a pagan. He may repeat his creed every day in the church, and go home to a private shrine dedicated to all the twelve gods. This is common enough. Important as a body of doctrine may be, it is not large enough to fill up the meaning of the living word *faith*.

Again the term is used to mean a mystical power which dwells in the very act of believing; so that miraculous results may be obtained in the material world, if we can only believe that those results will follow. This may be true; we know so very little of the power which the strong human soul may exert upon spiritual forces behind material things, that it would be presumptuous in us to deny the utmost that may be claimed for it. But this much is matter of experience; that such power does not lie in the control of the ordinary man—as we all of us can testify who have wrestled with an Angel of Calamity coming in at our door, and suffered bitter defeat there.

What we want is the definition of a faith which is at once the entrance into the religious life; which every modern man is able immediately to exert, and which immediately and always condemns him if he does not so exert it.

In the first verse of the eleventh chapter of the Epistle to the Hebrews, we find such a definition. "Faith," so the inspired author says, "faith is the substance of things hoped for, the evidence of things unseen."

We live in a universe of things unseen. To begin with, life itself is unseen; we see only what life does to visible things. Beauty is unseen; something wonderful shines out through form and color and sound, but that is all that we know about it. All nature flows out from sources unseen, and drops into a gulf beyond our sight. Our very bodies are made and unmade by forces which we cannot see. Unseen purposes are all the time doing something to our thoughts and acts, and to our ways and wills. Our nearest friends presently pass us by and pass on, and become themselves a part and portion of the unseen. History itself has been likened to a carpet woven by invisible hands on an invisible loom.

Now what is demanded of us in such a universe of the unseen? We are all given some glimmering sense of the presence of things unseen, and we are given a human will to act in some relationship with them. We are asked to test these things unseen, to prove these things unseen, by willing to act upon the assumption that these things unseen exist. To act, that is the vital requirement; a worthy task to lay upon a man; a task fundamental in his development, a task which any man, which any most ignorant, most tempted, most miserable, doubting, despairing man is able to attempt, a task which it is an eternal discredit to him if he does not attempt. And this faith we may name the faith of the working hypothesis.

We all know what a working hypothesis is. A certain state of things is assumed to be true, in order to form a basis for certain operations; then, in proportion as these operations work out successfully on the lines of our hypothesis, we conclude that our assumption corresponds with actual fact. In other words, we test, we prove, things unseen by their effect in things seen. And the process, according to our text, is faith.

We first learn to apply this method to our every-day life. Every man wants a healthy body and an alert mind; he wants activity and satisfaction and happiness; he wants to strive and to get ahead and to excel. But not by accident are these things gained and kept; they are earned, and guarded when earned. And they are earned and they are guarded by going into partnership with invisible co-laborers, the laws of nature. By observation and by induction we infer a probable set of conditions underlying health and success in this life. They are not over-evident and absolutely convincing, in the arrogant assertion of things immediately seen; men are forever tempted to rely upon lucky chances, and upon some fortunate possession of an Aladdin's lamp.

But here is a life to be lived; and how shall we live it?

If we are worth anything at all, we resolve to follow resolutely the most probable roads we can discover to worthy living. This attitude is fundamental, and leads us to perceive that the most probable roads always seem to be moral roads. And so we take as a working hypothesis the assumption that moral roads are the right roads for us, and we proceed to live perseveringly upon that assumption. This is a kind of living which any man has it within his own power to choose for himself; and it is a discredit to him if he does not so choose it. Thus is faith applied to conduct.

The next great fact of life is death. It is rather the fashion not to speak of this more often than necessary, but it is a coward's fashion. Since it is the most inevitable thing we know, we ought to face it bravely, and to take it into account in our conduct of life. What we continuously see is a procession of living beings like ourselves, and many of them dearer to us than ourselves, disappearing into the place of things unseen; but it is the place whence life itself has come, along with beauty, truth, and goodness, and all the potencies behind this visible world.

And as our eyes follow this vanishing procession with love and desire, we feel an energy arising in our souls to deny that death ends all. It inspires us to take as a working hypothesis of life the assumption that death is but a doorway in a House of Life, a Father's House of many mansions, and we will proceed to act upon this assumption. The best kind of life in this world cannot be best, unless it is lived in the hope of another. To act upon this assumption, to live as if it were true, this is within every man's power, and it is a discredit to him if he does not so act and if he does not so live. Thus is faith applied to the fact of death.

The next great fact of life is God. Our tendency is perhaps not to doubt nor deny the existence of God. His name, heard from earliest childhood, becomes interwoven in our thought, and a part of the texture of our mind. If we speculate about him, the farther we project our speculations into the region of things unseen, the more we feel the necessity of a unifying mystery there. But it is never by thinking that we find out God. We may postulate him, and define him, but he ever remains, to thought, that which is most unseen—the innermost essence of things unseen.

What we crave is a Personal Sympathy in the unseen. The question of all questions most important to us is this: Is the Universe friendly to us? It is the omnipresent tragedy in creation which makes us doubt. Not only vast war, but the dead sparrow in the woods suggests to us forever that God the Infinite is also God the Infinite Indifference.

But such a thought is fatal to our soul's growth. The soul withers under it, and sinks to the level of things seen to fill the vacuity of its unfulfilled desires. We know that. And so we will prove a God of love by living as if a God of love exists. This much is possible for any man to attempt, and it is to his discredit if he fails to make this supreme adventure of faith. Thus we apply faith to our idea of God.

The next great fact of life, in Christian countries, is the Gospel. In truth, the Gospel gathers up into itself the questions of conduct, of immortality, and of God. For in it there is presented the story of a perfect man, one who solved, with unerring instinct, every problem of human conduct; one who claimed that human life, taking hold upon divine life, is carried over by it across death into immortality; and, finally, one who claimed so to represent God Himself to men, that men, reading the record of him, are compelled to say, "Yes, God is like that!"

Now the most significant possession in a man's soul is the picture there of the man that he would like to be. It is an absolute obligation resting upon every man's conscience, just because he is man, to become the highest kind of man that he is able in any way to conceive of. Here in the Gospel stands that ideal for him. There are problems, intellectual, which a man may stop to dally over—but they are beside the mark. Sweep them all away. You can prove that Jesus the Christ lived and lives, that he was and is, all that he claimed to be; you can prove it all—but only in one way.

Make a working hypothesis of his life; assume its truth, and then act upon the ground that it is true, making its standards our standards, and its hope our hope, and its conception of God our own conception of Him. We take to be the pattern of our own life the best pattern of life we know, and this every man has it within his power to do. And it is a discredit to him if he does not do it.

Thus is faith applied to the Gospel; a kind of faith which everyone may have. Not everyone can hold, honestly, all the items of an intellectual creed. Not everyone can experience an emotional faith. But the faith of a working theory, the faith which is based upon will, this every human being with a will can have.

And now begins the miracle. As soon as one acts, processes start invisibly, following the lines of the act. The conduct which is true to a principle, begins to make real to the mind that principle's truth. The life which assumes immortality, begins to have a sense of a wider horizon and a freer air. The soul which acts in loyalty to a God whom it does not yet know begins certainly to feel him drawing near. And the man who swears allegiance to a Friendship in the Gospel story which he does not yet realize, presently raises no more his old complaint that the Universe is not friendly to him. For it has begun to have a heart.

There is nothing new in all this. "Live the life and you shall know the doctrine," was a promise spoken long ago. Live mentally in the company of things hoped for, and soon you begin to feel the substance, the essence, the influence, of things hoped for welling up in the secret places of your thought. Faith becomes the evidence of things unseen.

Kenyon College Chapel
January 28, 1917.

CHAPTER 17

The Formation of Conscience

A LONG TIME AGO, before any kind of men had appeared in the trees and in the caves, strange races of animals lived on this earth. Monstrous animals, most like the pictures which children draw on their slates, wallowed and floundered in the marshes, flapped low and heavily through the air, or dragged enormous tails along the shores of the warm primeval seas. Imagine toad-like creatures as big as an ox; flying creatures with bat wings like schooner sails; huge crawling creatures half bird, and huge flying creatures half lizard—you could hardly make them more fantastic than the truth. It was as if Nature, still a child, were playing with her clay, experimenting whimsically with the vague creative dreams that she felt stirring in her mind.

We know these grotesque beasts from broken skeletons dug out of the rocks, pieced together and set up in museum halls; sometimes only a bone or two, but providing implications by which skilful anatomists reconstruct the entire frame. Strange names the scientific recollections of these strange animals bear, moving ponderously in geological books as their possessors moved ponderously on earth so long ago: the Ichthyosaurus and the Megalosaurus, the Dinoceras, the Pterodactyl, and the Ornithoscelidan.

These malformed and disproportioned beasts have long since disappeared, as Evolution recorded their grade of accomplishment and then threw them aside in the scrap-heap. But one wonders whether the monstrous lop-sided souls of them, dispossessed of dwelling-place, may not have taken refuge in the bodies of men, when men arrived, so that they still pursue abnormal activities upon the earth: strange souls still deserving their strange primeval names, though masquerading now in human ones. Perhaps their roarings and hootings may still be heard in the mortal battles of these beast-souls in our own century: sea-beasts and air-beasts and terrible scale-armored land-beasts, renewing more vastly in men their ancient war.

If we were able to see souls as we are able to see bodies, doubtless just such monstrous growths would still be visible in the jungles and caverns of earth; enormous egotisms and ambitions armed with teeth and claws; bulky selfishnesses spreading leathery wings; over-grown passions stretching up long serpent necks; extraordinary combinations of perverse development producing dragon-like creatures of ugliness and dread. So that even that most divine thing, the human Conscience, might appear as a great vampire, drinking the blood of men, and hanging head-downward in the dimness of a cave.

This is a startling fancy; for what is the Conscience, if there is a possibility of its being a dangerous thing, hanging by hooked wings in a dark cavern, upside down?

We are accustomed to think of the Conscience as a Divine Voice speaking in the very center of our soul, pointing out to us what is right and what is wrong, and commanding us to do what is right. It is a voice whose decisions are ultimate; when they are given they over-ride every outside command whatsoever. We feel that in a crisis we might even refuse to obey the ordinances of any society or government, and be justified in our refusal by simply taking the ground that God, through our Conscience, has made a higher demand.

But when we hear men declaring solemnly that they take up arms and wage war at the summons of Conscience, and other men declaring quite as solemnly that they will not fight at all because Conscience forbids, we realize that the judgments of Conscience are not incontestable, are not absolute, since we see them pulling in opposite ways. And we are impelled to ask, in perplexity: "How much, then, of the Conscience is divine? How far is the Conscience infallible?

How far is the Conscience subject to the Will? How far are we responsible for the decisions of our Conscience?"

A while ago I found in a certain book a phrase which was unfamiliar and even startling. The author spoke of the efforts that he made "in the formation of his conscience." The *formation* of conscience. We often hear of the "formation of character"; but what is the "formation of conscience"?

The phrase will do for a text, by making it sum up the ideas implied in certain expressions used to describe a conscience in the New Testament—such as "a weak conscience"; "a defiled conscience"; "a conscience seared with a hot iron"; "hearts washed from an evil conscience"; and "a conscience cleansed from dead works by the blood of Christ to serve the living God."

These are expressions which imply that the conscience may be imperfect, that the conscience may be entirely wrong, that the state of the conscience may be determined by the will, and, above all, that a wrong conscience may be made right through the processes of religion. So these ideas we will gather together under the head of the phrase above quoted: "the formation of conscience."

Our proposition is this: that the conscience is still of divine origin and authority, in spite of the fact that it may be weak and defiled and perverted. Although it is formed within us, it grows and develops from a divine germ. It still is a divine voice within the human breast. But what it says is this, and only this: "Do right!" And we may describe the entire moral history of every man, and the entire moral history of the human race, in the shape of a little drama, a dialogue between Every-man and his Conscience.

Conscience begins in a whisper: "Do right."

Everyman asks, in much perplexity: "What is right?"

Conscience replies: "Go and find out."

And so Everyman goes and inquires and experiments and struggles and suffers and thinks and at last decides:

"*This* is right."

And Conscience commands: "Then do that."

But Everyman, just because he is a growing, developing creature, making his growth through repeated experiment and long toil, may be mistaken in any given conclusion about what is right or wrong. He very often has been that.

In the first place, our sense of what is right and wrong is influenced greatly by the opinion of the community in which we are born and grow up. Much of this opinion is inevitably true, the inheritance of accumulated wisdom and experience of the past. But some of it is temporary and local. We are sometimes taught a conscientious distinction at one period of life which our developing reason may afterward reverse. Perhaps we all of us have considered certain things to be sins in our childhood, in which we see no harm now; an experience which leads us justly to suspect that certain things may now seem wrong to us which a clearer light in the future may reveal as things indifferent. And conversely, it is very possible, it is very probable, that much of our present living and thinking has a moral significance which we do not now appreciate, and which will be felt to be wrong when we grow more sensitive to right and wrong. So the fact stands out that the boundary line of conscience is a changing one, taking the general direction of the common conscience of the people among whom we live.

In the second place, Everyman's endeavor to find out what is right is always handicapped by what he prefers to find right—that is, by his selfish desires. We want our own way to be the right way. We want our own pleasure to have the approval of our conscience. We want to be worldly, and yet we want at the same time to feel unworldly and saintly. We want our greed and our self-love and our harsh treatment of other people to be labeled prudence and self-respect and justice, so that we may pass unsuspected and unchallenged through the custom-house of conscience—smugglers of righteousness. We want our faultfinding and our officious meddling in other people's affairs to be taken as a godly zeal for reform. We want to be disagreeable—for your own good.

We want to peddle scandal—in the interests of truth. We want our bad temper to be called righteous indignation. We want our lying to be called tact. We want our sensuality to be called natural instincts. And Everyman compels his conscience to agree to all these things. Small chance has the conscience to flow forth pure, when it has to filter through our selfishness. Probably few of us there are who cannot recall, in hours of honest self-examination, some selfish act, or some mean act, or some cruel and unjust act, which we have deliberately done in the sacred name of conscience.

And a third difficulty is the difficulty of reasoning out, into practical application to our every-day life, the rules of conduct which have been delivered to us from the past. The Ten Commandments seem to be very elementary, the A-B-C's of morality; but the words they spell grow more and more extensive as our moral nature becomes more and more mature. For instance, where are the graven images which we shall not bow down before? By any chance have we set them up in secret shrines in our own house? Are we using a holy Name in an unholy way, stamping the Name of God upon things belonging to Satan? How shall we observe a Sabbath-day—what is our "sabbath-day," indeed? Does it fall under the freedom of the Gospel, left to each man's conscience how he shall keep it holy? To honor father and mother, how far in principle does this command extend in a democratic state? Are we committing murder every day, stabbing men with secret daggers in our thought? Are we stealing every day—other things than money, in other ways than by picking pockets? Are we bearing false witness against our neighbor, even by telling what we call the truth about him? And what is the dead-line between covetousness and that desire which is the lawful spur to energy? This was the fatal knife, we remember, which pierced the conscience of that Saul who became Saint Paul: "Thou shalt not desire."

All these are questions of the conscience, but that they are difficult to solve in any final way is demonstrated by the diversity of opinion and practice. But there are questions more

143

difficult still, as we proceed to search the Scriptures for the instruction—for the formation—of conscience. The first and great commandment, "Thou shalt love the Lord thy God with all thy heart and mind and soul"—this is an absolutely unqualified command; but how shall we apply it, how are we applying it, in its countless points of contact with life? What does it mean, even, to love God?

Or the second commandment, like unto the first, "Thou shalt love thy neighbor as thyself"—what does it involve to love even our friends, as ourselves? And then to love our enemies, those who slander us and wrong us, what does that involve? Shall we endure them patiently, always turning the other cheek? Just at what point may we strike back—"for their own good"?

All this is only the beginning of questionings; and there is no Mount Sinai to answer them. They have to be worked out with prayer and fasting, with thought and patient experiment. That is the way we have to learn in God's college; it is the method of God's revelation, the method of Experience.

Taking it altogether, then, we may compare that which we call our conscience to a magnet, whose attractive force has drawn a mass of things around it, iron filings, metal scraps, and rusty nails. So the soul of us has a magnet within it, vitalized with a divine attractive force. But it draws to itself many things which have little that is divine in them: selfish desires, old prejudices, and strange superstitions, and even such things as envies and angers and hates. And this conglomerate mass of things we name our Conscience!

And it *is* our conscience; all that is alive in it is our conscience: an original divine impulse at its center, an impulse to find and to do the right, by which we bring the knowledge we have to bear upon questions of right and wrong. But since our knowledge may be inadequate, and our reason may have used a false logic, and our purposes may be twisted by selfishness, it appears that our conscience cannot be regarded as infallible.

We must follow our conscience, but at the same time we must be held responsible for its movements, as far as we are responsible for our knowledge and our reason. And in a democracy we have also a community-conscience to reckon with; our conscience may oblige us to stand out against the community-conscience—but then let it be upon our own feet. It is cowardice, if not blasphemy, to throw the responsibility for a possibly perverted conscience upon God.

Now since we take it that the formation of conscience is subject, in large degree, to our own will, the most practical question arises of how to form it. The method is simple enough to state, but at the same time it is broad enough and solid enough for the foundations of Solomon's Temple.

There are three elements in the method. The first is that of purpose. We must resolve that the right is the pearl of great price, to be gained at any cost. This is absolutely fundamental. We may even say that it is one expression of the first and great commandment, to love God with all one's heart and mind and soul. It surely is the first step in the true love of God, determination to know what is his will, for his will is the Right.

The second element is that of search. We must look everywhere and always for indications and manifestations of the right, to build them into our own conceptions of Right. In the pages of our holy books; in the tides of human history; in the wonderful discoveries of science; in the harmonious revelations of beauty, in music and poetry and art; in the lives of the saints; in the hearts of our friends; in the highest longings and aspirations of our own souls. And the more we look, the more we shall see; until the whole world appears full of the operations of the right, busily weaving order out of chaos, and holiness out of sin.

And the third element is that of action. We must establish it as a law of our life to make every thought and every word and every deed of ours a right thought and right word and right deed. Never to make a compromise with what seems wrong, never to be disloyal to what seems right; to watch our motives sharply, to see our duty clearly, and then to act decisively—like an arrow from Saint Michael's bow.

Now two steep precipices drop, one on this side and one on that side of the narrow path of conscience.

The first is the Precipice of Indifference. To hear the judgment of conscience and then to disregard it, this is to weaken the conscience; over against its formation, this is the beginning of its disintegration. Whether we plead that we are too weak to follow out its demands—the pitiful plea of the spineless—or whether we boldly declare that we must have our own way and take the risk, the result is just the same: a gradual indifference to the distinctions of right and wrong, a gradual obliteration of conscience, and a gradual relapse into purely material living, where the tyranny of sense supplants the gentle urge of conscience, and the balanced peace of Eden becomes Babylon and Tyre.

And the second precipice is deeper and steeper yet. If there is a Bottomless Pit, down into it this descent goes. For it is the Perversion of Conscience. It is to establish the habit of transposing right and wrong; calling right whatever wrong things we desire to have or to do, and using ingenious arguments to make them fall within the permissions of conscience. It is a process of self-deception, a deliberate substitution of falsehood for truth; worse than that, it is naming falsehood truth, cloaking it with the garments of truth, and proceeding to live as if it were the truth. So, finally, for that cheating and cheated soul, so work creation's laws, the falsehood becomes the truth, and the whole world becomes false.

And this must be the terrible Unpardonable Sin, the Sin against the Holy Spirit, which our Lord declared may not be forgiven, neither in this world nor in the next. For when a soul's standards are reversed, when wrong becomes right to it, and when right becomes wrong to it—if such a state may be imagined—there is no sense of a need of forgiveness; the Holy Spirit's light is seen as darkness, the soul hanging thus, bat-like, head down, in the dim cavern of its own creation and choice.

We hear a great cry for peace in the world. The whole world is longing for peace; it is praying for peace; it is fighting a great war for peace—so it says. And yet peace there shall never be. It is not the way of this world. We may change the battle-field, but we cannot stop the war. We may sign treaties of peace on one frontier, but new foes invade on another, forever. Man was born to be a soldier; it is the business of his life to forge swords, and then to wield them. There is no escape for him—except to become not-man. He may prefer to drag a chain and be a slave—and still his arrogant masters compel him to fight in battles not his own. He may migrate to a South-Sea Island, dreaming there to eat the lotus through the golden afternoons, and to repel every enemy by conscientiously objecting to their approach —and still he must fight, or die.

The very flag we follow we ourselves, with difficulty, must weave. The very lantern which guides us through the dim trenches of life, we ourselves, with difficulty, must light. Yet we need not fear that we are left alone, without God, to meet our fate, to fight through life, and fighting still, to die. For God himself is in the strife, he is a very part of the strife, since God himself has become Man. Not for nothing is God named the Lord of Hosts, the God of battles; not for nothing was it said that there was war in heaven. To live is to fight; to grow is to strive; there is no peace but death. All that we are that is worth anything, is something that we have won.

So let us listen again to the dialogue between Everyman and his Conscience, for it is the drama of life.

Conscience, in a whisper, speaks: "Do right."

Everyman, much troubled, speaks: "What is right?"

Conscience answers, inexorably: "Go and find out."

And Everyman goes and returns at last and says: "I have sought and fought and suffered and thought, and I believe, I believe, that *this* is right."

And Conscience says: "Then do that."

Kenyon College Chapel
(1917-18.)

CHAPTER 18

Honor

"Again, the kingdom of heaven is like unto a merchant-man, seeking goodly pearls;
"Who, when he had found one pearl of great price, went and sold all that he had, and bought it."
                                        Matt. xiii:45-46.

IT WAS IN a crowded railroad car, one winter's day, where miscellaneous wanderers—some of them merchants, perhaps, seeking goodly pearls—were packed together in the temporary intimacy of travel. Four of the men, to relieve the tediousness of the journey, had thrown two seats together and were busy playing cards. The game made a center of excitement in the car. Other men gathered around, and stood watching the vicissitudes of the play, adding their comments and their jokes to the running talk of the players. Noisy disputes ofttimes arose, and it was in the course of one of these disputes that something happened. Above the confusion of voices one voice suddenly sounded clear. Through the heavy, tainted air, filled with protests and recriminations and oaths, a shining phrase fell—like a goodly pearl. "Upon my honor!"—that is what the voice said—"Upon my honor!" And straightway, at that magic word "honor" the sides of the narrow railroad car began expanding east and west, and its low and dingy roof was swelling out into a dome. And I saw men facing each other with pistols and swords, death in their eyes, to defend or to avenge their honor. There moved before my memory splendid tales of what men have dared and suffered and sacrificed, for honor. And I saw the

149

idea of honor, so highly esteemed by men, extended from themselves to a vague and magnificent personification of their country, and symbolized by a flag; so that great populations have reverenced a stripe of color like a cross, and armies have fought innumerable battles in its name. Millions of men have died for that intangible, that spiritual, that most precious thing—their country's Honor.

And yet, a country has no honor except that of the people who live in it. If they have no honor, then the country in which they live has none. In fact, a country's honor actually lies on a level far below that of its men of highest honor, because it represents a composite result, an average. If we judge a nation's honor by its behavior among other nations of the earth, we shall find little to claim our respect. A citizen's notion of his country's honor is really his sense of his own personal honor partially transferred to it. He is thinking poetry. He is throwing a spectrum of himself upon a screen: a screen which is the glorified map of his native land. He is bearing testimony to his own deep sense of the ultimate value of honor.

For it is the ultimate thing in a man, and every man instinctively feels that this is true; he must feel it even if honor has but a weak and stunted growth in him. Tell a man that he is wicked, and he may even take it as a kind of compliment; but tell him that he has no honor, tell him that he is no gentleman, and that will be an insult which he must resent in his own way. And not so long ago there was but one proper way, and that was the way of crossed swords. To doubt one's honor was a crime worthy of death.

There is no hope for a man without honor. If he assumes to have what he calls patriotism, it is an empty, selfish thing. If he claims to have what he calls religion, it is a whited sepulcher. Patriotism can do nothing for him; religion can do nothing for him, unless it first may start a sense of honor. He can be moved to action only by bribes or by kicks.

A sense of honor, then, lies at the very roots of a man's

character. It is worth while, therefore, to ask ourselves what honor really means and implies. It is worth while to define for ourselves some of its necessary parts. Rude and crude such a process must be—to attempt to dissect honor: the only excuse for it is that it is done for honor's own sake.

The first constituent of honor is what we name Self-respect. It is the feeling which a man ought to have that he possesses value, and a value which depends upon nothing else at all than what he actually is. He naturally will desire that this value shall be acknowledged by other men; but that is not the necessary thing: the necessary thing is that his value shall be acknowledged by himself. It is a distressing experience to be called a coward; but it is an experience more incurably painful to realize that one is a coward in one's own heart. For this wounds self-respect still more deeply, and self-respect bleeds miserably until it is healed by courage. For courage, fortunately, is a matter of will, and will is the back-bone of self-respect. To be afraid is not a matter of will, but of nerves; and what makes courage most praiseworthy is that it is able to overcome fear—or, rather, it is able to drive the body on in spite of fear.

But there are other things to be afraid of than guns and rattlesnakes and high places and ghosts. There is fear of people's criticism and ridicule, fear of failure, fear of the untried and the unknown, a multitude of fears which hinder us from being our true selves, and living the free life that we ought to live. And to be afraid and to allow one's actions to yield to fear, this is a poison-gas in which self-respect wilts, and the sense of honor droops. Even hell, it has been said, was not built for rabbits.

But self-respect has other enemies besides fear; every man knows what peculiar vampires may suck the blood of his own heart. And one such enemy is lying. So truly is this felt to be a foe to self-respect, that although there are many liars in this world, no liar will allow another man to call him one. It is felt to be a blow at his self-respect, and so to be a wound dealt his honor, even to be named what he really is. And the insult is worth a duel, to wipe out the stain of it in blood—if that could be!

Perhaps one element in the disgrace of a lie is the fact that it is allied to cowardice. He who tells a lie usually is running away from a situation, afraid to face it by telling the truth. Like the cuttle-fish, he emits an inky secretion out of his cowardice, and muddles facts, and so he hopes to sneak away in the obscurity which he himself has made.

But a lie has its own inherent ugliness. It is a crawling, traitor thing, in a world which is trying so painfully to find and to follow truth. It is tares in a field of facts. It is a false entry in a column of figures. A fact is respected just because it is a fact, and can be depended upon when men want to use it in their daily lives. And a true man is respected because he is true, and can be trusted in a society of men. So a man's promise ought to be a fact to be depended upon like a law of nature. His word ought to be as good as his bond, we say. If a man is less than this, knowing that his promise is always subject to discount, and that his word is below par, he feels, or he ought to feel, that he is by that much unworthy of the society of true men, and his self-respect is lowered, and his honor is abased.

As every virtue can be twisted into a vice, so self-respect can be twisted into self-conceit, self-righteousness, and pride. What saves it from this is a twin quality, a second constituent in the sense of Honor, which is Respect for other men. It grows out of an acknowledgment that all men share in the same humanity, the same divinity. All being compelled by some strange fate to be forever in conflict with their fellow-men, it is a fine attitude in each if he insists that the conflict shall always be on equal terms. So the man of honor must have a keen sense of fair play. If life is a game, the rules of it are to be respected at least as scrupulously as those of a game of cards. He cannot cheat, of course, in any competition, nor win by any sleight of hand. He can never take a crooked advantage in any clash of interests, for that is not playing the game.

Consequently, with this grounded demand for fair play in him, his impulse is always to try to mend unfair conditions wherever he meets them; to protest against injustice, to take the side of the unfortunate, to lend a hand. In the old tales of chivalry, this is the real business of the knight errant, to ride forth into the forest to find someone to help. To be unfair, to be discourteous, to slight the distress even of a beggar or a child—these things are stains upon honor.

The third constituent in the sense of honor is Loyalty. Note that the core of the word *loyalty* is the word *law*. Loyalty, then, is the steadfast devotion to a principle, or to a person, or to an institution, with an obedience as faithful as a law. It is the one indispensable virtue in any association of men. The strength of any society is in the loyalty of its members; its weakness is in their lack of loyalty. On our public buildings you often see carved a bundle of rods bound together by a cord: that cord will represent loyalty. A good citizen is measured by his loyalties; a bad citizen is condemned by his disloyalties—when they develop beyond a certain point they create a capital crime. And loyalty has its widest sphere in the smallest circle—the circle of the present hour.

For a man's whole life is filled with the urgent calls of duty, and his honor or his dishonor is involved in the loyalty with which he answers them: loyalty to his family, to his friends, to his work, to his country, loyalty to those intimations, more interior and more starry, which he will call his religion, equivalent to loyalty to God.

Now Honor has a motto. It is written in the language of that country whose history has been, more than that of any other land, the history of Honor. Those tales of chivalry which, told us in our boyhood, arise again in memory whenever we think of Honor, were first told around the camp-fires and the castle-hearths of France, when France, in its own radiant boyhood, was dreaming first of chivalry. And the entire history of France has been that dream, more or less coming true. There were the enchanted towers, and the imprisoned princesses, and the dreadful fiery dragons, throughout that history; and the knight was always there, not always victorious, indeed, but always brave.

And a motto took shape to express the soul of France, a proud and splendid motto. Not only was it the motto of nobles and knights, and the motto of Joan of Arc; peasants on their little farms, laboriously making France rich; sewing-women of Paris, composing fashions for all the world to wear; masons on the church-towers drawing Gothic architecture out of their prayers; and poets and writers of prose creating a beautiful language of clear running water and flowers and fire;—they all embody this motto, the motto of pride and humility, the motto of purpose and loyalty. It does not need to be translated, even if that were possible; for it has slipped, in the form in which it was born, into the speech of every civilized land: *"Noblesse oblige."*

It is very evident that Honor is not a gift nor an inheritance; it is an achievement. It cannot be put on like a uniform; it must become a part of one's self. It is very evident, likewise, that Honor cannot be attained piecemeal, by saying that this year we will learn courage, and next year we will learn fair play, and the year after that we will learn loyalty. We need a single ideal and a single enthusiasm which will carry on all the processes of Honor's growth simultaneously—something like life, which keeps weaving all at once bone and muscle, and brain and heart.

Suppose we raise Honor to its highest power by making it religious. Then we find that single ideal and enthusiasm —that force which is like life, for it is life—when we kneel, just as knelt the knights of old, before an altar, swearing allegiance to a perfect life, loyalty to an over-lord, who now is Christ, and service to men. Then currents begin to run through all the forms of Honor, as the rain fills the sluices of the fields. What can more inspire self-respect than to believe in the indwelling Spirit of God? What can more inspire courage and eliminate fear, than to believe that God drew the line of his good purpose around mankind before the world began? What can more inspire fair play than to believe in universal Love and the Communion of the Saints? And what can more inspire loyalty than the heroic example and the world-wide implications of the Cross?

Back from a battle came a message once: "All is lost but honor." But if honor really were not lost, then nothing was lost—of much account. For honor expresses the completeness of the things worth keeping, the sum of the things of a man that endure. Call it a pearl of great price, or call it a plume of chivalry, it represents the only thing that a man can carry away with him out of this world. "Honor and splendor in my heart abide."

Perhaps some of us have read the play, made famous here by Richard Mansfield, of *Cyrano de Bergerac*. And perhaps we remember how Cyrano, old and sick, stood against a tree in the park at the end of the play, defying death, while the yellow leaves kept falling all the time. The friends of Cyrano reminded him how vain a fight it was.

"But who fights only hoping for success?"
he said.
"I always fought for a lost cause—am fighting still.
You strip from me the laurel and the rose;
And yet, in spite of you, there is one thing
I hold against you all. And when, tonight,
I enter Christ's fair courts, one thing is left
Which, without smirch or stain, I bear away
In spite of all the world."

His friends asked Cyrano what that one thing was. It was his plume, he told them; it was his honor.

His words remind us of the dying words of another stout soldier of Honor, words which had still more to justify them:

155

"I have fought a good fight," said Saint Paul, as he bowed his head to the sword; "I have fought a good fight. I have kept the faith."

Kenyon College Chapel
March 30, 1919.
The present, printed text
is a later revision.

CHAPTER 19

Reform

"And it came to pass in those days that King Joash was minded to repair the house of the Lord."
II Chron. xxiv:4

KING JOASH IN these days is minded not only to repair the house of the Lord, but everybody's house. The voice of the reformer is loud in the land; many voices of many reformers are loud in the land. There is a long scale of reforms demanding attention, from the reform of international relations down in the bass, up to the shrill voice in the treble advocating reform of dolls. No one can feel himself a serious member of society who has not a pet reform to advertise.

There is for instance the spelling reform. We all of us know what thin ice we walk upon whenever we sit down to write a letter; and some statistical person has figured out how many millions of dollars business loses every year on account of the superfluous characters we are obliged to learn and to use in our English words. But shall we merely simplify spelling on old lines, or shall we reconstruct the alphabet, giving it forty letters instead of twenty-six, and so going down to the root of the matter?

Then there is the language reform. A common language to be learned in the schools of all civilized countries as a part of the common education, would bring about a far more extended intercourse among nations, and so facilitate the exchange of their offerings to civilization. But shall this common language be the ancient Latin, as some demand, or a simplified Latin, as others suggest, or shall it be Volapuk, or Esperanto, or Ido, or what?

Then there is the Calendar reform. How absurd it is that some months should contain thirty-one days, and others thirty days, while one has only twenty-eight. Again the statistical person has computed the millions of dollars which business loses every year on account of our illogical Calendar. There is an association which you may join if you wish, whose aim is to equalize the months. But shall we have twelve months of thirty days each, with five uncounted holidays; or shall we have thirteen months of four weeks each, with only one day left over for a New Year's holiday? It is the latter plan which appeals to Americans, for the thirteen months will correspond with the thirteen stripes in our flag, and the new month may be named *Liberty*.

Then there is the feminist reform, which is a series of reforms, now in process of triumphant accomplishment. And the end thereof is out of sight. The other day a meeting of women in England demanded admission into the orders of the Church, with privilege of becoming priests and bishops. And they are sure to get it. It is a sign of the times.

For the democratic spirit which now possesses humanity conceives of no door through which it may not enter. It is a strong and strenuous spirit, sometimes speaking like an archangel, and sometimes acting like the devil; but this is its own day, let none mistake, and it will try its experiments and experiment with its reforms, whether the conservative spirit likes it or not.

And this is only the beginning in a catalogue of reforms. Why should we go on to speak of the public utilities reform, and the city-government reform, and the tariff reform, and the tax reform, and the weights and measures reform, and the time reform? Why should we go on to enumerate the reforms proposed in our theology and in our worship and in our Church frontiers; and those reforms besieging the citadels of our education, demanding new subjects of study and new methods, stipulating for the blood of Latin and Greek, and dragging again the dead body of Hector around the walls of Troy?

Now one clear fact emerges out of this shrieking pit of reforms, and that fact is this, that the reform impulse is in the very make-up of man; it is part of our human nature. If man is the animal that laughs, man is also the animal that reforms. The bird makes the same nest forever, each species of bird its own style of nest, forever. But if man built a nest to live in, he would soon be tinkering at it to improve it. The next generation would probably cover it with a roof, and the next might add a little porch. And so the process would go on until there resulted, possibly, a ten-roomed abode with a furnace and a bath and a telephone. And man will not stop there, no matter where he begins nor where he ends. He is convinced that perfection always lies ahead. What kind of house man will build tomorrow no one can foretell, but it is inevitable that it shall be different. When the Greeks erected the Parthenon, one might have thought that, having attained perfection, they would build Parthenons forever; but not so. When men created Gothic architecture in France, one might have thought that, having attained perfection again, they would be satisfied with that miraculous result, and build nothing but Gothic forever; but not so, indeed. They kept on changing the forms their fore-fathers gave them; pursuing their own ideals; and if they lost beauty, in our judgment, they at least gained what they desired, the utterance of their own souls.

For that is the great thing, the all-important thing, the utterance of our own souls, the expression of ourselves. We want to leave some kind of impression upon the world as we find it, to show that we have lived in it. And this impulse of ours is at the bottom of all progress. If no man had ever wanted to improve upon the world as his fore-fathers had left it to him, we should never have got beyond the Stone Age; indeed, we should never have reached it. Civilization is like a great coral reef, made up of what millions of people have kept on adding to it. And add to it we must, in spite of what we euphemistically call the conservative side of us. Something in human nature drives us. Even conservatives in religion and politics invent a better plowshare, or a better business method, or contribute some valve to a steam-engine. We may reject or deride many of the reforms that are proposed, but let us respect the reformer; for the spirit that impels him is the spirit that impels civilization, just as the force which makes the tea-kettle boil over is the same force that drives the *Aquitania* across the sea.

And indeed the reformer usually has a hard row to hoe. One reason is that the great structures which were built by the past and in which we live, have a sacredness for us, and we do not like to see them changed. And another reason is that we do not want to be bothered with other people's reforms: we have our own. And another reason is simply inertia, commonly called laziness, which makes us prefer to run, or rather slide, in a well-beloved groove. So the reformer, if he is in earnest, must be prepared to become a martyr in his cause.

But that is not the worst of it. The reformer's soul is itself in danger. Precipices lie on each side of the path of the reformer's soul. Not only is he in danger of self-righteousness and spiritual pride and intolerance, developed by the constant assertion which he has to make that he is more right than his fellows; not only is he in danger of losing his perspective and magnifying his own reform into the one and only thing that will save the world and bring the Millennium to our gates; but he is in danger of making the end he strives for so important that all methods are legitimate in the pursuit of it, and he may become an immoral moralist, an inhuman humanitarian. Hawthorne, in one of his novels, shows vividly how a man may be cruel and unscrupulous in as good a cause as the prison-reform.

So a man may do well to hesitate to become a public reformer, unless he feels quite sure that he is strong enough for his mission. But such a warning need shut no man out from a reformer's work, or quench in no man's soul a reformer's zeal. There is one field of reform in which every man may proceed at once to labor—a field in which it is all-important that every man should labor, for that field is himself and his own life. It is very kind in a man to want to clean up other people's back-yards; but if there are difficulties in the way of doing that, why, always there remains his own back-yard.

In the Roman Catholic Church its members are expected to take stock of themselves at regular intervals, and to make a report thereon to their priests in the confessional. Protestantism has abandoned this method on several accounts; but this much, at least, may be said for it, that it encourages the custom of self-examination, a good thing from which we all, for natural reasons, shrink. We protest that we are afraid of morbid introspection; but this, which is self-examination overdone, few of us in our busy, practical modern life need fear. It surely would be a healthful habit if we all could sit down at regular times and look at ourselves as impartially as possible to see in what respects we might be improved, or in what respects our daily actions might be reformed. Our friends could help us here, no doubt; but unhappily friendship could never stand the strain. We have got to do the work of investigation ourselves.

It is small wonder that we are slow about undertaking the task, for it is one which is very repugnant to our self-satisfaction. Suppose we begin low down, in our common speech. How do we use our lordly English—murder it every hour? How about our grammar, our pronunciation, in the wonderful gift of talk? How about our conversation? Do we really know how to converse? They even say that conversation is a lost art. We are able to deliver monologues, and to exchange funny stories; but real conversation, which is as reciprocal as a tennis-game, is something which is rarely heard. The new education might well urge a course in conversation in its reformed college schedules.

Let us proceed. How about our manners? Are we fault-finding and irritable at home, the vice of the saints? Do we observe with any scrupulousness the ordinary courtesies of polite behavior, or do we even very much care whether we do or not? Back of that, is it a matter of much concern to us to show careful regard for the sensibilities of our neighbors in little things? We have a fine scorn for little things. But a polite Chinaman will pass you the sugar with both his hands, just to prove to you that he is glad to give himself entirely to your need; to use one hand in the service would betoken such carelessness as to be almost an insult. But we Americans—somehow we are afraid that we might possibly be thought too polite; and we take good care that we shall never be so misjudged.

Let us go on with our questions. How do we do our work, the daily task which is set for us in the order of things? Do we make it a matter of pride, a matter of self-respect, to do it well, to make it perfect, "to sweep a floor as by God's laws"; or do we do as little as we can for as much pay as we can get, do we shirk and skimp and watch the clock? Such a disposition has a dire effect upon the character: an effect only imperfectly symbolized by the careless rivet which the workman put in the air-plane and which cost a man his life.

Let us go on. We are members of a democratic State, so-called; that is, we vote. But how much do we really know about the policies which our votes help to settle for the time? How far are we merely members of parties, and applauders of catch-words, and how far are we really intelligent supporters of intelligent opinions? Do we carefully read both sides of every problem, and think over them, and pray over them, and cast our votes, as we ought to cast them, as if we were performing a sacred sacrament?

We are members of a Church: an institution founded by our Lord himself as a stately institution of unity not only to symbolize but also to preserve the unity of his followers with himself. How loyal are we to that unity? How much do we do to preserve it and to extend it? Is it the central living-room in our lives; or is it the musty parlor to be opened only on Sundays—if even then—and for weddings and for funerals? What kind of Church members are we?

Back of that, what kind of Christians are we? How do we keep our Lord's two great commands, to love God with all our heart and mind and soul and strength, and to love our neighbor as ourselves? In the monotonous rounds of commonplace duties and pleasures which fill up our days, what kind of a sky do we keep over our souls? How much do we remember that our earthly life is only half of our life—is not even that, if we only knew—and that it soon will pass away, leaving what as its blossom and outcome and result? How much do we remember that the spirt within us, aspiring and striving, is the Spirit of God himself, and that all our most ecstatic moments and all our bitterest hours are due to that one fact alone—the Spirit of God within us crying up to God in his heaven with groanings which cannot be uttered?

So, then, ourselves, our souls and bodies, are the Temple of the Spirit of God, dwelling invisible in the Holy of Holies there, and our daily lives are—or they ought to be—appropriate priestly service which we offer to him. It is not a new thought. Saint Paul said it with the utmost emphasis: "Know you not that your body is a Temple of the Holy Spirit which is in you, which you have from God? and you are not your own; you were bought with a price. Glorify God, therefore, in your body."

Evidently to glorify God in our body is to try to live the kind of lives we were born to live; with bodies and minds developed to the utmost perfection which we can attain and keep; the instruments of the highest thinking we can compass in a world so full of wonderful things to think about, and the instruments of the most unselfish service of humanity which we may find in our lot to attempt.

Here, then, is reason enough and incentive enough to look most carefully over our habits of living, in every part of our living, where nothing is to be considered small, nothing of no account. Dust and disorder we are sure to find somewhere within us and around us, if nothing worse. Habits of health, habits of social intercourse, habits of thought, habits of

163

work, habits of spiritual outlook, they all must be made elements of a real service in a real Temple. They all belong to the service of the Altar: they all are proper subjects of reform.

Here is reason enough and incentive enough, to do ourselves what old King Joash did, who, so it came to pass, was minded to repair the House of the Lord.

CHAPTER 20

The Seven Seals

THE ROLL OF a book, sealed shut with seven seals: that is what Saint John saw when he looked through the open door into heaven. This book, sealed with seven seals, was held in the right hand of God, the Maker of all things, who sat on his great white throne in heaven. And Saint John heard in heaven, which is the world of the meanings of things, a strong angel proclaiming, with a great voice, "Who is worthy to open the book, and to loose the seals thereof?"

And no one came to open the book, no one in heaven and no one on the earth. And then it was told Saint John that no one was worthy to open the book, except him who was able, through great overcoming, to loose the seals of the book; *he* was worthy to open the book and to read what was written therein. And it was told Saint John that one such there was who was able to loose the seals and to open the book and to read what was written therein. And that one was the Man who was made in the image of God, the Man who had overcome like a Lion and had shed his blood like a Lamb of sacrifice; his great overcoming had made him able to loose the seals and to open the book and to read what was written therein.

And so the Man arose in heaven, which is the world of the meanings of things, and he came to the throne, and God gave the book to him. And the Man, Man as he was made in the image of God, took the book; and then he broke the seven seals, one by one. And as each seal was broken, there appeared the picture of a separate Wonder: swift horses, white or red or black or pale, each bearing a fateful rider; clouds of much incense rising, the visible forms of earth's prayers; thunderstorms and dazzling glimpses into the sun.

So flashed these pictures before Saint John's eyes, as the seven seals were loosed; as if he caught sight of initial letters, splendidly and symbolically illuminated with strange forms of color and gold, to illustrate the mysterious meanings contained in the writing of the book. They were mysterious meanings given to none but the Man to read, the Man who was able, through great overcoming, to loose the seven seals.

And now, since he is the representative Man, the Man to whom all men are related, these mysteries are given to all men to read, in so far as they may be able, through overcoming, to loose the seven seals.

For this is the Book of human living, sealed with seven seals of mystery; and the only way to open the seals is to live the human life. So we ourselves hold in our hands this summer day the Book with the seven seals. It was given to us when we were born; it was given to us to read. And it is to recall our thought to this wonderful Book, this divine Book, and to its supernatural interest, that we take a half-hour today to count the Seven Seals.

The First Seal is the Seal of Nature. Since the Seven Seals are the locks of knowledge, and, therefore, may be thought of as Seven primitive Ignorances, the First Seal is ignorance of the world in which we live, ignorance of Nature. When we enter this world as children, such ignorance is complete, and the first quarter of our life is spent largely in learning enough about Nature for us to manage to live the remaining three-fourths without serious accident. And even so, serious accident is rarely escaped; indeed, only a fraction of the human race live through the four-fourths of their allotted time, the rest of them falling victims to ignorance of Nature somewhere along the road.

Man has been named the animal that laughs; but he quite as well might be named the animal that asks questions. And this is both his shame and his glory. He must ask questions, if only to find out what he safely may eat—and what apples he may not eat in his Garden of Eden. We learn to walk and run—but find out that it is dangerous to fall. We learn to

166

make a fire—but find out that it hurts us to touch the attractive flame. We learn that we may make pets of certain animals—but we must choose most heedfully our snakes. We learn how to plant a garden, and we learn incidentally that we must keep an eye on the seasons and the weather, and that we must maintain an everlasting war with insects and weeds. We learn a thousand facts about Nature, hardly realizing that we are finding out secrets of Nature, because it is not our curiosity that urges us here, but our necessity. We are obliged to know something about Nature, if we are going to live in Nature's house at all.

But suppose we let loose our God-given curiosity and try to learn more about Nature than necessity demands, simply for the satisfaction of knowing. There is such a satisfaction. Many human beings feel it, and many always have felt it, and all may feel it—if they will but allow it room. It is an element in the make-up of the human soul, the desire to know about things. Out of it all that we call Science has grown. To verify facts and classifications already recorded, and then to add some observation of our own, if possible, this is a pleasure which may easily become a passion. To wake up to the realization that there are worlds all around us waiting to be explored by us, this is almost to be born again. But that there are such worlds offering us both day and night occupations of the greatest interest, this is a literal fact. In every direction paths lead away into unknown continents, and every one of us is free—for every one of us can conquer a certain leisure—free to choose a path and enter thus the most fascinating regions. The study of plants, the study of animals and birds, the study of rocks, the study of air and water and fire and light, the study of atoms, the study of stars—all of these things are open to every one of us, and any one of them is worth all the time and all the labor we can possibly give to it. Any one of them will lead us—I will not say how far, lest you think I am tending to poetry. But at the very least and most literally, it will lead us into fairy-land,—yes, where dragons and sea-serpents thrash around in every drop of stagnant water, and tropical forests flourish in every spot of mildew.

So is the First Seal loosed, and the first page, the page of Science, lies open for all of us to read in the Book of Life —if we will.

The Second Seal is the Seal of Humanity. We are not only born into a world of Nature, but we are born also into a world of men and women; and as we are a vital part of the one, so also are we a vital part of the other. Indeed, so much must we learn from the people among whom we find ourselves born, that without the help they give us, we should never come to know anything at all, more than the beasts. A child growing up alone, grows up little more than a kind of ape; this dreadful thing has been. We have no instinct deeper than the instinct that draws us into association with other people; our health and our wealth and our salvation depend upon it. The very God we worship must have the form and the nature of a man. And so, also, Satan must be a man, though with hoofs and horns to show that he is an unhuman kind of man.

Our greatest happiness and our greatest misery both are produced by our relations with the men and women around us. They are our friends and our enemies. They delight us and they torture us. They inspire us to do our finest deeds, and bring to the front the best in us; and they also betray the worst in us and paralyze us and drive us to despair. And yet, always and forever, whatever else they are, they are all of them interesting to us, just because they are human.

You find a queer-shaped stone down by the river, and it has no value for you until you begin to suspect that its strange form was given it by some ancient man, who once drilled a hole in it for the handle of an axe. Then it becomes immediately a sacred relic, worthy to keep on your desk. And whenever your eye falls upon it, the poor water-worn pebble, you wonder and wonder about its ancient owner, and dream of the kind of life he led.

There is a human occupation called "gossip," and we are prone to speak scornfully of it; but we need not, for it is simply human interest. Our scorn of it must arise from the mean and common things our curiosity fastens upon, when it might choose larger and finer ones.

And what larger, finer human subjects there are! All we have to do is to open books to learn what important things our fellow-men have been doing all the time, the accumulation of which is our inheritance. Men of the Old Stone Age, men of the ancient Empires, men of Greece and Rome, men of the romantic ages, men of modern times; kings and queens and soldiers and builders and explorers and revolutionists and martyrs and saints—what people to gossip about! The history of the human race is the gossip of the gods. And all this human history is fascinating to us, just because we see in it the same qualities and the same passions which we ourselves possess, presented upon a far grander scale. We see ourselves acting upon a far wider stage, and we expand in spirit as we watch the thrilling pageant, for it is we ourselves who wear the crown and draw the sword, or suffer the magnificent tragedy.

And if men's actions charm us, what about their very thoughts, preserved in the books of the world,—their bold and daring thoughts, their delicate and jeweled thoughts, their wild and passionate thoughts? Vastly more interest is here, because in books we come closer to the hearts and minds of those who wrote them. What the best human beings have felt and thought in the past, we ourselves can think and feel along with them. And if the highest, noblest pleasure we know is to feel and think with another human being—that rare experience we call friendship—then we have something in literature akin to that precious thing. To think and to feel—however thinly but sincerely—with Homer and Shakespeare, Shelley and Keats, and all that brilliant company of men and women who have thought and felt to the wisest and most beautiful purpose on earth: this is, in a way, to enter into this select company and be greeted by them as friends.

And this privilege is the privilege of any one of us, as

far as we ourselves may choose, when we break the Second Seal of the Book of Life.

The Third Seal is the Seal of Self, the Seal of one's own self. The human being begins to be a human being only when he begins to say "I"; and his growth as a human being is the growth of the "I," or the Self, within him. Through the senses of its body, in which it lives, it begins at once to reach out and gather in knowledge of the world around. And this knowledge is assimilated by the Self and becomes a part of itself, and so the Self grows.

As a matter of fact, the Self of every human being is a thread woven in along with countless other threads to make the human race, but it is difficult for the Self to realize this. Its sense of isolation and uniqueness is fundamental in its nature. It seems to itself to be the center of the world; and so it is, the center of its own world. It is as if the Self were dwelling in a dark tower, watching through narrow windows the landscape and the passing people outside, and painting upon the walls of its rooms pictures of what it thinks it sees. And in this way the world outside becomes for the Self a world inside. But the truth of this inner world depends upon the manner in which the Self sees the outside world. It depends upon its own capacity for seeing. The windows through which it looks out at the world may be filled with little panes of colored or crinkled glass, so that the people passing by may be distorted into monsters, and the bright world may seem to be red or brown or blue. Knowledge of the world depends upon the Self's knowledge of itself.

We all of us think that we know ourselves, even if we know little else; but such is not the fact. We may find ourselves very dull company, excluding ourselves from our social circle, and refusing to be left alone with ourselves any more than we can help. At the very same time we may have exaggerated opinions of ourselves, thinking ourselves more and better than we really are, priding ourselves on virtues we do not possess. In other moods we may imagine ourselves less and worse than we really are, bewailing sins and weaknesses

170

that are not ours. We look at ourselves through crinkled glass.

The first and great commandment of the old Greeks was, "Know thyself." And obedience to this commandment takes shape in our modern time in a new science, the science of Psychology. It is a fascinating science, we find, and the most wonderful fact which it makes known, is that in us there is far more than we ever imagined. Each one of us, it declares, is like a man carrying a lantern through a dark forest. The narrow circle of light in which we walk is our consciousness; but the unknown forest is also a part of ourselves.

To know ourselves, progressively, is to widen our circle of light, and so to include the knowledge of greater things, and thus to expand our spiritual habitation. It is a kind of spiritual architecture. As Oliver Wendell Holmes expressed it, in verses treasured in old scrapbooks:

"Build thee more stately mansions, O my soul,
 As the swift seasons roll!
 Leave thy low-vaulted past!
 Let each new temple, loftier than the last,
 Shut thee from heaven with a dome more vast."

The knowledge of Self, slowly unfolding, is the opening of the Third Seal of the Book of Life.

The Fourth Seal is the Seal of Pain. The great complaint we have to make against this world is that there is in it so much of pain. In fact, no life can be without it in some form. It exists wherever life exists. "The shadow of life is pain," said the Hindoo philosopher:

"The shadow of life is pain, infallibly
 Moving as life doth move."

And it is true. We are all the time suffering some pain, or suffering from the fear of it. There is no escape. It may be like stinging flies; or like a rat gnawing in the night; or like a snake coiled in the garden; or like a tiger leaping out of the wood; or it may be like a ghost haunting the dim galleries of the mind; but in some unwelcome shape we always

171

feel the presence of pain. We flee from it, of course; we are all the time aiming to evade it, but we have only to look behind us to find it at our heels. We can never escape. And we try to fight it, of course. Much of the effort of science is to defend us against pain, or to drive it away when it attacks. And the last desperate endeavor of the human sufferer, in his conflict with pain, is to deny that it exists. "There is no pain," he bravely insists, even while he is writhing with it.

But in spite of all alleviation or defense or denial, pain still dwells in our house of life with us. The human race is married to pain, and there is no divorce.

"The babe is wise," said the old Hindoo philosopher again; "the babe is wise that weepeth, being born."

But this is not the way to deal with pain: simply to resign ourselves to it as to an inevitable curse of our human lot. Nor is the way to deny its existence, for that is not facing facts. The true way is the way of knowledge, to find out, if in any sort we can, what pain means.

The first function of pain is—and this is very clear—its activity as a kind of sharp alarm-bell to warn us of danger. Some thief is trying to pick the lock of our home of life; some enemy is trying to climb in at the window, and pain urgently wakens us to be up and on our guard. Surely here we can understand that pain is constant and is kind. And since Nature shows her good-will so unmistakably here in this first function of pain, we may take it as the key to unlock the secret of its other functions also. Nature is kind, even when most inexorable; her purpose is always good, even when seeming most charged with punishment. This is our starting-point of courage and hope in any effort to gain knowledge of pain. And as we pick our way along the thorny road, we may even be able to adapt for ourselves the Endymion Sorrow-song:

> To Sorrow we bade good morrow
> And thought to leave her far away behind.
> But cheerly, cheerly,
> She loves us dearly,

> She is so very constant—and so kind.
>   We would deceive her,
>   And so leave her;
> But ah! she is so constant—and so kind.

So we will not try to run away from pain. We will face it and grapple with it and compel it, if we can, to give up to us its meaning and its message. It is the only way to conquer pain, the way of understanding it; and, perhaps, as our knowledge grows wider, we shall see how it was that the most rapturous song was one that was sung in the furnace of fire.

It is a difficult Seal to break, but it is one of the Book of Life; the Fourth Seal is the Seal of Pain.

The Fifth Seal is the Seal of Beauty. The presence of beauty in the world is as constant as that of pain; and far more evidently kind; perhaps even more mysteriously kind. For pain drives us with whips to discover its meaning in life, while beauty does nothing but woo us and delight us, and we are quite willing to think that beauty's sole function is to give us delight, and to let it go at that. And so beauty's mystery remains unsolved, and its message undelivered. Perhaps we hardly know that it has a meaning.

The spring arrives and fills the earth with beauty, spreading countless green leaves to the air, and hanging the trees with bright, fragrant bloom. We are told that the leaves are the lungs of the tree—no more—and that the color and perfume of the flowers are to call the bees to serve as Nature's errand-boys—no more. But we are attracted as well as the bees, and we cannot think that our inevitable response is an accident and not a purpose. Nature is kind, we say, and the beauty of spring is for our pleasure. It is the bees that enjoy an accident.

We listen to the music of violins or to the honeysweet voices of song; and as we listen our soul is like a harp, whose strings vibrate harmonically in reply. But men tell us that music's first function was to keep time for a dance, and that our response is due simply to the dance in our blood, never extinct. We may admit the origin, but we extend the result. The genius which expressed itself through developed music must have a broader purpose. Nature is kind, we say; the beauty of music must have been given for our pleasure.

But there is no sign that Nature ever does anything for our mere pleasure. She is not concerned, it seems, with our pleasure, but only with our best welfare. The same Nature that gives us beauty, also gives us pain. The same Nature that uses beauty to attract the bees for her serious purposes of life, must also attract us with beauty for something far more serious than our mere pleasure in life. Pleasure for pleasure's sake is one of Satan's snares.

"Beauty is truth, truth beauty," said an ardent disciple of beauty, whose devotion to beauty consumed his life like a fire: "Beauty is truth, truth beauty." And if this is so, then beauty's attraction must be an attraction meant to draw us to knowledge. Philosophers have tried to analyze beauty, and have classified certain elements of it, such as symmetry, proportion, and relation to life. But there always remains something which escapes observation and definition; something mysterious and essential which makes beauty to be beauty; without which beauty would be gone. It seems trite to quote it, because it is quoted so often, but there is no better figure at hand. The essential thing in beauty is "the light that never was on sea or land." It is a light falling on earth from heaven itself, and in our pursuit of truth by way of beauty this is the light that we must follow; and what we shall see in the grace of that light will be a new page laid open, and a new revelation made, by the loosing of the Fifth Seal of the Book of Life.

The Sixth Seal is the Seal of Religion. The human race is born religious. As man is the animal that laughs—and weeps; as man is the animal that asks questions—and forgets the answers; so man is also the animal that prays. That is, he is the animal that suspects that there is an invisible world behind this visible world, all the time reaching out invisible hands to interfere, to play, to mend, or to destroy. And man's endeavor to see into this invisible region and to make the invisible powers there his friends: this is his religion. Whether he rises to light a fire to the dawn, or hangs a horse-shoe up over his door, or consults mediums, or makes the sign of the cross, it all means the same thing; it is a gesture made toward the invisible world.

But we do not well describe this world behind our visible world by saying that it is invisible. Indeed, it can hardly be called invisible when its presence is so very evident in the visible world; we have only to look to see that the visible world does not explain itself. Behind the moving curtains of creation, forms are forever passing to and fro, betrayed by the waving movement. A real world stands behind our visible world of shows and shadows, and men's religion is their allegiance to realities.

So our problem is to find realities. The secret of salvation is knowledge again: to know the truth (the reality), and the truth (the reality) shall make us free. And there is no difficulty in finding the road to this knowledge, and no fear that a man may miss it, if he is sincere. The cause of truth is safe, and no skepticism will long lead a man astray if he is honestly in search of truth. We need not be anxious about the infidel who really wants to live a true life. For the desire of reality draws reality to itself, as the magnet draws the iron. The dangerous doubt is the doubt of reality, the doubt of goodness, the doubt of justice, the doubt of honor, the doubt of love.

They say that the religion of the future will more closely combine science, the endeavor and achievement of the intellect, and mysticism, the endeavor and achievement of the soul. The passion of both is the truth. The aim of both is knowledge. The intellect starts with things seen, and every road leads it ultimately into the unseen. The soul starts with living the true life, with living the every-day life in fidelity to truth, and so it arrives at its beatific vision. It seems, indeed, as if the intellect and the soul together might walk arm in arm as they set forth on their great adventure to find reality.

175

And so this is the Sixth Seal, the Seal of Religion, which opens the page of realities in the Book of Life.

The Seventh Seal is the Seal of Death. It seems a harsh note to strike, especially in the season of the spring, when life is so vivid and so bright, and hope is so dominant in the earth. But it is one of the Seven Seals; it is one of the facts of life, and it will be a witless thing, if not a cowardly thing, to refuse to look it in the face. Oh, we always shrink from looking it in the face. And yet we cannot see its face. Perhaps that is why it seems so terrible to us. A fold of its dark mantle droops over its brow and casts a heavy shadow over the features we fear to gaze upon. And so it is our imagination that creates the grim and cruel skull-face which is the horror of our dreams.

And yet we have our excuse. This unwelcome guest always appears so much the very enemy of life. There is no sweet relationship he does not ruthlessly tear apart. There is no earthly ambition he cares ever to respect. He breaks the pitcher at the fountain; he blasts the flower in its bloom; he pulls down the buttresses of faith and the banners of hope and the bowers of love. Yes, we have our excuse if we fear death and dread it, and refuse to talk about it, and try to forget it—until we hear it turning the handle of our door. Yes, we have our very good excuse.

And yet death is one of the facts of life. And as it is the one that seems most inevitable, so it is the one that demands most insistently to be faced. It is the fact of all facts about which men have always most longed and sought for knowledge.

But yet it does not seem good, in life, to think too much about death. It does not seem good for us to keep knocking at the door of the tomb to ask for knowledge. There is no reply. There never has been any reply, except hollow echoes that reverberate disastrously in the chambers of the soul. We must leave the grave-side and go out under the blessed living trees if we want to know as much as we can know about death. It is Nature who will whisper to us in lovely parables to suggest to us that death is not the end of life, but an

176

episode in life; that life is the most precious thing in the universe, and every seed must somehow grow, or somewhere; it cannot die. And if we read now the page which the loosing of the Seventh Seal has opened to us, we shall read that if life itself is so precious, most precious is the life which has drawn into itself the essences of beauty and truth out of the crucifixion of living. Eternal life is life that is worthy of return to the conscious Heart of the universe, there to enter unimaginable processes in the endless creation of forms of beauty and truth.

The ear will not hear when we call; the flying feet will not turn back. But we have all reason to believe that the young runner has gone into the bright fields of reality, and that "it is, it is a god-song he follows this many a mile."

So these are the Seven Seals of the Book of Life: the Seal of Nature, and the Seal of Humanity, and the Seal of Self, and the Seal of Beauty, and the Seal of Pain, and the Seal of Religion, and the Seal of Death. But how much we shall read in the open Book will depend altogether upon ourselves. And we know that there are very many things to draw us away from the reading, or to dim our eyes as we read: the modern rage for amusement, and the ancient curse of sloth, and the fascinating pursuit of soap-bubbles, as well as the bondage to machinery, and the paralysis of routine.

But knowledge is fundamental, and there are many things to know, and time is short for so much. But all we need is the will, for the Book of Life lies ever open, with a word for every hour, and a verse for every day.

"Knowledge is power," says an old aphorism, and nothing is more true. "Learn anything under the sun," said a wise old man, "but *learn* it, and you will find that some day it will fit into use, and be the very tool that you want."

"Knowledge is morality," said the Greek philosopher; "for to know the good is to follow the good." So the critical choice for the soul is to choose to know the good.

And "Knowledge," said our own Shakespeare, "knowledge is the wing wherewith we fly to heaven."

"Ignorance is the curse of God,
Knowledge the wing wherewith we fly to heaven."

"To heaven!" Dante the exile saw into Paradise as well
as Saint John the exile. And while Saint John saw the Seven
Seals of knowledge loosed on earth, Dante saw the consummation of knowledge in heaven. And what Dante saw was
this:

He saw Paradise as one vast white Rose, whose circumference reached the emerald walls on every side. And every
shining petal was a conscious flame of triumphant life expanding in joy. And the countless whorls of them, close-
ranked and ever-lapping, sank in diminishing circles into
the central burning vortex of life, in which lay the seeds
of all the infinite future manifestations of life, waiting for
their destined hour.

Oh, but it is splendid! And it is wonderful! The white rose
we pluck on earth and hold in our hand, noting how its
concentric petals are whorled down into the mysterious
heart of it: this white rose which we hold in our hand becomes a thing mystic, holy, as we dream of it as a symbol of
the great white Rose of Paradise—the symbol at once of
Nature's miraculous law; and the communion of saints; and
the mysterious unity of Self; and the beauty of holiness; and
the creative pain of a universal Cross; and the rooting of
Life in the invisible world; and the final transformations
of Death into such bloom of life as the eye hath not seen,
nor the ear heard, nor hath it entered into the heart of man to
conceive.

Harcourt Place School
June 6, 1922.

CHAPTER 21

Stewards of the Mysteries of God

ORDINATION SERMON

*"Let a man so account of us as of ministers of Christ,
and stewards of the mysteries of God."*

1 Cor. iv.:1

OLD WORDS, THEY say, are like old coins. They become worn by use and lose the sharp impress of their original image and superscription. The word "mystery" is such a word. It means to us now merely something secret, something involved in shadow, veiled and obscure; but Saint Paul meant by "mystery" a secret which was no longer a secret. It was a truth long hidden in the purposes of God, but now revealed and made known.

Very visible and definite was the religion of the busy Graeco-Roman world surrounding the Mediterranean Sea in the days of Saint Paul. Wherever people dwelt their white temples stood. Every little town by mountain or seashore had its green altar somewhere near. Every pious morn saw the priest leading the heifer to the sacrifice, "her silken flanks with garlands dressed." But the gods who received all this worship could not be regarded as mysterious, although unseen. They were too much like men. Their appearance, their family history, their personal characteristics and idiosyncrasies, were quite as well known to their worshipers—and their doings were often quite as scandalous—as those of the worshipers' next door neighbors. The worshipers knew their gods only too well.

This religion provided the setting of solemn ceremonial

179

for all events of the people's social and family life, and it gave poets and sculptors material for their imaginative work; but it was also a breeding-place, this ancient and pompous and worm-eaten religion, for all superstition and vice. As a religion, it was something at which philosophers laughed or sneered, and for which the virtuous apologized, even while they poured libations of wine to the gods at dinner every day, like a grace, and offered cocks to Aesculapius—like Socrates.

So it came about that more serious men, and more moral men, and men who craved reality in their religious life, settled into religious associations apart from the magnificent emptiness and glorified corruption of the State religion. Secret orders, organized societies, were founded, becoming vastly extended and powerful, composed of members who had proved themselves worthy of being taught a body of truth, facts of nature and of human existence, supposed to underlie the popular stories of the gods, those stories being only allegories when rightly understood. The candidate for initiation into these associations was required to pass some moral test— at the sight of which the emperor Nero, so we are told, fled in terror. The candidate confessed his sins; he fasted; his old life was washed away in a ceremonial bath, a baptism. And now he was ready to be admitted into the great hall of the order.

Here he witnessed a dramatic exhibition which we may call a pagan "miracle play," or a pagan "passion play." The tragic story of one of the gods was represented on a stage with splendid pageantry, and while the candidate gazed upon its successive scenes, his guide, always at his side, explained it to him, whispering into his ear the meaning, step by step, of what he saw: how life on earth forever passes through the death of winter to rise again into spring; how man on earth forever struggles, blindly, to become a god; and how he may indeed so become by learning the miraculous way. Something like this was whispered into the ear of the candidate while he watched the action of the drama which symbolically pictured it. And therefore it was called a *mystery*, something made known in a whisper. It was a secret to those outside, but

180

to those inside it was a mystery. So the meaning of the word *mystery,* as it was understood in Saint Paul's time, was *a secret revealed*—at least as far as one was able to comprehend it. And in this sense Saint Paul always employs the word: by the term *mystery* he always means something once secret, but now revealed to those initiated into Christianity.

And so the striking phrase of our text, "stewards of the mysteries of God," will have a clearer meaning for us if we retranslate it and make it read, "stewards of the revelations of God." "Let a man so account of us, as stewards of the revelations of God."

But what did Saint Paul have definitely in mind when he spoke of the mysteries, or the revelations of God? What secrets had been whispered into his ear by his divine Guide?

Saint Paul uses the word "mystery" eighteen times in his epistles, and always, except twice, to mean some aspect of the Gospel, as now, in the fulness of time, it was unfolded for men to know. And very impressive it is to note how the idea of unity is predominant in Saint Paul's thought: the whole universe summed up in Christ—in what unimaginable way! the Church the one bride of Christ; Jews and Gentiles becoming one people in Christ; the future life one with this earthly life in Christ, the soul changing its garment simply as it steps from one world to the next. And all these things are mysteries, or revelations of God.

Yet all these ideas were already scattered in the world in some form. Men had been groping after unity from the beginning—with certain approaches to it in places far apart. The Jews had found one God; the Greeks one inevitable Fate. The universe had been called "the Great Man." Followers of Mithra and Isis were striving to become one with divinity. Currents were setting in toward the Brotherhood of Man. And everywhere the world was seeking, however despairingly, to discover in death a door, and not a wall.

It was Saint Paul's great genius and inspiration that he saw all these things combined and made one in Christ. He summed up the universe, not as a philosopher or theologian, but as a lover. He seized the most perfect thought to be found

181

in the world anywhere, the aims of its utmost aspiration and the products of its most creative imagination, and with them all he clothed his Christ.

The Jewish Messiah, so long and so passionately awaited, he had arrived. The Greek creative Word, it was now made flesh in him. The Heavenly Man, humanity's pattern and ideal, here at last was he. The world's long-desired Savior from sin and guilt and death—behold him on the cross. The resurrection and the life, and the soul's indwelling divinity —learn this in the Mystery of Christ.

Whatever is good and true and beautiful, then, at any time or anywhere in the world, Saint Paul ascribes it all to the work of Christ, while never failing to proclaim that the ultimate source of it is in God. But the power to recognize these divine relationships between God and his creation, is due to a divine Spirit given to the Christian, so that the power of insight is the power of revelation. For let us read what he says:

God's wisdom appears in a mystery—that is, in a revelation —when we have the Spirit of God.

Things that the eye saw not—for the eye was dim; things that the ear heard not—for the ear was dull; things that entered not into the heart of man—for that heart was too dark—yet things which God has all along had ready for those who love him: these things God has revealed to us, lovers of Christ, through his Spirit. For the Spirit searches all things, yea, the deep things of God. And we have received this Spirit which is from God, in order that we may know those things which God has freely opened now to us.

Saint Paul's "mysteries," drawn out thus from the deep things of God, still stand at the head of all that we call revelation today. In number they are five:

First: What Saint Paul names the "Mystery of Christ" will surely be that Length and Breadth and Depth and Height which includes, as supreme for us, the love of God which Christ reveals, the love of God for men.

Second: Saint Paul's Mystery of the Great Consummation, the universe summed up in Christ, contains the vision also of a redeemed humanity sharing in his destiny, fellow-heirs with him in his inheritance of glory. Here is the magnificent assertion of a hope for mankind which our theory of Evolution can only suggest, pointing out a rough and climbing road which vanishes ahead—with precipices on either hand.

Third: Saint Paul's Mystery of the Indwelling Christ, so often repeated and stressed, this is for Saint Paul the basis of our divine sonship. We are sons of God because the Son of God abides in us, who admit him into our hearts through faith, and our sufferings are a part of his, and his victory is ours. It signifies something, anyway, that we cry instinctively, "Abba, Father!" And the soul's inarticulate sighings and groanings for something—it does not clearly know for what— is it not the groping spirit of sonship greatly desiring love?

Fourth: Saint Paul's Mystery of the Reasonableness of the Future Life is clinched by an argument from analogy. The bird with its wings for the air, the fish with its fins for the stream, the quadruped with feet for the ground, all suggest a body equally fit for the soul in any sphere to which it may come. The argument still holds good. We still believe that as life creates its own proper organs of connection with its environment, so we need have no fear that a spiritual being will not find itself at home in a spiritual world.

Fifth: Saint Paul's Mystery of the Equality of Men, vivid to him as an issue in relations between Jews and Gentiles, still remains as an issue in other forms today. Slowly, slowly, grows, in practice, the Brotherhood of Man.

Mysteries, or Revelations, then, are deep things of God as looked into by men, but by men who have the spirit of God. They are nature as the man sees it who sees God in it. They are the history of the nations as the man studies it who traces out God's movements through it: Greece his golden harp and Rome his iron plowshare; the Goths and Huns his whip of scorpions, and America, perhaps, his new experiment-room. They are any system of knowledge as the man knows it who discerns something of God's methods therein. They are the experiences of human living, made revelation by the eye which sees their import. The Ten Commandments were hammered out by a thousand years of human experiment beside the Euphrates, before they were thundered from Mount Sinai and carved upon tables of stone. And doubtless we all have some secret record of strange processes in our own microcosmic lives.

So humanity is limited to its own plane and circle in its glimpses into the deep things of God; but even that limited region is one whose horizon we cannot measure. It is a continent as yet without a map, upon whose mysterious shores we find ourselves as adventurers and explorers, with many a doubt and many a fear—but not without a compass, a hope, and a high resolve. With many a valley and wild wood between, we yet can see light on the mountain tops.

And now we come to the question which is of special interest for us today: What is it to be a steward of the Mysteries, or Revelations, of God? What are those functions to which Saint Paul appeals, faithfulness to which he begs may always be the rule that men shall judge him by?

A steward, of course, is an officer in a great house who has in his charge the care of its daily needs. In to him from the family's resources come the requisite supplies, and out from his directing hand goes the due measurement, day by day, of what the family requires. He is obliged to look two ways: that is, to watch the daily need, and to provide the daily supply.

The steward of the revelations of God, then, must first of all know the revelations of God; they must be his study night and day. He must make, as the basis and substance of all his supplies of knowledge, the five great Mysteries of Saint Paul: God's Love revealed in Jesus Christ; Humanity's ultimate Hope in Christ; the Spirit of Christ in the human heart; the Victory over the fear of death; and the Brotherhood of Man.

These things the steward of God's Mysteries must know, buttressed with every possible resource of the intellect, and with every possible experience of the soul; for he has been appointed to be other men's eyes in the fields of revelation. And to know these things aright—else are they but mere book-knowledge—he must have in his own heart the Spirit of Revelation. He must have his own vision of the deep things of God.

So the steward of the Mysteries of God will look out over the world, and everything he sees will be a Mystery; that is, it will reveal to him something divine. And in order to widen his outlook upon Revelation, he should make his outlook over the world as wide as may be. In other words, the candidate for stewardship of God's Mysteries, the student for the ministry, should have a preliminary education as comprehensive as possible, in order to know as much as possible about the wonderful world in which he lives. He cannot learn too many things for his purpose, since out of the all he shall spin nothing but silk.

He should study the Sciences: Biology, Geology, Astronomy, Mathematics, to get marvelous glimpses into the very workshop of God.

He should study human history and its related subjects, to realize the fact of progress, and to trace out the intricate curves of its direction, and to see, in gigantic shadow-pictures, great principles put to proof. Human history is full of the footprints of God.

And the student should know the field of literature, to associate with the noblest thinkers the human race has gendered, and to dream over with them their loveliest dreams. For the Spirit of God is blooming here in thoughts, as elsewhere in flowers and stars, Lord and Maker of Beauty, as Lord and Giver of Life.

And the student should have knowledge of Sociology and its related themes, for they open up to him perhaps the most living region of human activity in all this living day. For Society is here consciously concerned in its own development, and consciously considering its own discipline. And so significant is this present energy that men are calling ours the Holy Spirit's own peculiar age. Maybe it is. But anyway, the world is drifting swiftly toward momentous changes, and the steward of God's Mysteries will desire to act a worthy part therein.

Revelation is as wide as knowledge, when once you have

185

the prophet's eye. A narrow conception of God it is, that which represents him as sitting afar, doling out his revelations frugally, crumb by crumb. Rather, God has spread open all his books, and here they lie before us. Nothing but secrets they contain, so long as we cannot read them. Nothing but secrets they contain, so long as we conceive of God as separate from his world. But when we see that the Seven Days of creation are never past, but are here and now, creation still in process organizing chaos, with the Spirit of God, who is the Spirit of Life, beating like a heart in every cell of it, then books of science, books of poetry, books of history, books of music, and all books printed with the life-blood of man—every stray volume picked up at any stall on any street: they all are Sacred Scriptures now, because we have learned to read them. Remember the wise old Welsh triad:

"Devoutly read; all books shall edify you.
Devoutly look, and naught but wonders shall pass by.

And now you, as a steward of the Revelations of God, are not likely to forget that you are also a minister of Christ. Whatever is yours of knowledge and of wisdom and of vision is not yours to keep. What the steward possesses is his only to give. And if objection should ever rise that too much is demanded of you, in the continued study of subjects commonly called secular, while your path of life shall often lie through dim places where such subjects will seem very far away, the answer shall be implied in that same old Welsh triad: "Devoutly read; all books shall edify you." As you must regard them, there are no subjects secular—just as the Bible is not religious if one reads it with a secular mind. You must keep the greatest range of knowledge possible behind your simple life. Our Lord had all heaven behind him as he talked with the woman at the well; and he could converse with the doctors in the Temple as well as with the fishermen of Galilee.

And so, when some young man, having studied a little science, shall say to you, as he will: "The world is only a vast machine, and no man deserves either praise or blame"—

When some old man, with his heart burnt out, shall ask you, with pathetic cynicism: "Can water spring again, and can green leaves grow again, in desert sands?"—

When some soul shall stretch a hand to you, out of the currents dragging him down, and shall say to you: "Is this Fate? Can there be, anywhere, help for me?"—

When some father or mother shall say to you, and it will be said: "All my faith in God is buried in the grave of my child"—

When someone with failing breath shall clutch at you as he sinks into the dark, asking you: "Does death end all?"—

When others shall mock and deride, and shall call you a dealer in delusions and dreams, bitterly accusing you of having nothing but wine mingled with myrrh for humanity on its cross of pain—

When you shall often stand perplexed with difficult problems, sorely tried between the shows and the realities of things, asking yourself what is the true decision of an honest man—

Then, as a steward of the Revelations of God, and as a minister of Christ, you shall have great need to bring forth out of your treasures things both new and old.

But we all of us have a question to ask of you, as one who, being a steward of the Revelations of God is also a witness of the resurrection of Christ; and most glad shall we be, we questioners, whenever you can take us aside and say, whispering it into our ears as something most sacred and wonderful:

"Yes, I know! Very large is the knowledge that has no knowledge of him, and very dark is the doubt men cannot see him through! Angels and principalities and thrones and dominions and powers all declare that they themselves fill all life's hemisphere. And yet—I know it is not true! Because last night I heard his voice; this morn I felt his hand!"

That, that, is the message we long to hear from you. It is the message that all men, everywhere, with longings inexpressible, long to hear.

It is a sorrowful world into which you go; but yet not a world of despair. Remember what the good old pope once said: "Some are weeping, and others laugh, and the world is full of smiles and tears. So shall it be and continue. No one can save mankind from their sorrows; but much shall be forgiven to him who brings us courage to bear them."

Courage and hope! they are the world's great need; and that—oh, blessed privilege!—it shall be your life-work to give. Stewards of the Revelations of God have often been taught—strangely taught!—that vinegar and vitriol are proper remedies to pour into human wounds. May you never be deluded into such therapeutics, as a minister of Christ. And you will not, if you can keep clear your revelations of God. And you will learn that by far the most of those whom we name sinners in this world are hapless men without vision, and men tormented with doubt, and men in despair. Help them to see, for you are a steward of the Revelations of God. But, in order to do it, you must keep your own vision burning steadfast in your sight. Whoever doubts, it must never be you! Whoever despairs, it must never be you! In the face of all the stupidities and the perversities and the piteous tragedies of earth, you must maintain a brave front—although your soul may be fainting and your heart may be bleeding within you. For you are a steward of the Revelations of God. In the face of the black Pit itself you must hold up a bright hope—even as Prince Love in the poem, who rode forth to find hell, and who returned to say that he could find nothing but a meadow full of flowers.

Yet one must face facts; and, so facing them, one may hardly sing now the song of the happy Italian silk-girl, on her spring holiday:

> "God's in his heaven—
> All's right with the world."

But we, if we have the Spirit of Christ, we must maintain and declare, under the windows of every darkly-curtained

188

chamber where sin may seem to be magnificent, and where Death may seem to be King:

> "God's in his earth,
> To make—in the fulness of time—
> All right with the world."

June, 1922.

CHAPTER 22

Fellow-Citizens With the Saints

"We are fellow-citizens with the saints."
Eph. ii.:19.

THERE IS A certain picture of the Deluge which has become typical, so expressive it is of the most rudimentary bond which binds animal natures together, the bond of a common danger driving them to a common safety. Upon a rock in the midst of raging waters are men, women, and children in close company with the most dangerous of beasts—lions, tigers, and snakes. For the moment they are all friends, because they are all clinging precariously to the one friendly refuge.

Now this strange company upon the rock may be fancifully considered an incipient society; it is the conception of a society composed of such antagonistic elements that the very existence of such a society draws instant attention to the cause of it, and makes more vivid and tremendous to the mind the force of the cause. How terrific must be the fear which makes the lion and the lamb to lie down together!

But, after all, it is a truce between citizens which will last no longer than the common danger threatens. As soon as the waters begin to subside, the lion feels his lust for blood arising again, and the man looks about him for a weapon of defense.

In the last century a certain philosopher saw in this picture of animals made friends by a flood a vision of all human society. Social institutions, so he said, rest entirely upon human selfishness; they are the methods which intelligent selfishness has found the best for the attainment of its ends. Society is the compromise between the attempts of greed.

190

Each individual has a better chance of getting more, by combining forces and dividing the spoil. Manners are the conventional veils by which motives are concealed. Etiquette is the mutual agreement not to drive a dagger into one another's back. Politeness is the fawning for some sort of favor. All mankind are in reality wild beasts, each bent on getting the best of the world for himself, kept simply by various necessities from following his primal instincts of biting and tearing his neighbors. Men submit to military association and rule, in order to keep invaders on the opposite side of the mountains—they are friends through a common fear. They compare experiences in order to accumulate a science, through which each may profit from the observations of all. They maintain peace among themselves in order to create an organism of combined muscle-fiber and brain force which shall be stronger than all hostile power of nature and man, and enable them to win dominion and conquer spoil to divide; so internal dissension must be guarded against as a weakening of the common armament.

But suppose every man were suddenly to feel himself independent of his fellow men, immediately all society would resolve into primitive anarchy and chaos.

Now there is a great truth in all this; there is in reality such a bond—we might call it an iron bond—which does so bind men together by means of an appeal to selfishness. It is a necessary bond, it is a divine and beneficent bond, for it brings raw mankind together and makes possible the gradual growth of better relations and the welding of a better and a brighter bond—we might call it the golden bond—the bond of love.

I saw a cask made once, and noted how the staves were all held together, barrel-wise, by means of a rough, strong temporary hoop, while the workman fitted on more leisurely the lighter and more elegant hoops, more perfectly contrived and more ingeniously intertwisted, which were to be permanent. So selfishness holds the staves of society together until the hoops of love can be hammered on, when the first rude and ugly hoop will be no longer needed.

But the bonds which hold society together are still largely external. They bind together both loosely and closely the most heterogeneous elements: the good and the bad and the indifferent, the learned and the ignorant, the refined and the rude, the clean and the unclean, the rich and the poor —these all dwell in a common country, speak one common tongue, observe certain common customs, and that is all.

Two men or two women ride together for a mile in a street-car; they submit to be companions for the sake of a common convenience. They do not speak to each other. They both want to be transferred quickly to another place. That is their common bond, riding in the same car—a bond which breaks with the end of the journey.

Two men or two women eat at the same table in the railroad dining-room. They take food from the same dish, and then go east and go west, separating forever.

Two men enter into partnership to make money. But when the mutual advantage ceases, they may pass apart, to remember one another no more.

Two men may grow up in one family, rocked in the same cradle and watched by the same love, and yet go forth into the world strangers at last.

Most inexplicable of all, man and woman may be man and wife, and yet the sources of the Nile in old days were no more mysteries to civilized Europe than the nature of this woman and of this man to each other.

But there is one bond which really unites men, and that is to love and desire the same things. We are fellow-citizens with millions of human beings, but how many of them should we find congenial to our companionship? We are drawn to those who have the same tastes with ourselves, who think the same thoughts, and who have the same ideals. Slaves used to be chained together sometimes, when they were put to work. Perhaps the only bond between them was their chain. They might be deadly enemies, keeping time together at the stroke of the oar, or bending down together to pick the cotton—linked together in body, but far apart in mind and soul. It is so sometimes with our own environment: those with whom we are most intimately associated are no more a part of that which we consider our real life— the life of our mind and soul—than if we dwelt in foreign lands, with a sea between.

We refuse to be limited in the things of our real existence to the spot where our bodies are chained.

Our friend goes away, he or she with whom we found such satisfaction for the best in us, who stimulated our aspirations and quickened our resolves and fed our high ideals. Perhaps our friend dies. But does our friend go out of our life as the light goes out of the chamber when the lamp is withdrawn? Not at all; we have his form with all his excellences to be admired and imitated, set up within the shrine of our hearts, and we live there with him still, in a far truer sense than we live outside with uncongenial things.

Nor does the process stop here. We need not have known our friend in the flesh at all. Suppose that he has left the products of his wise and beautiful thought, and the records of his noble life, embalmed in books. You read, and you discern a character who was in many respects what you yourself would like to be; who has carried on more eagerly or more courageously an ideal of living such as you would like to live; who has had thoughts which you yourself would like to think. Does he not become more real to you than many of the men and women who go in and out at your door? Does he not become a part of your real life? Do you not call him a friend, and are you not proud of the fact? Look within! Is Shakespeare an abtraction to you? or Browning or Tennyson or Shelley or Keats? or Thomas à Kempis, or Anselm, or John Bunyan, or Emerson, or Phillips Brooks? or William of Orange or Abraham Lincoln? or Giotto or Raphael or Beethoven or Shubert or Bach? or a whole glorious company of earth's noblest and best who will come at your invitation and sit down and sup with you in the "secret garden" of your mind? They belong to all mankind now, as far as mankind will understand them. They commune with all who will appreciate and love them. They have become universal by passing out of our pent-up, physical life. They have become a part of the Kingdom of Heaven, the Kingdom of the Skies, to which they each one have contributed a share in the building. For every man and every woman and every child who ever lived on this earth and ever spoke a word or performed an act of unselfishness and love; who in the least degree made life brighter and more full of meaning to other men and women coming after; who ever exhibited, in earthly living, traits of bravery and self-denial and gentleness and love—each one, in passing into the place of shadows, is not extinguished like a lamp, although our eyes behold him no more. On the contrary, that region of ideals toward which our souls are bound to turn when we grow sick over earth's unfulfilled promises,—that region, invisible yet real, along the boundaries of which our earthly path lies from the cradle to the grave, so near and yet so far,—that region gains something in definiteness, in beauty, in richness, to our minds, from each one who enters it, bearing something away with him rich and rare in his character. As far as we can see into heaven at all, it is adorned only with the precious gems which death has stolen away from earth. All that we can see of the architecture of heaven is that it is made up of those souls which have displayed some heavenly loveliness, or some striving thereafter, on this earth.

There they are, in multitude no man can number:— Saint John, at the very climax of prophetic sight, looked into heaven and saw:—there they stand, with their white robes and harps and palms, environed with righteousness and harmony and victory, in the wind which is holy influences blowing everywhere, from the central source of the great white throne; the goodly fellowship of the prophets and the glorious company of the apostles, and the heroic host of the martyrs, all the saints of all the ages—but all of them outshone, in our own sad sight, by the dear eyes of those whom we ourselves have loved and lost.

But we, looking after them this day, lay our claim to be counted in with them, fellow-citizens of the saints. That country is our country, far more than this earthly land in which we live—our true country because it is the country of our soul's choice, the Land of our Heart's Desire. The residents of that land are our true fellow-citizens, because it is not an external bond which binds us together, but the law of the heart's attraction.

Great souls of the earth, poets and painters and warriors and saints, with those beloved souls which we ourselves have known here on earth—we shall not be shut out from them, nor from their fair place above, as long as we can love what they loved, and aspire to be something of what they were.

Love is the sole bond between earth and heaven. To love heavenly things: *that* is to establish and maintain our citizenship there in heaven. To love things which are immortal: this is to drink the Water of Life and so to become ourselves immortal. To love what the great saints loved is to be fellow-citizens, with them, in the kingdom of our King, theirs and ours, our Lord and Savior, Jesus Christ.

February 11, 1924.

CHAPTER 23

The Fourth Commandment

"And it came to pass that while the children of Israel were in the wilderness, a man was found gathering sticks on the sabbath day."

Numbers xv:32.

IT WAS a simple thing to find a man out gathering sticks to cook his pint of manna. And yet there would be a certain ominousness in this scene, for the man was so definitely alone, out of sight of the tribe, the community, whose black tents would be just around the corner of the sand-hill. And the man himself must have felt a sinister something in the solitude, for he no doubt kept glancing to right and left as he went stooping along to pick up the dried stalks of shrubs and the dead twigs of trees, and he no doubt kept his growing bundle hidden in a fold of his goat's-hair cloak.

And he might well hide his findings, and he might well feel afraid, for he was committing a capital crime. The crime was not that he was gathering a handful of fuel for his little fire, but that what he did he was doing on the sabbath day. It was a capital crime to do any manner of work on the sabbath day. And so presently someone spied him, and his horrified fellow-tribesmen caught him, and they brought him to trial and condemned him, and then they took him out into a desert place and stoned him to death. Such was the price of a handful of sticks.

This example, rather stringent to our modern minds, was intended to illustrate the holiness of the sabbath day. Now the sabbath day was one of the distinguishing marks of the Jewish religion. Just as every Israelite had a special mark made upon his physical body, to show that he belonged to

196

Jehovah, so likewise every Israelite had a mark placed upon his time, to show that his life belonged to Jehovah. The sabbath day was Jehovah's name branded upon the body of the year.

The sabbath day was the seventh day of every week; and, originally, the week was a natural division of days measured off by the changes of the moon. So the seventh day was not given an arbitrary and artificial importance among the days of the week, but had its own inherent distinction in being located at a turn of the moon, from new moon to quarter, and from quarter to full, and from full to quarter, and from quarter to new moon again. And this day was honored by being made a rest-day, a day of privilege, when men dropped their toil, and were free for twenty-four hours to do the things that pleased them best.

This seventh day, this rest-day, the Hebrew tribes inherited, and they proceeded to do with it that which pleased them best.

So the Hebrews, being the most religious of people, naturally began by stamping the seventh day with a supernatural sign. It was a day offered as a sacrifice to Jehovah, a day of rest from work to commemorate the rest which Jehovah had given them from their slavery in Egypt. Then, later in their history, in order to establish the holiness of the day upon a basis more primitive and fundamental, it was conceived that the seventh day was a rest-day sacred to Jehovah, because, after six days of labor in creating the world, on the seventh day he rested from his work.

The religious observance of the seventh day, therefore, consisted above all things else in rest; that is, in cessation from work. What was at first a happy privilege, became at last a rigid law, and was incorporated in the Ten Commandments: "Six days shalt thou labor and do all that thou hast to do; but the seventh day is the Sabbath of the Lord thy God. In it thou shalt do no manner of work."

So runs the commandment still read in our churches every Sunday. We take it quite lightly, but not so the old Hebrew rabbis. As time went on, their thought became more and more concentrated, and more and more microscopically concentrated, upon this central point: Just how much did the word *work* include?

Of course all ordinary occupations of the field and shop were prohibited: all sowing, reaping, threshing, and grinding; all shearing of sheep, all spinning and weaving; all working in metal or in wood; all cooking and baking and preparing of food—even an egg might not be eaten if it had been laid on the sabbath day. All this was clear; but outside of daily routine labor there were innumerable acts to be carefully weighed by the rabbis in order to decide whether or not they fell under the head of work.

Plainly you must not carry a burden, but might you not drag it along the ground? No, for if you scratched the earth, that would be plowing. And likewise you must not pick a flower or a blade of grass, for that would be reaping. You must not kindle a fire in your stove, nor light nor extinguish a lamp; even if your house is on fire you must let it burn. If you break a bone of your arm or leg, you cannot have it set on the sabbath day; nor may you take medicine—unless you assume that you take it for pleasure and so place it outside of the sphere of work. No woman is allowed to look into a mirror on the sabbath day, and no one may tie a knot— with the exception that you are permitted to tie your shoes in the morning; but whether, if a shoe-string breaks in the course of the day, you may tie it again, is a question about which there is great difference of opinion among the rabbis.

It was into a society all tangled up in spider webs of this sort that our Lord Jesus Christ came, and for himself and for his disciples he broke them through with a careless hand. No reformer's broom he wielded against the sabbath itself, but wherever the sabbath law stood in his way he put it aside with a lordly unconcern. And when he was challenged to justify his defiance of an ancient institution, his simple reply was this: "The sabbath was made for man, and not man for the sabbath."

This saying is supplemented by another which an ancient New Testament manuscript preserves in the Gospel of Saint

Luke. As Jesus was walking one sabbath day, he saw a man busy at work. And Jesus stopped and said to him: "Man, if you know what you are doing, blessed are you; but if you do not know, cursed are you, and a transgressor of the law."

That is, the justification of the man's action depended entirely upon the motives which underlay his audacity. If he was defying the scribes and the Pharisees from the vantage of a principle, Jesus approved his freedom; but if he felt that he was breaking a law, yet ran the risk for the sake, perhaps, of another penny in his purse, Jesus could look upon him only as a man acting against his conscience, and so doing injury to his soul.

So the new religion which Jesus founded ignored not only the sabbath law, as it was developed, but the whole elaborate structure of which that law was a rigid part. Before the very gates of Jerusalem's splendid temple, both the symbol and the tomb of Jerusalem's religion, Jesus said, magnificently prophesying, "This temple will I destroy, and in three days I will build it up again."

And he did it. He destroyed the old temple by drawing out of it the divine meanings which its heavy, gold-plated masonry had imprisoned, and in the lack of which its pretentious too-visible mass grew pale and spectral, and crumbled down into dust.

And he started his new temple to be built out of men, men cemented together into one body by a new spirit, filled with enthusiasm by a new hope, and forcing, by a new force named faith, ideals to become reality.

Inevitably new forms shaped themselves around the old meanings; but these meanings, so drawn forth by our Lord and planted in humanity, can never again be completely obscured, and they have ever striven, and still are striving, to root themselves triumphantly in the lives of men.

And our struggle is still the struggle which has been that of earnest men all down the ages, to understand these meanings, and then to be loyal to them when they are understood.

Now one such meaning was the meaning behind the

199

sabbath day. Christianity repudiated the Jewish sabbath, along with other Jewish things, but it took the essential meaning of it, the consecration of time, and set it into a new day of its own, stamping the Christian year with the sign of the cross. The Christians' holy day is not the sabbath of the Jews, and never has been, least of all in the early age of the Church, when the Christian day was established, alongside, in fact, of the declining sabbath day of Judaism. The Christian Sunday is not the Jewish sabbath, as appears in four observations. In the first place, it occupies a new relation to the week; it begins the week instead of closing it. In the second place, it was given a new name; instead of being called the sabbath day by the early Christians, it was called, contrastingly, the Lord's Day. In the third place, it has a new reference; instead of commemorating the completion of creation, it commemorates the beginning of a new creation, a new life. It is a weekly Easter day, insisting that the Christian promise and hope of life's constant renewal and ultimate triumph, shall never drop out of our consciousness of time. And in the last place, it has ever been the instinct of Christianity to celebrate its own different day in its own different manner.

How shall we keep our Sunday, our Lord's Day? That we keep it shabbily and unworthily, is our constant reproach and shame. The Sabbath Commandment has had its inductive influence, no doubt, sometimes very strong. But the Sabbath Commandment and Christian liberty have not reacted well upon each other. The stoppage of labor, very good in itself, is not the true celebration of the sacred day; it is merely clearing a free space for the day's real purpose. And the day's real purpose is to allow every human being a time each week for the pursuit of the best thing in life he knows. What that best thing shall be, and by what method that pursuit shall be made, is left, in Christianity's characteristic manner, to the decision of each individual soul. No one has a right to impose upon another, except by example, his own religious ways. To try to do so, is to revert to the religion of a schedule, and to show a symptom of the fatal cancer of Judaism.

But, exulting in this freedom of Christianity, let us recall to ourselves the sobering fact that a religion of freedom is not a thing more easy than a schedule of rules and regulations; on the contrary, it is far more difficult, for the soul is thrown upon its own responsibility, and lies wide open to the danger of choosing lines of the least resistance. But it is so, the highest spiritual roads are also the most perilous. And today, with the wonder of God's presence to be perceived in a thousand ways in this wonderful world of ours, today, the Lord's Day, multitudes of Christians are out in the desert gathering sticks.

But the Lord's Day, as we have seen, means more than itself; it is the sign of the cross upon the whole week. It consecrates all time; all days are really the Lord's days. Our responsibility for the way we recognize and use the privileges it offers us, is a responsibility which extends through the whole week. Each day is full of opportunities and surprises, compelling choice and action, so that every day is in itself a valley of decision. There is a little poem of Emerson's on "The Days," which is a parable. The poet stood in his garden, watching the procession of the days go by, "marching single in an endless file." And each day had her hands full of gifts, all kinds of gifts for mortals to choose: bread, diadems, kingdoms, stars; yes, and faggots are in the enumeration—bundles of sticks. The poet, as he watched the pomp, forgot his morning's wishes, hastily took a few herbs and apples—and the Day turned and departed silent. "And I, too late"—the poem concludes—"and I, too late,

Under her solemn fillet saw the scorn."

No one can read the New Testament seriously, without being struck by the reiterated note of warning:
"Watch, for the Lord is at hand!"
"Watch, lest he find you sleeping."
"Watch, lest he come to find you a slothful and unprofitable servant."
The long centuries which have passed since these warnings were uttered, suggest to us that they refer not so much to

some "far-off, divine event" as to some crisis which each man may expect to meet him any day. That there are such crises, we all of us know, together with the humiliation of their having found us unprepared. The Lord comes every day, and we must be ashamed that he should find us occupied with trifles. The parable of the Wise and Foolish Virgins seems to mean just this. The foolish virgins were foolish because they thought that their lighted lamps were the important thing at the wedding, and so went blundering off at midnight to buy a supply of oil, and thereby missed the bridegroom's coming when he came. The important thing was to be there at the door when he arrived.

The important thing is to be doing one's duty in the place where one is. The wise man in this world is always on guard. He aims, by the daily doing of the daily duty, to develop a character which shall be proof against surprise. For it is in the unguarded hour that the character betrays its inmost quality. This is illustrated by another saying of our Lord's, not in the New Testament, but handed down to us in another way, and it is this:

"By that in which I shall find you, by that will I judge you."

And suppose, when the Lord comes and looks to meet us in the glory of the tabernacle, where the pillar of fire has settled at home and cannot be hidden behind the heavy, waving curtains embroidered with the purple, the scarlet, and the blue, suppose that the Lord find us out in the desert, stupidly gathering sticks. And suppose that then he shall say,

"By that in which I find you, by that I judge you."

Winter of 1924-5.

CHAPTER 24

Who Is This That Cometh from Edom?

"Who is this that cometh from Edom, with dyed garments from Bozrah?"

Isaiah lxiii:1.

ABOUT THIRTY YEARS ago, in the Island of Java, there were found embedded in the sandstone a few bones of what turned out to be a very ancient man; only a shattered skull and a thigh-bone, but they were enough to classify the find. He was not quite a man, it appeared after due measurement; something of an ape he was, but still more man than ape, for he had more brain than an ape, and he walked erect, as the thigh-bone proved. And so they named him the Ape-Man That Walked Erect, and they made a model of him which you may see any day in the Museum of Natural History in New York.

There are ways of estimating the age of such relics discovered in the strata of the earth, and this Ape-Man, after careful calculation, has been given a date somewhere about 500,000 years ago, the earliest trace of mankind in this world. And yet he must already have come a long distance; for it requires much time for a skull to expand to accommodate a growing brain, and it requires much time for a thigh-bone to straighten in answer to a desire to walk upright. So this Ape-Man who walked erect 500,000 years ago must already have come, they figure, at least another 500,000 years up the road from Edom, the long, long road from the place of his beginning in Bozrah.

"But wherefore is thine apparel red," one in Isaiah's parable asks, "and thy garments like his that treadeth in the wine-vat?"

"I have trodden the wine-press alone," the mysterious traveler replies; "it is my enemies I have trodden in my anger, and it is their life-blood that is splashed upon my garments."

It is true. A primary fact we may lay down as certain in the life of the ancient Ape-Man of Java, is that he was a fighter. As his fathers had been for 500,000 years, so also was he; and as he was, so his children have been for 500,000 years. Having come down out of the trees, his natural home, he has had to fight for the right to dwell on the ground. All about him were wild beasts, fiercer and stronger than he, and hungry for his flesh. And he too was hungry, and compelled to be alert for prey. Always on the watch, this side and that, always obliged to run or to fight, his life swung between two passions, fear and rage. But wild animals were not his only enemies; far from it. He had to fight wild men as well, his brothers, desiring the same warm cave or the same good food. He lived in constant tragedy, as all other creatures did; but he had one vital advantage: he was able to learn from experience. That is why his brain grew, although so slowly through the centuries: he was trying to think, trying to scheme and plan and to invent weapons. His never-ending battle was the price of his progress. And that, too, is why his garments are red; they are red with the life-blood of his enemies, as well as with his own, as he comes up the long road from Bozrah.

This mysterious stranger coming up the road from Edom with blood-stained garments and a shout of exultation, we perceive as the figure of the human race, Man climbing up the stony stages of his development, Man working his way up through the processes of his evolution. To be sure, the strict interpreters maintain that the figure is that of God himself, returning as a victorious warrior from the slaughter of his enemies in savage Edom. Very well! But it is in the works of God that we see God; and it is in the highest work of God that we see him most clearly; and the highest work of God that we know is most evidently Man; and it is in the method we name Evolution that we see God most wonderfully working; and it is in the evolution of Man that we see Evolution at its supreme level and promise. So the prophet, with insight into the realities of things, might well see God himself advancing with a shout of human triumph and pathos, in the form of a Man marching up the road of progress. The mystery of Evolution is the latest revelation of God. Here we see him in his very workshop; here we see his invisible hands weaving a universe out of living cells. And he has given us thus, in the secret of Evolution, a master-key to unlock many doors of knowledge. So when men today not merely deny, but perversely strive to extinguish this divine revelation, it is as if they, frightened by the adventure of life, would turn back again to Edom, and retrace again the well-worn road to Bozrah.

To us, living in the freer atmosphere of our Church, the reports of this strange revolt against scientific truth outside come like echoes of an alien age, when the operators of the rack could dictate to Galileo the limits of his research and his thought. To us these men seem like old King Canute, sitting on his throne by the sea-shore and commanding the tide to retire. And yet they have their followers, not a few; for they base their contention upon the necessary defense of religion, and claim to be the champions of certain fundamental truths which no man may deny, and which, they hold, the theory of Evolution implicitly contradicts. So they are known as Fundamentalists, these men, although the term is a loose one, for it includes adherents of differing ideas as to what these fundamental propositions are. Indeed, we are all Fundamentalists, no doubt, in that we all believe that there are certain truths elementary and basic in our religion, which every man must accept when he sets out to live a religious life, truths which it is a discredit to him if he does not so accept. And these fundamental truths are three.

Now it happens that these three fundamental truths of religion are involved in the life-history of the human traveler whom we see coming up from Edom; developing in him step by step as he developed, along the difficult road from Bozrah.

The first Fundamental is concerned with the relations existing between ourselves and the world in which we find ourselves. For our first practical question in life is this: Is the universe friendly to us? Is the God of Nature a God of love? And our natural answer to this question is one of suspicion. We have inherited ancient apprehensions and fears. We are still afraid of the dark; we are afraid of the unknown. We have also inherited ancient antagonisms. We know very well how Nature is red in tooth and claw, and we ourselves still feel the instinct to scratch and to bite. We suspect hostility in the very earth out of which we sprang. At the same time our newly-acquired self-consciousness increases the sense of separation. So we do not feel quite at home on our earth. This feeling crops out darkly in old theologies, which represented men as related to the earth in ways evil and dangerous, and as destined, mostly, to be swept off into a certain garbage-can of existence which they called "hell." This sense of separateness takes also another shape, when we regard the laws of the earth, the laws of nature, as like the laws of our social state, and we treat them as not applicable to us if we are clever enough to evade them. For some reason or reasons we do not feel ourselves interlocking smoothly with the scheme of things. We grow weary on the road from Bozrah.

But let us remind ourselves that no closer relationship can be thought of than that between the earth and us. Well is she named our Mother Earth. We are built out of her substance, and every cell in us beats in unison with her heart. And all earth's geologic ages are recorded in what we now are. As the glaciers left their writing upon the rocks of Put-in-Bay, so they left their grooves also upon the nature of man. And our pedigree is written down in our very bodies, a record running back through the long procession of earth's millions of years, back to the foam which floated on earth's primeval sea. We are not only brothers to the Ape-Man of Java, but we are close kin to all earth's beasts, and we are cousins of the noble race of trees.

Now when Man comes up on the road from Edom, a road

implies direction; and direction implies purpose; and purpose implies intelligence. Creation unrolls like an endless manuscript, and that which unrolls is the product of thought. But thought implies a Thinker, and we name this thinker God. It is an argument as old as Saint Paul. So whatever the creation of earth means to God, we mean that to him, and more. So our salvation and our peace will rest upon the realization of this our intimacy with creation and its Creator, and upon our will to learn and to help, and not to ignore and to hinder, the purposes of his vast and magnificent work. It is the First Fundamental, thus expressed in an ancient Book:

"Thou shalt love the Lord thy God with all thy heart, and with all thy soul, and with all thy mind. This is the first and great commandment."

And it is also the first and great Fundamental.

The Second Fundamental is concerned with the relations between ourselves and our fellow-men; relations which are gathered up and woven together and organized into what we call Society. We have said that no closer bond can be imagined than that which unites us to the earth and its Maker; but surely a bond akin to it in its closeness will be that which binds us to our fellow-men. This fact appears vividly if we fancy for a moment what a child would grow up to be if he grew up among the animals of the wood or field. Adopted by the wolves, like Romulus and Remus, or like Mowgli in *The Jungle Book,* he must become himself a kind of wolf, with no language, no knowledge, no morals, no religion. Literally we are the heirs of all the ages, owing all that we are to the accumulated wealth of the whole human race from the beginning; an inheritance which becomes our own to use only through the society into which we are born. Every word of our talk, so fluently slipping into its exact place in our sentences, has been filed and fitted and polished by millions of men, since the time it was merely a grunt or a squeal in the forest. Every article of commonest use has a lengthened history, representing the ingenious thought and experiment of generations of inventors. For example, imagine the many human hands and brains that have developed a knife, a wheel, a lock, a piece of cloth, a sheet of paper, a pen, or an alphabet.

And all our customs have the same story behind them. And the very thoughts that we think, and that seem to be so intimately our own, are thoughts which already have passed through millions of other brains, and are blowing through millions of other brains today.

This is all because men live together. Society develops by means of the co-operation of its members, struggling against common enemies. And this co-operation is kept stimulated by constant conflict and battle. Race against race, and tribe against tribe, and party against party, every generation shows its garments stained with blood. But the co-operation which at first is compelled by necessity, presently induces a sense of obligation—each member feels that he owes certain duties to his tribe. And this sense of obligation presently unfolds finer issues, in Evolution's mysterious manner; conscience appears, and justice, and an impulse to help the weak, independent of self-interest. We begin to realize that we owe the best efforts of our lives to the furthering of a process vastly larger than pursuit of our own personal safety and pleasure. We do not belong to ourselves. And presently this new sense of obligation will take the form of the Second Fundamental of our religion, also written down in an ancient Book:

"Thou shalt love thy neighbor as thyself."

But this means more than that we are to love others in the same manner, or to the same degree, that we love ourselves; it means rather that we are to love others as being part of ourselves, as we are part of them. Not only are we bone of the same bone and flesh of the same flesh, but we are brain of the same brain and heart of the same heart; so that the hurt of one is the hurt of all, and the joy of all is the joy of each. Regarding thy neighbor's rights, his personality, his happiness, as the apple of thine own eye, "Thou shalt love thy neighbor as being thyself."

And this is the Second Fundamental.

208

And now we have come to the Third Fundamental of faith. They tell us of an ancient people in the West, a remnant of whom still cherish the embers of an expiring civilization, who watch, and have watched from time immemorial, for a hero, a leader, who shall come one day to restore them to energy and dominion. What planted that expectation in their souls at first, they themselves could tell the least of all, for it must have grown out of the very substance of their hearts, a hope born of endless desire and defeat, as they fought their way up along their human road; a dream that the green earth might reach upward and the blue sky might bend down, until, at the point where they touched, a man might spring who was also a god, and a god might descend who was also a man, to make life new for them. It is the universal dream of humanity. And so, there they sit through the years and wait, weaving bright-colored woolen blankets as they wait, in whose zigzag patterns of red and black and green and blue they try to express dim thoughts of the earth below and the sky above. And every morning, from times unknown, a watchman climbs to the top of a tower and gazes forth over the plain to the east, to see whether, at last, the horses and chariot of their long-awaited leader may not now be descried coming toward them from afar. With his hand over his eyes, the watchman strains his sight along the shining road into the sunrise. And then, seeing nothing in all the wide plain, he climbs wearily down for another day.

Why does he linger so long in coming from Edom? And why does he so long delay upon the road from Bozrah?

Ah, well! He has already come—if they only knew. And that he has come, and that every human creature owes to him his oath of allegiance and loyalty, is the Third Fundamental of our religion. For it is in him that earth and sky have met. Men's passion to reach God could never rest until they saw him as perfect Man, for man is the only being that men can understand; and men's inborn hero-worship could never stop until they saw their hero as divine, for God is the only being that they can fitly worship. And here he is, our Lord Jesus Christ, who lived and died and lives again. Men can no more explain him than they can explain life. And men can no more ignore him than they can ignore goodness and beauty and truth.

When men ask, as they always ask, what God is—can it be that he is friendly?—here is the answer: God is like that. And when men ask, as they always ask, what kind of men they themselves ought to be, here also is the answer: Become like him.

And love is the essential force in both aspects. Love God, as we so learn to know him, and we are at home at last on this our beautiful earth. Love men, as we so learn to love them, and the co-operation which creates and preserves Society becomes a heavenly thing. And the time will come, it is drawing nearer—slowly, slowly, it still is drawing nearer— when men will make this transfigured co-operation dominate the world; and they will see their true enemies to be, in the eternal war which it is their destiny to wage, no more their fellow-men, but disease and ignorance and superstition and anarchy and chaos and everything that maketh a lie. And they will combine to exterminate such enemies, beating their swords into plowshares, and their spears into pruning-hooks.

And so these are our three Fundamentals: (1) Love God; (2) love man; (3) love God and love man together, as we see God both loved and loving, and as we see man both loved and loving, in him who knows entirely how rough is the road from Edom, his own garments dyed with the blood of Bozrah, our Lord and Savior, Jesus Christ.

(After 1925.)

CHAPTER 25

The Veil of the Temple Was Rent

"And behold, the veil of the Temple was rent in two from the top to the bottom."

Matt. xxii:51.

IN JERUSALEM, WHERE our Lord died, a magnificent Temple stood. In the Temple a great curtain hung. Full thirty feet in height it was, and the width was thirty feet. It was woven of linen and wool, very heavy and thick, so that it was like a soft, hanging wall. And it was in fact a kind of wall, for it closed the end of the Holy Place opposite the entrance door, separating it from the inmost shrine of the Temple, the Most Holy Place called the Holy of Holies. The sacred colors of the Law were woven into this curtain, scarlet and purple and blue and gold. And these colors took mystic, symbolic forms over the field of the curtain, figures of cherubim with wide-spread wings, and checker-work, and inter-twisted vines, and pomegranates, and grapes.

This great curtain was called the Veil of the Temple, and it hid from sight the dark, cube-shaped chamber behind, where the Lord Jehovah was thought to dwell. In mysterious darkness, behind the veil, God dwelt in his Temple. And into this dark chamber, behind the veil, only one man out of all the people was ever allowed to enter. This one man was the high-priest, the official representative of the people, and even he was allowed to enter there on only one day out of the whole year. And he himself could enter the Holy of Holies, behind the veil, for only one purpose, to sprinkle there upon the sacred rock the blood of a bullock and a goat as an atonement for the sins of himself and of the people. So this great curtain represented a fundamental fact of

211

separation between God and man. It represented a wall between God and man.

Now one afternoon, about three o'clock, a very strange thing happened, we are told. Suddenly, while the priests were engaged in the evening sacrifice, perhaps offering the incense before the great curtain, it was torn in two, from the top to the bottom. The great curtain was suddenly torn in two. And if the two torn halves of it blew aside, the terrified priests could see, if they dared to look, into the very Holy of Holies, where God himself dwelt.

But the priests could not have known what it meant. By no possibilty could they have connected this strange happening with a man who was just then dying, as a criminal on a cross, outside the city gate. But the history which at once began to flow from the man's life and death, revealed, in due time, to other men, at least, what it meant. The history of Christianity explained what the strange miracle meant. Indeed, it has been surmised that the miracle itself is only the poetical statement of the history, a symbolic explanation of the history. However that may be, the fact remains that this man's life and death tore open the veil conceived to be between God and his humankind, so that all men may now enter, without priest and without sacrifice, into the Holy of Holies where God dwells.

For the new covenant is written on the hearts of men, and not on tables of stone. The new Holy of Holies is man's own heart, and the only veil between God and man is the veil which man himself may weave. But man, above all things, is a weaver of veils.

Therefore, see now what comes to pass. Hardly had men recovered from their Pentecostal joy, out of their heads for a time with joy over the new revelation, that their Lord was alive and with them again, than they began on the warp of their new materials to weave a new veil out of the very threads of the old. But this was on a far grander scale. It hung from the sky and was as wide as East and West. And on it presently, in all colors, were embroidered cities and domes; the lust of the eye and the pride of life; processions and armies and banners and flags; heathen gods with new names, and heathen superstitions marked with the sign of the cross; a hierarchy of priests to underwrite passports to heaven, and heretics burning at the stake; angels and arch-angels above, and a red lake of fire below, in which swam the souls of the everlastingly damned.

Here was a veil sufficient to hide God. But this was not all. Behind this veil was another veil, woven out of ancient philosophies, vast spider-webs, heavy with the brown dust of the ages, not lacking spiders, too, on the watch for heresy.

But even this was not all. The old high-priest of Jeru-salem went with fear and trembling behind the veil once a year, afraid lest some unperceived spot of sin in himself might make his approach a fatal presumption; but the new high-priest, no longer the humble representative of men but the master of their bodies and souls, strode unabashed into the Holy of Holies with his triple crown upon his head, and sat down on the very throne of God.

And this claimed to be that Christianity which rent in two the veil of the Temple, signifying that man no longer needs a representative to intercede with God for him, but that he himself must enter alone into the Presence of God, there to make his own plea and present his own case; that our Lord, who taught us to say "Our Father," declared thereby that the way into the presence of a father is open to all his sons; that he who rent the veil of the Temple, at the same time spoke to all the children of men and said: "Come unto me all ye that are weary and heavy-laden," so that the most miserable sinner now has as much right to enter into the Presence of God as the Pope of Rome. All mediation, except the mediation of Christ himself in rending the veil, is forever swept away. And all means and all methods of religion are good now only as they help us to realize the universal Presence of God in his world.

But now let us not stand aloof and condemn the Church of a thousand years because of the veil which it wove and hung in the Temple to hide God; for the Church always was, and is, the Church of that mankind to which we ourselves belong;

and the Church has always been, and is, what we ourselves have made it. And men, as we have said, above all things are weavers of veils. Just as the ancient Jews themselves wove the great veil of the Temple and hung it up to hide the Holy of Holies where their Lord Jehovah dwelt; so men are always engaged in weaving veils which hide a spiritual world and a God who is Spirit, from their spiritual sight.

We ourselves are doing it continually. Through some strange hereditary impulses, of shame for our nakedness, or fear of the vast unknown, or even the cave-man's instinct to hide in the earth; or through some backwardness in development, or through some sluggishness in learning what our Lord made it his great aim to teach and to manifest in his life and death; we shrink from the thought of meeting God face to face. At least we act as if we so shrank; and so we keep our shuttles flying day and night, weaving veils which shall hide him from our eyes. And yet we know not what we do; and so perhaps it may be well to remind ourselves of a few of those veils which we, poor weavers, weave.

In reality these veils are all one; they are simply our inability to realize the Presence of God in the world. And obviously the first form of that veil to meet us will be that which is created by our own wrong-doing. When we ignore our conscience, at once we feel something intervening between ourselves and God. Something hangs intangible and inevitable between ourselves and our free approach to him. It is something that we ourselves have made, and yet we do not know how to unmake it, nor how to grope a way through its perplexing folds. Our first impulse is to try the methods we try with an earthly superior,—we used to say a king. We will send him a present, we will make for him a sacrifice; we will persuade someone, or bribe someone, to go in to him in our stead, and intercede for us.

But our Lord shows us a better way; he himself tears the separating veil in two; and he invites us to enter and to say there in our own person that we are sorry for our sin, and that we promise a better will for the time to come, and ask for the aid of his love to help us against ourselves. The way through the veil is our own personal plea of repentance, addressed as sons to a father, and not as criminals to a judge,—which is indeed all that is meant by the difficult theological phrase, "Justification by Faith." The only true confessional-box is in our own heart, and there we whisper always into an attentive ear. "When thou prayest," said our Lord, "enter into thy closet, and shut thy door, and then in secret pray to thy Father who heareth in secret."

Another veil is the veil of the every-day life, out of which we weave a curtain to hide the Holy of Holies from our eyes. The world in which we live is so very visible, it is so very evident, it is so very insistent, that we are prone to think it is the only world there is. The pictures embroidered on the curtain of life and nature, are so pleasant to look at that we forget that they are only symbolic pictures, meant to convey meanings that are more real and more important. The return of the spring, for instance, is very beautiful, and we enjoy it as it recurs, with our gratified senses, year after year; but we rarely stop to think that it preaches, whenever it returns, a Gospel of Resurrection, year after year.

The lives we lead are very full of interest, so many subjects of fascinating study, so many friends to meet for the solace of our heart, so many pleasures to enjoy, so many ambitions we deem worthy of our work; but we are very apt not to think far back of our interest. Art for art's sake, life for life's sake, we say. And so our politics tend to become partisanship; and our duties tend to become routine and drudgery; and our methods tend to become machinery; and our talk tends to become cant; and our religion tends to become mere formalism. And then, when interests fail, as interests ever may, our lives settle down into the deadly level of the commonplace, and become drab-colored and narrow and mean.

Thus in our every-day life two tendencies contend; one makes it worth too much, and one makes it worth not enough. And both work side by side, in the same soul. We are both too busy, and at the same time too unoccupied; and so in this most active age of the world, we hear the most voices of discontent. We see two sides of the same veil, the veil which hides God from our eyes.

But our Lord has torn this veil in two. When he lived our common human life, he turned it forever into something heavenly. He transfigured human life in all its smallest details, so that nothing in it should ever again be deemed common or unclean. And the reason was that he saw it all in the light of the Presence of God. And in such a light there is nothing small that is real.

He saw in common children members of the Kingdom of heaven; he saw in publicans and sinners his companions and friends; he saw riches in a poor widow's copper pennies; and on the Mount of Transfiguration his coarse peasant's garments became raiment white and glistering. And the reason was that he saw everything in the light of the Presence of God. And in such a light there is nothing common that is real.

"Devoutly look, devoutly look, and naught but wonders shall pass by."

But another veil that we constantly weave is the veil of doubt. It is doubt of the Presence of God in the affairs of the world, because so much is active there that seems not to be divine. When we see nature "red in tooth and claw," and when we see men driven by the same instincts; when we see so much suffering and sorrow, suffering and sorrow that the innocent have to endure; when we see so much deprivation and poverty and loss, when we see so much human life going to waste, and so much promise never coming to bloom; when we see so much tragedy, and tragedy seeming to fall by chance, without reason or design; when we see the ideals of materialism so victorious in the battles of men; and when we see a great war for noble ends, as we thought, leaving the world in a quagmire of selfishness and cross-purposes, where the only haven of peace seems to be the stupidity of Main Street; then it is no wonder that we feel oftentimes that a veil is hung between God and the world, and that He who sits behind the veil is well named the "Great Indifference."

But even this veil has been rent in two by the hands of

our Lord. And this is declared and guaranteed by his very name, his prophetic name, "Immanuel," which means, "God is with us." If we could but remember this difficult name, "Immanuel," *God is with us,* it would be the cure of all our woe. If God be with us, and if we realize that this is so, we can run and not be weary, and we can walk and not faint.

And when Immanuel came and dwelt among us, pitched his tent among us, as the Gospel says, that we might catch, through its crevices, the glory of God; when Immanuel came and dwelt among us, he saw low ideals sitting in high places, even as now, absolutely deaf to his appeal. He knew poverty and injustice and misunderstanding and treachery and loss, even as we. He felt all the loneliness and all the pain and all the tragedy and the death—we keep each Passion Week in memory of it. And he even knew the bitterness of our doubt, so it seems, when he cried from the cross, "My God, my God, why hast thou forsaken me?"

That he whose name is Immanuel, God is with us, that he knew all these things, is our way through the veil of doubt. He knew them then, he knows them now. And remembering that he knows them, we still may not be able to sing, as the girl Pippa did, in Browning's poem, on her happy holiday,

> "God's in his heaven—
> All's right with the world."

But we *are* able to say, on the supreme authority of our Lord, "God's in his earth, and in all the suffering and in all the strife of it." The way of evolution, or of salvation, is the way of crucifixion. Man, like God, must endure the cross. Not a sparrow can fall to the ground without our Father —the Father of sparrows, and so, still more, the Father of us men. So God is in all our common life.

Our Lord, before he died, sat down to a common meal with his disciples; and he took the common food, bread and wine. "Eat and drink this in remembrance of me," he said. And this his disciples have ever done.

But men are above all things weavers, as we have said. And so they took this very remembrance, and they wove out of it another veil to hide the Presence of God. The Holy Communion itself, strange to say, may be made, and has been made, into the great veil of the Temple, to hide the Holy of Holies from men's eyes. And this is done by confining the sight to the symbols, and by riveting the thought on the bread and wine.

For what is true remembrance of our Lord, but remembrance of how he made a sacrament out of human life, out of all of human life, its daily task, its simple family relationships, its humble friendships, its hungers and its thirsts, its aches and its pains, and the inevitable tragedy at the end of it?

He made every meal a sacrament. It is as if he said: "So near is God to you, that he is in the bread and wine you eat and drink, and in the human companionship of those who sit around the same table to partake of it."

No, there is no true remembrance of him, unless our every-day life, fed on such food, becomes itself a sacrament: an outward visible sign of a resurrection and a life beyond this world.

There is one more veil which hangs between God and man, and that is the veil of Death. There it hangs, and there it has always hung, so inevitable and so final, and so apparently the end of all things; so impenetrable and so indifferent to human hearts, that men have always found it difficult to reconcile their ideas of a living God with the fact of this enemy of life. From behind the dark, smothering folds of this veil never, never has there come one authentic whisper to tell us that life is not extinguished but only hidden by it. Never, never have we heard one single syllable to let us know what lives behind the veil.

Three thousand and five hundred years ago, they laid a young Egyptian king in his granite tomb. They made his poor, dead body ready for a long, long journey, and they placed beside it plenty of food for the traveler's need. There they left him in the perfumed darkness, and there he has lain quiet for three thousand and five hundred years. Three thousand and five hundred years! And still his waiting feet have not yet started on their journey, and still the food prepared for him we find is all untouched. And all that we can guess from this pathetic experiment is that the king set out on his road long ages ago in fact, and that the veil of Death divides him irrevocably from all the things of this earth.

But our Lord Jesus Christ passed through this veil of death. He tore it in two from the bottom to the top. We cannot see within. But we do know that our Lord still lives, and that his Presence fills the world, and that it issues from behind the veil. This is all that we know about death, that it is not necessarily final. And this is the glory of the Christian religon: the faith that neither things present nor things to come, that neither height nor depth, nor life nor death, nor any other created thing, can be woven into a temple-veil to separate us from the love of God which is in Christ Jesus our Lord.

(1929)

Chapter 26

A Door Was Opened in Heaven

"After this I looked, and behold, a door was opened in heaven."

Rev. iv:1.

IN FRONT OF the south porch of Kokosing, the Bishop's House in the woods yonder, you see the trees drawn back in a semicircular wall around an open slope of grass. Through this defensive rampart of trees three tunnels have been cut, with design to give three glimpses into the outside world. On the left hand you look down the leafy passage and catch at the end the spire of the Chapel of the Holy Spirit, clear-cut against the east a mile away. On the right hand you get a distant view of farms and folded hills across the valley, with a soft horizon fading to the west. And now in front, facing you to the south, is the third opening through the foliage of the girdling trees. Downward it slopes with the slope of the hill, and at the farther end below you see the bright mirror of the river, reflecting to your eyes a shining blue which is itself out of sight. It is your reason alone that tells you that what you see is the river; for if you trusted your senses you might well believe that you were looking through a long telescope of leaves into the very sky. And it was while gazing down this leafy telescope one day, on the south porch of Kokosing, that someone said: "It is like a window looking out into heaven, on the other side of the world."

Now this remark, so casual, so fanciful, nevertheless expressed the most poignant question humanity ever asks: "What is on the other side of life?" And as I thought afterward over this remark, so casual and yet so significant, I felt that the vivid man who made it might himself be such a window as we long for, looking out into heaven on the other side of the world. He himself represented so finely a fact which is omnipresent with humanity. For in the very heart of man is the magic casement—"opening on the foam of perilous seas," indeed, but mysterious seas in the world beyond the world.

It is the world beyond the world that is the object of our ceaseless wonder, hope, and fear. Like Christopher Columbus men stand forever on the shore of Spain, gazing west so wistfully, and asking the question over again and again, "Can there be land beyond the far horizon line?"

But Christopher Columbus never saw, as we see, ship after ship set sail continually, never to return, never to send back the faintest word of what they found. It would have made him despair; but here we dare not despair, although we often may doubt. Our entire being is too deeply involved for despair. We cannot know, but neither can we admit that there is nothing to know. Our fatal mistake most often is this, that we gaze to the west for our certainties, instead of toward the east.

We picture the world beyond the world as a glorified duplicate of this. It is inevitable that we should do so; and yet Nature takes utmost pains to destroy all ground for such imaginings. In the midst of this physical world in which we have so much delight, a world so tangible, so visible, so apparently permanent and real, suddenly one who walks intimately beside us pauses to listen to a call he alone can hear, turns to see something he alone can see. He drops whatever his hands may hold; he drops his cup or his book, and he throws aside his cloak and he flees away, unearthly swift, into the silence and into the dark.

It is surely not another material world into which he goes without material baggage. We acknowledge that, but nevertheless we think of him as living in similar earthly scenes. Of course we are not able to think of him otherwise, but it rouses puzzling contradictions. He walks amid unfading flowers, we say, but unfading flowers are wax flowers. He lives where now there is no death, we say, but a world without death is a dead world.

Very childish, and very pathetic, too, are the ways in which we try to get into touch with him—for they are physical ways. And oftentimes we peer into dark cellar-windows, mistaking them, alas! for windows into the sky! But is there, then, no evidence at all of a world beyond this world? Yes, such evidence is ours to find. But let us look east instead of west.

Actually we live all the time in a world that is not a material world. That is, we men live in such a world, although the animals and trees, our fellow-creatures, do not; we do because we are men. We have pleasures and pains, like the animals, which belong to the body; but we have also pleasures and pains, motives and aspirations, which belong to the soul, and soul-life is life of another world, strangely involved with this. We may call it the spiritual world, or we may call it the world beyond or behind the world, but we live in it, here and now, although hardly realizing its signs for what they truly are.

It is somewhat as when we move about in the sunshine, very busy with our work and our play, but forgetting that the light of the stars is mingled with the sunlight, though drowned by it for the time. But the stars are all there, the zodiac binding the sphere and the North Star holding the pole, with all the mysterious unknown influences which the constellations exert, operating just the same. So we live and move and have our being in two worlds, each one drawing us with tragic counteractions. The sense of the inner is overwhelmed by the insistence of the outer, though oftentimes we flee into it for refuge or for ecstasy. It is as wide and as little realized as the starry firmament, but for our present practical purpose we may give it this much of a name: "The Starry Firmament of the True, the Beautiful, and the Good."

Truth comes first. Truth belongs to the spiritual world, because it belongs to mind. Truth is the relation between mind and the things perceived by it. It is the harmony between what a thing appears in the mind to be, and what it actually is. So all our human activities, our sanity, our development, our very existence on earth, depend upon the degree in which the mind perceives the real nature of the world outside the mind. It is no wonder, therefore, that one of our Lord's names in heaven is "Faithful and True." It is no wonder that what was conceived to be Falsehood in the highest affairs was branded as Heresy and punished as a capital crime. The instinct was right, although Falsehood often has posed as the champion of Truth, and in the name of Truth tried to shut up Truth in prison. To man's entire being, as far as man is mind, Truth is necessary, fundamental, immutable, ultimate, so that the human mind's search for Truth is the real Quest of the Holy Grail.

And now the wonderful result is this, that the farther and farther this quest advances, the more what seems to be material reality melts and vaporizes, revealing more and more distinctly a universe of force and life behind. In other words, the bond of Truth which ties the mind to the outer world proves to be something organic, like arteries and nerves, which unites it to the world beyond the world.

The sign, then, which the flying soul sees and follows, is the finger of reality, beckoning it home.

The second window into the spiritual world is Beauty. The pilgrim spoke more truly than probably he meant when he stood in rapture before the great east window of the French cathedral, and called it a descent of the Holy Ghost. And perhaps the poet meant all he said when he exclaimed that in Beauty he drank "the bright wine of immortality." For Beauty is a universal miracle whose power we all feel, and our response to which we all suspect may measure some essential element of soul.

Beauty cannot be analyzed as we analyze other phenomena. That which makes it Beauty always remains mystic, wonderful. Chemistry explains the painted trees of autumn, but it cannot explain why our eyes see fairly-land. Optics will explain the sunset, but not how the sunset becomes to us an apocalypse. Physics and mathematics explain music, but not why music starts harps to playing and gracious presences to moving in the inmost chambers of the heart.

Patterns of sound and color in themselves are not Beauty; Beauty is what the mind does to patterns of color and sound. Like Truth, Beauty is the relation between something outside and something inside the soul. There is a bond reciprocal between what we perceive as beautiful, and that within us which perceives it. If Beauty belongs to the spiritual world, so also do we, in whom is the power to recognize and love the beautiful. Is it a figure too extravagant to say that Beauty is a bright wine of immortality, for immortal souls to drink? Is it too much to say that Beauty, like Truth, is a light shining out from heaven's open door? Is it too much to say that the call which the flying soul hears and follows is a god-song luring it home?

The third window into the spiritual world is Goodness. Goodness is inseparable from Truth and Beauty, Truth being the essential basis of it, as of everything, and Beauty being the manifestation of it, although wrought now in a different material, the material of human character. Goodness, therefore, might be named the Beauty of Holiness. And Goodness has this pre-eminent distinction, that it belongs only to persons. It is seen only in a person, and by a person only can it be seen. It creates human companionship, without which this world, with all its illimitable interest and loveliness, would be but a desert of Sahara. The value, the delight, the endurance, of human companionship are in exact proportion to the fidelity, the nobility, the goodness of companions.

We say, and we say truly, that the most precious flower of creation is personality. So high is the estimate we place upon it, that we are obliged to think of God himself as a Person, with supreme personal attributes of will and wisdom and love. So the great Spirit of the spiritual world, the great Personality, is with a special closeness the God of persons. And wherever we see the fruits of the Spirit, as listed by Saint Paul—love, joy, peace, patience, kindness, courtesy, fidelity, humility, and self-control—we see the light of the spiritual world, where the glory of the Lord is the light thereof, shining through the colored glass of human lives.

And the unending procession of good men and women passing away from earth and out of sight, does not leave us without a hope. For, if Truth be Truth, and if Beauty be the radiance of immortality, and if Goodness be the character of God, they must be traveling on to "the world on the other side of the world," where—so we dare to believe—the companionship of souls will be their meat and drink, their varied landscape and their evening tent, with the sky of God's infinite companionship above them all.

Gambier, Ohio
October 12, 1930

CHAPTER 27

And Isaac Went Out to Meditate

*"And Isaac went out to meditate in the field at the
eventide; and he lifted up his eyes, and saw, and, behold,
there were camels coming.*

Gen. xxiv:63.

THE HOUR OF evening always invites to meditation. The
busy day is over, and all nature begins to settle itself for the
mysterious calm of the approaching night. A definite space
of time is ended, a definite stint of work is finished, and another step has been taken on the stairway of life. So the quiet
hour of evening invites the thought to look back upon the
day to estimate its worth, and to cast a glance forward to the
possibilities of the morrow.

Isaac, son of Abraham, wished to be alone to meditate. He
had left his father's tents, in which evening-talk and prepara-
tions for rest were distracting, and was walking in the field,
where the open sky above him gave space for the winging of
his thoughts. And Isaac was a young man, with much to think
about. Being a young man, his thoughts were "long, long
thoughts," flying into the future rather than brooding upon
the past. His father Abraham had sent a trusted servant into
a far country to bring back, if it might be, a fitting wife for
him, a wife of his own kindred. For it was time for Isaac to
marry, and it was not well, Abraham knew, that Isaac should
take a wife from the alien Canaanites among whom they
dwelt.

It was this fateful embassy to Mesopotamia that must have
been the subject of Isaac's meditation. It could not have
been otherwise, for the outcome of it must color all the years
ahead. If there were doubts and fears for him, they would be

226

the inevitable shadows that lurk in all that is unknown; but Isaac was a young man, and hope must have been the sky of his soul, with stars beginning to shine in it, and with a prophetic breeze to blow beautiful dreams through it, as the winds of the desert often bring fragrance from far-away flowers and lemon-groves.

Then, in the midst of such meditation, Isaac, watching continually, no doubt, the dim horizon-line, lifted up his eyes and saw a caravan of camels in the distance. We are able to imagine, from designs on Christmas cards and other creations of artists' fancy, something approximate to the picture that Isaac saw: a long procession of camels, one behind another, carrying riders and baggage, all in sharp silhouette against the gold of the evening sky.

Were they merchants coming from Gilead, their camels loaded with spicery, balm, and myrrh to carry down into Egypt, or were they his father's servants returning from Mesopotamia? What were those camels bringing to him, disappointment or a bride? And Isaac girded up his heart, and walked forward across the field to meet the caravan.

This idyllic story, set down with so much detail in the Book of Genesis, was not composed for entertainment of the dwellers in the nomads' tents; it was to mark its importance in the history of Israel. For the eyes of the inspired writer, seeing the future as the present in one wide view, might perceive what those camels were actually bearing out of the East and over the rocks and sand to Isaac. Not only the veiled Rebekah, with her jewels of silver and jewels of gold, and her store of costly raiment, but centuries of wonderful history were hidden in those corded packs:

Jacob's dream of a stair that reached from earth to heaven, with angels going up and down; Joseph's dreams in Canaan and in Egypt; the visions of Moses on Mount Sinai; the forty-years' wandering in the desert, with its delusive mirages and its dreams of a Promised Land; the musical harp and the conquering sword of King David; the Temple with its Holy of Holies where Jehovah might dwell, in perfumed darkness, among his people; the visions of the great prophets, foretelling doom and marvelous restorations; wars and exile and yet more wars; a new Temple, more magnificent, but in whose Holy of Holies the ark of the covenant no longer was; always strife and agony, yet always a desperate star of hope; until, at last, another caravan should come out of the East, bearing to a stable-door gifts of gold and frankincense and myrrh.

Nothing of all this could Isaac possibly know, as he led Rebekah proudly to his mother's tent; and yet, to the eyes of the prophet, it all was there. And that it was so, is the very reason why the beautiful story is told.

We very often in these days have melancholy hours like the shade of eventide, in which the sinking of hope is the setting sun, when we take a little time alone with heavy thoughts, and meditate on what is coming out of the future upon our land. The doubts and fears that always have hiding places in what is unknown, have grown bolder and more terrifying in the past few years, and men who maintain a brave front before the world often whisper in confidence that they are afraid. Institutions that we considered permanent and founded upon rock now show ominous cracks in their walls. Wealth that seemed as real as anything material can be, has suddenly been found, when men unlocked their safety deposit boxes, to be like fairy gold that turns, when counted, into brown and withered leaves. Doctrines of religion, which we were taught in our youth to be fixed and unchanging, have little by little been crumbling away, making many people apprehensive that religion itself is doomed to disintegrate. And the enforced idleness of millions of men is sowing seeds of multiplied evils to be harvested in sorrow in due time.

Well, as we meditate upon these portents, which truly would seem to have been long ago foretold: "Upon the earth distress of nations, in perplexity for the roaring of the sea and the billows, men's hearts failing them for fear, and for expectation of the things which are coming on the world" —as we meditate upon what would seem to be fulfilment of these words, let us not forget the climax for which this dark prophecy was but the preparation: "When these things begin to come to pass, then look up, and lift up your heads; for your redemption draweth nigh. And ye shall see the Son of Man coming upon the clouds, with power and great glory."

Now these words, which are the very words of our Lord, have lost their vivid force for us, because we have been taught to look far into the future for their accomplishment, in one unique spectacular event. But the truth is—and may we keep it well in mind—that the Coming of the Son of Man is a process extending through the centuries. The clouds upon which he comes are not the shining thunder-heads we see these summer afternoons, but they are phenomena of the spirtual world, the region of our ideas of goodness, beauty, and truth. And the periods of confusion that precede these successive episodes of his Coming, are the breaking of bonds with which men have tried to confine into rigid permanence the expanding forms that Life is forever creating.

Men cannot—they cannot—much as we long for something fixed and stable in a tragic world of change, they cannot shut up life in institutions and covenants and codes and creeds, and expect them to last forever. Life is in its very nature change—do we not know it! Its symbol is not a granite pyramid—which is only a tomb; its symbol is rather a growing tree. And the only part of a tree that is alive is the part that keeps changing, the leaves and fruit that come and go, and the slowly increasing circumference. Conditions change: climate and population, for instance, modes of thought, scientific method and discovery, inventions of machinery; but life adapts itself undauntedly, making of these very things its own instruments; yet unless the institutions of society, the protective armor that society has devised for itself, unless these institutions are elastic and allow for growth, there is distress and trouble, shortness of breath and heart-disease.

All this is plain enough in the political world. Think, too, of the field of religion. What has become of the old doctrines preached more or less everywhere only fifty years ago? What has become of the flaming hell, and the terrific divine decisions of fore-ordination, and the mercantile "plan of salvation," and other things that I might name? They have disappeared—or almost disappeared—of themselves, so it would seem, as salt dissolves in water.

Now changes occur, never without reason. They occur to make way for something coming. Always that. They are the pressure of the future. And although there is stress and pain and perplexity in the process, and although we may fear that what the future brings us is something worse than the past, yet it is shame for us to allow our faith to let go its grip upon certain fundamental assurances. The first is the ultimate victory of Freedom, meaning by Freedom the possession, by every soul that God has made, of the opportunity to attain a complete and happy life, and to achieve that destiny for which we believe that God created souls. We know that that state of things has not yet arrived. The selfishness of men has forever been erecting barriers in the way of this heavenly idea, and ignorance of how to strive for it has always been in alliance with the enemies of its progress. For just as the foes of Freedom are obliged to wave the flag of freedom and masquerade as friends, so the partisans of Freedom borrow both the weapons and the spirit of Despotism, and win, when they chance to win, a doubtful victory.

Nevertheless, the cause of Freedom advances, though never so slowly, like the tide, of which the waves recede and return incessantly, to add painful inch to inch in their gradual progress up the shore. It was only yesterday that the Declaration of Independence was printed again in the papers, to remind us that Freedom is still a living idea, an idea that cannot die. And it may well remind us, too, that the war for Freedom on this side of the world had only begun at Yorktown.

And the second fundamental assurance is this: that there is a principle in the world called Good, and it is stronger than a principle called Evil; that men are in the world for that which is good—something larger and better, after all, than their own individual happiness, though men find their true happiness only in serving it. And that assurance is religion. Doctrines and creeds may lose their validity and fade into relics preserved for their ancient sacredness, but religion remains as an essential element in men's lives. Its forms of expression may change, and its methods change—they do change—but that is no reason for despair. "God's in his heaven," and while it is hard for us to see that "all's right with the world," yet our faith must hold fast to the thought that all's *going* to be right with the world. It is on the way. It is coming. Creation was not finished in seven days; it is still in process. And we all of us are, in Saint Paul's words, fellow-laborers with God, in his difficult task of creating a good world out of chaos. We walk by faith and not by sight; which means that our road is precarious, but it is also adventurous and wonderful, with the stimulus always of an earnest upward-looking expectation—for hope has been called the rainbow over faith.

"Say not the struggle naught availeth,
   The labor and the wounds are vain,
The enemy fainteth not nor faileth,
   And as things have been they remain.

"For not through eastern windows only,
   When morning comes, comes in the light;
In front the sun climbs slow—how slowly!
   But westward, look, the land is bright."

(*1930-33.*)

Chapter 28

While I Was Musing, the Fire Burned

"While I was musing, the fire burned."
Psalm xxxix:3.

ONE DAY, IN the railroad station at Columbus, my attention was drawn to a small boy who was trailing along in the stream of passengers flowing through the gates. He was in fact inviting the attention of everybody in his immediate neighborhood by repeating in a clear, chanting voice a very remarkable declaration. For he was saying, over and over again, these exact words:

"Day by day, in every way, I am growing better and better."

But such joy as we who heard him might have felt over this encouraging announcement, was discounted as soon as we noted the expression in the boy's face. There was something so impudent in the poise of his head, and there was something so impish in the glint of his eye, as led us to suspect that a more truthful confession might have been the complete opposite: "Day by day, in every way, I am growing worse and worse."

The secret of this exhibition lay, of course, in the adult environment in which the boy's days had been cast. It was from grown-up people that he must have learned his very improbable affirmation, and it must have been from their own flippant remarks that he had caught this particular method of raising a laugh. For the time of this episode was the time when the French psychologist, Professor Coué, was visiting this country, and thousands of honest, respectable, middle-aged Americans, taught by him, were practising a new magic, and were repeating exactly twenty times each night, "Day by day, in every way, I am growing better and better."

Now this new magic was based upon a new discovery in the human mind. Just as on the other side of the earth Europe found at last another continent which had lain so long unknown—although tropic flowers and fragments of carved driftwood had long been washed up on the shores of Spain, to set the sailor-boys to dreaming—so, a while ago, in the curious Nineteenth Century, the accumulated notes of mental activities unexplained by the current "mental philosophy," led to the theory—perhaps we may call it the discovery—of another continent of mind beyond that mind whose geography—or, rather, whose psychography—we had studied in our schools. This new continent of mind was named the "Subliminal Mind" or the "Subconscious Mind," by which was meant that it lies below the threshold, or surface, of our every-day consciousness. Romantic imagination at once began to paint the wonders of this new continent, attracting bold adventurers. Here was the true El Dorado, and here the real Fountain of Youth, within us, like the Kingdom of Heaven.

More sober investigators, however, trying to chart a reliable map of this new territory, have ignored the fancies of the earlier romancers, but even so their drawings are sufficiently marvelous. For they locate here that department of mind which carries on those varied physiological operations which maintain our life and health in the body—like the intricate machinery of a ship, unknown to passengers in the cabin.

And here lies, like the ooze in the bottom of the sea, a bed of ancient heredities and animalisms, stirred up, now and then, to cloud the clearer regions of the consciousness above. And here are the safety deposit boxes in which are stored away the many things we never realize we remember until they turn up in strange abnormal states. And here is that noiseless apparatus whose existence appears not only in the solution of difficult problems in dreams sometimes, but also and especially in the inspirations of genius.

All this is sufficiently marvelous; but the activities of the subliminal mind are brought into far closer relationship with what we call normal life, by a further teaching of the psychologists, which is this: that the subliminal mind originates nothing, and can make no discoveries of its own. It can only use what is given to it by the Conscious Mind. In dreams it plays with the materials of memory—as if a child were let loose in an office and should proceed to build castles and palaces with the cards of the card-catalogue. The subliminal mind of genius can do no more than that—although now it is not a child but an angel that is playing with the cards. And in the miracles of faith the process is still the same; the subliminal mind is now like the Slave of Aladdin's Lamp, working wonders, indeed, but only under strong command. And that is why Professor Coué was able to set so many people to rubbing Aladdin's wonderful Lamp, as it were, repeating twenty times over, before going to sleep each night,

"Day by day, in every way, I am growing better and better."

The idea is that by making, through repetition, a deep impression upon the subconscious mind as you go to sleep, the subconscious mind is driven to realize that impression and to work with it through the dark hours, so that on the next day you actually do grow better and better. Suspicion arises, however, that although the positive thought is twenty times repeated, it may be unable to counteract the current of negative thoughts, not to say evil thoughts, which has been pouring into the subconscious mind during all the long day.

For that is the truth, a truth so familiar that its force is forgotten; but our consciousness may be conceived of as a stream of thoughts springing from what we see and hear, and from sources more remote, to sparkle for a moment and then to disappear as other thoughts flow in to take their place. But as they pass they do something, or they carry something into the subconscious with them: that is the important fact which nowadays we are taught. While we are thinking, something is happening, some process is going on. The thought-flow may be likened to a river, carrying silt to the gulf to add a fringe to a continent. Or to the constant fall of snow-flakes on a mountain, accumulating glaciers. Or to the work of coral-insects, building reefs and future islands. Or to the laying of bricks by invisible masons in some invisible wall. These pictures all represent a fact. While we are thinking, something is happening. What we are thinking, the Fates are weaving into a weird. While we are musing, the fire burns.

The quantity of our thinking will the more astonish us the more we estimate its continual flow through all the years of a life-time. But what about its quality?

We take great pains that the fabrics of our clothing shall be such as may wear well. We ravel out a thread of cloth to be sure that it is all-wool. We give much care that the articles of our food shall not be adulterated nor injurious to our health. We demand that milk shall be Pasteurized, and we want to know the date of our eggs. If we build a house, overseers will be paid to watch the fidelity of construction and the honesty of the wood and stone, the mortar and the plaster, the metal and the glass, in order that no inferior materials nor workmanship may impair the durability or the strength or the beauty of our projected building. And in politics we make enormous pretense of scrupulousness in the selection of men for office; and if persons slip into place who disappoint our hopes, it is not from lack of microscopes and discreet use of key-holes. Yes, we are very careful about everything—everything except our thoughts, the stuff out of which our lives are made.

And here, where our souls are at home, in dishabille, as it were, we do not realize that we are in the very laboratory of life and the factory of fate. While we muse, the fire burns; but what we mistake for a pleasant hearth-fire to lounge and loaf before, is far more like an engine-furnace and a blow-pipe's dagger of flame. And our thoughts are all, and at the same time, both the fuel and the fire and the ore.

One of our familiar hymns contains this line, "Our foes press on from every side"; but very little meaning can it usually have for us. Certainly in no literal sense are we ever surrounded by enemies. There perhaps are many people who dislike us, for various reasons which we consider inadequate, but there must be few who wish to do us actual harm. Never are they so many that they can be said to be pressing on from every side. Such a situation may occur in dreams sometimes, where one is pursued by a mob or hunted by bands of savages; but that predicament belongs to nightmare rather than to real life.

Realizing this, we commonly turn the "foes" of our hymn into temptations. It is the temptations of the world that press on from every side, we say. But even so the picture represented to our mind is still so much exaggerated that it remains unreal to us. We are never conscious of being assailed by temptations in large number and on every side. We do, indeed, now and then meet those critical problems of choice which we name temptations, and we ought to be always on our guard against them—so well and so often are we warned. But temptations worthy to be personified as armed foes, come one at a time and seldom. We conceive of them as starting up from some ambush in the outer world, disguised as beggars or as lovers, perhaps, but our encounter with them is a duel. If they came pressing on from every side, we should, indeed, be in a perilous state.

But the line in the hymn will represent a very real condition of human life when we wake to an appreciation that these foes so numerous and so insistent may be thoughts. No need to emphasize the fact that thoughts press on from every side. How often they deny us sleep that they may make of our minds a circus-ring or a battle-field or a Yucatan jungle to be explored! We know them then as foes to sleep, to be sure, but we are not so apt to recognize their hostile quality in the bright day. But that there are certain thoughts to be marked as mortal foes, we have the testimony of our Lord himself, who declared with the utmost emphasis that thoughts of anger and enmity and contempt will make us deserving of jail and gallows and hell-fire. But such unsocial thoughts do not by any means exhaust the list. Our Lord simply quoted thoughts of hate and sensuality to illustrate for us the portentous fact that "thoughts are things," and that they accomplish a deadly work although shut up within our heart and denied all outward expression in word and deed. If we desire a fuller catalogue we may turn to Saint Paul's enumeration of friendly thoughts and substitute for them their opposites:

"Whatsoever things are false, whatsoever things are dishonorable, whatsoever things are unjust, whatsoever things are impure, whatsoever things are ugly, whatsoever things are of evil report, if there be any fault and if there be any blame —think not on these things."

The enemies of men, the objects of their daily fear, used to be, aside from neighboring human tribes, lions and tigers and venomous snakes. As these have become more rare, other foes of our physical well-being arrive to take their place: swarms of insects to attack our food, our fruit and grain, and, more subtle and more fearsome still, innumerable germs and microbes to infect our blood and afflict us with disease. Invisible foes do press on from every side, of which we are still lamentably careless, in spite of the warnings of science.

But no less dangerous are the omnipresent microbes of the mental world; false thoughts and cynical thoughts and unjust snap-judgments hatched out of irritability and prejudice; resentful and ill-natured and uncharitable thoughts; gloomy thoughts, complaining thoughts, and thoughts of discouragement and pessimism; envious thoughts, suspicious thoughts, thoughts of self-pity, self-depreciation, or self-glorification—all these things are like microbes in the soul. And there are other thoughts, thoughts which produce no active poison to paralyze the red corpuscles of the mind, but which multiply incredibly and smother our ideals of a better life. They are the trivial thoughts about trivial things, lazy and inert thoughts, aimless and drab-colored thoughts, commonplace, negative thoughts, blown like dust from the earth out of which they rise, to choke our lungs and blind our sight.

To control our thoughts—a difficult task it is, to be sure, as we all of us know if we have ever attempted it— truly a man's job! Nevertheless, it has got to be done, and the first step in our purpose is to settle upon a method. The

resolve first and most natural is to sit on guard against unwelcome thoughts and eliminate them as they arrive. But
we soon discover that to fight them thus is like killing mos-
quitoes in the Canadian woods. Moreover, not only is this
method futile, but our introspective attitude is one not good
for our health. So perhaps we come to see that our true defense will be to try to live in an atmosphere in which our
enemies cannot breathe, an atmosphere which they cannot
enter, or where, at least, they cannot long survive. Such an
atmosphere should be found in the upper levels of our minds.
Abbé Dimnet urges us to live as far as possible upstairs on
the higher floors of our being, where our ideals of goodness,
truth, and beauty are. We are often obliged to go down-
stairs to deal with the postman or the grocer, but we are not
compelled to live on the ground-floor—still less are we
obliged to live down in the cellar!

There is a picture painted by Rembrandt which is called
"The Philosopher." It represents a man sitting absorbed
in deep meditation. Behind him rises the curve of a stair
which winds upward to regions out of sight. This stair is clearly a device to suggest the way up which the man's climbing
thought goes. But such a spiral stair belongs not only to the
philosopher but to every human soul. In every one of us there
is a private stair which winds up into chambers where our
true Self dwells. There is the hearth where the fire ever
burns. There is the work-shop where the blow-pipe glows.
There is the upper room into which we retreat continually,
for refuge or for recompense. For that is where we treasure
those images that are to us most intimate and most sacred.
There are the formless poems we make on the beauty of the
world; the questionings we shape on the mystery of the
world; our hero-worship and our human ideals, the hidden
patterns that we cherish in our hearts of what we desire
ourselves to be; the memory of our dead and our hopes of
re-union with them; the gods we secretly worship, and the
things we really love—here they all are gathered, at the top
of the spiral stair, and we withdraw into company with them
when we will. And there is nothing we know more surely

than that there we are living at our best, and that there we are most safe, and that there we are most truly ourselves.

To call this withdrawal "Prayer" might seem to be too much, and yet it approaches near to it and naturally that is what it is. For the essence of prayer is an upward reaching toward the best we know, and the desire to absorb its truth and beauty into our own being. Prayer is far more than simply asking for things. If Saint Paul means *that* when he urges us to "pray without ceasing," he demands the impossible; but if he means that we are to live always on the higher levels of consciousness, in an atmosphere of faith and hope and good-will, then that is an attitude of soul which we may attain. It will take different forms in different men—for there are many mansions in the House of the Spirit—but the old monk we know as "Brother Lawrence" called it the "Practice of the Presence of God." "Whatever I do," he said, "if I only stoop down to pick up a straw, I do it in the thought of the Presence of God." With such a thought made habitual, a thought becoming a color of consciousness, as it were, pervading all one's life, all one's work and all one's play, unworthy thoughts as they blow in upon us must shrivel and die before they are able to do us harm.

Even so, the control of the world of thought is a summons to a man's best efforts and to everything heroic in him. We may apply to this very real adventure the words of Thomas Carlyle:

"O thou who pinest in the prison of the Actual, and criest bitterly to the gods for a kingdom in which to rule and to create, know this of a truth: that which thou desirest is already with thee—is already within thee—here or nowhere, couldst thou only see!"

Kenyon College Chapel
December, 1932.

CHAPTER 29

Nathanael, Saint Bartholomew

*"Nathanael answered him and said, 'Rabbi, thou art
the Son of God, thou art the King of Israel.'"*

John i:49.

IN THE CITY of Paris there is a church which stands opposite the front of a great palace. The palace windows look
across at the church; the windows of the church look across
at the palace. A weak boy king and a strong, proud queen
and a gay, bad court once looked across at that church; the
saints in the stained-glass windows of that church still look
across at the empty palace. Kings and queens are gone; the
saints remain. I do not know whether the figure of Saint
Bartholomew is among the saints in those church windows or
not; or whether, once there, he faded out in sorrow and
shame one dreadful night, leaving a crimson smear in the
glass. I do not know. But the church bell still strikes twelve
on the Eve of St. Bartholomew's Day, just as it still strikes
twelve on every midnight and every noon. And you can
never hear it, even in the bright sunshine, with the voices
and footsteps of happy people all around, without feeling
your blood run cold and your heart grow faint, as you see
ghosts, with your mind's eye, pursuing other ghosts up and
down that busy street, and as you hear, with your mind's
ear, the firing of guns and shrieks of fear and yells of hate.
For when that very bell struck twelve, one St. Bartholomew's
Eve three hundred and sixty years ago and more, it was the
signal for the palace doors to open, like gates of hell, letting
loose devils to begin that bloody murder of unsuspecting men
and women which has been known in history ever since
as the Massacre of St. Bartholomew. Twenty-five or thirty

240

thousand of the best citizens of France died a bloody death on that St. Bartholomew's Day.

It is customary to call the Massacre of St. Bartholomew a religious deed, and to charge it up against that ancient Church that had married the World to reform the World, and has ever since been suffering the troubles that such marriages usually bring. Indeed, if the Massacre of St. Bartholomew had not been political as well as religious, it could never have occurred at all. Politics drew and wielded the sword which Religion had ground sharp; and men's hate was more bitter and their vengeance was more cruel just because, strange to say, they signed it all with the sign of the cross. Religion is like fire, which may blaze on a hearth to warm a home, or which may burn you, with intolerable pain, to death.

It is difficult to think of the Democratic Party or the Republican Party plotting, and carrying out the plot, to diminish the vote of the opposition by wholesale murder. But imagine the members of the Democratic Party all belonging to one Church and the members of the Republican Party all belonging to another, each Church believing the other to be the wilful enemy of all good, and considerable bitterness in their treatment of one another is conceivable still in our own time. But move this situation back some three hundred and sixty years, when the fierce Old Order woke up to the fact that it had to fight for its life, and we arrive at something like the condition of things on St. Bartholomew's Day, in the year of grace 1572.

We have recalled the Massacre of St. Bartholomew in order to make the real meaning of St. Bartholomew's Day shine out more clearly by contrast. For Saint Bartholomew stands, as we shall see, for the very essential principles of Christianity, and that men could have perpetrated such a cold-blooded and treacherous slaughter of their neighbors and kinsmen, as a kind of celebration of St. Bartholomew's Day, shows that they had no slightest conception of the nature of that religion which they professed to defend.

But this is the reason why we observe the day: it is the

reason why we observe all saints' days, and all the days of the Church Year: it is to keep ourselves reminded of the fundamental directions of Christianity, by setting up mile-posts at intervals through the seasons; or by erecting sacred shrines along the way, like those roadside shrines in foreign lands, where a lamp may be kept burning before a faith or a hope or a love. St. Bartholomew's Day is one of these shrines. Saint Bartholomew was one of the twelve apostles. And each apostle has his appointed day, on which the Church asks us to pay some attention to him; that is, to think about him in some particular way which will be of benefit to us in our Christian living. Tomorrow the Church asks us to think about Saint Bartholomew, and this, therefore, is St. Bartholomew's Eve.

Who was Saint Bartholomew? And what did he do on earth? The answer is easy: under the name of Bartholomew we know only that he was one of our Lord's twelve disciples, and that is all we know. In the three Gospels of Saint Matthew, Saint Mark, and Saint Luke, his name appears in every list of the twelve disciples, but beyond his name not one single detail, not a single word or act, is recorded of him. We might take notice, however, that in every one of these lists the name of Bartholomew is always coupled with the name of Philip. James and John are always linked together; so also are Philip and Bartholomew.

But in the Gospel of Saint John, the Fourth Gospel, the name of Bartholomew does not occur at all. But we do find there the name Nathanael, which, on its side, never appears in the Gospels of Saint Matthew, Saint Mark, and Saint Luke. Moreover, in the Fourth Gospel, we find Nathanael associated with Philip, just as we find Bartholomew joined with Philip in the other three Gospels. The conclusion, therefore, reasonably is that Nathanael and Bartholomew are the two names of one and the same man—just as Simon and Peter were the two names of one man, and as Joseph and Barnabas were the two names of another. It was not at all unusual for a man to have two names. So the Church has always considered the Nathanael of the Gospel of Saint John to have been also the Bartholomew of the Gospels of Saint Matthew, Saint Mark, and Saint Luke.

But all we know about Nathanael in the Fourth Gospel is what we read in the first chapter of it:

On the morrow Jesus was minded to go forth into Galilee, and he findeth Philip and he saith unto him, "Follow me."

And Philip findeth Nathanael and saith unto him, "We have found him of whom Moses in the Law, and the prophets, wrote, Jesus of Nazareth."

And Nathanael said unto him, "Can any good thing come out of Nazareth?" Philip saith unto him, "Come and see."

Jesus saw Nathanael coming unto him, and he saith of him, "Behold an Israelite indeed, in whom there is no guile."

Nathanael saith unto him, "Whence knowest thou me?" Jesus answered and said unto him, "Before Philip called thee, when thou wast under the fig-tree, I saw thee."

Nathanael answered him, "Rabbi, thou art the Son of God! thou art the King of Israel!"

We may note first the Lord's testimony to the character of Nathanael: "Behold, a true Israelite, in whom there is no guile." "But how do you know anything about me?" Nathanael exclaims, astonished. And Jesus answered, "I saw you before Philip called you. I saw you under the fig-tree." There must have been some peculiar significance or peculiar reference in this answer of Jesus, for Nathanael at once cries out, with emphasis upon the pronoun, "Then *thou* art the Son of God! *Thou* art the King of Israel!"

This short interview, to which we shall return presently, furnishes absolutely all that we know about Nathanael. We do not know, with any certainty, where he went, nor what he did, nor what became of him. There is a tradition, indeed, that he preached the Gospel in India and suffered a cruel martyrdom there. It may be true; but unfortunately such traditions in the lives of the saints do not rest upon evidence considered good by students of history today. There was a glamour about martyrdom in the earlier ages of the Church, and every one of the twelve apostles was given a martyr's crown in the Book of the Saints. But it is not safe to see in these stories any more solid substance than in the haloes which the painters drew around their sacred heads. The stories themselves amount to a kind of halo.

So we will come back to what we really know about Nathanael, his interview with Jesus, and try to find something in it that will be helpful to us. In the first place, why was Nathanael so astonished when Jesus told him he had seen him under the fig-tree? If the fig-tree was at a great distance, beyond the range of ordinary human sight, the incident was surprising, certainly, but not so surprising as to account for Nathanael's immediate recognition of Jesus as the Son of God and King of Israel.

But if Nathanael was praying under the fig-tree—praying for the Christ to come, the Son of God, the King of Israel— then the words of Jesus would have a startling force for him. They would mean that Jesus saw into his heart and read his thoughts there under the fig-tree. That was a divine thing, to see into his heart, and Nathanael cries out, "Lord, my prayer is answered: *thou* art the Son of God! Thou art the King of Israel!"

There is nothing forced in such an explanation. It was an obligation laid upon every Israelite to pray for the coming of the Christ, the King of Israel. It was said by the rabbis that an Israelite's prayer was no prayer at all unless it included a prayer for the coming of the Christ. And we have an echo of this ancient Israelite's prayer in our own Lord's Prayer: "Thy Kingdom come," we pray.

Now Nathanael recognized his Lord in his answer, and he recognized him in two aspects corresponding to the two titles with which he addressed him. Nathanael called him "Son of God," and he also called him "King of Israel." What these two titles meant to Nathanael could not have been exactly what they now mean for us. But they meant enough for Nathanael, as we shall see.

First, the title "Son of God" was a title often given to the expected Christ; but it had no metaphysical meaning to the Jews, such as it now has for us, and such as it has in our Creed. The word *son* was much used in a Jewish idiom to

244

express quality or character. James and John were "Sons of thunder." Disorderly men were "sons of Belial"—full of the spirit of Satan. So a "son of God" would be one filled with the spirit of God. And *the* Son of God would be the one in whom the spirit of God and the character of God were supremely to be manifested—in his Christ. And Nathanael had the spiritual insight to recognize the spirit in Jesus: God was in this man. It was not by argument that Nathanael sprang to his great conclusion. He had a sudden glimpse, a glimpse we call "faith," into the heart of this man who had looked into his own heart and read what he was thinking there. He had a glimpse into the character of Jesus, and he knew that what he saw was divine. He was the long-expected Man from God; and Nathanael cried, "Rabbi, *thou* art the Son of God."

Nathanael here shows insight, spiritual vision. Not everyone thereafter who saw Christ, saw him for what he was. Quite the contrary; only a few, a very few, saw in him the Christ of God. Only a few, comparatively, are able to see the divine in this world, even now. The difference is a difference in spiritual vision—a difference which is faith.

Second: Nathanael, having recognized Jesus as the Christ so long expected, and having given him his Messianic title, "Son of God," proceeds to add another title, also Messianic; he calls him "King of Israel." This title was more vivid and more clear-cut to the Israelites than it is to us. The nation's great longing, never extinguished by any calamity, slavery or exile, was the longing to live in a Kingdom over which their God should personally reign—a kingdom not Babylon's kingdom, nor Rome's kingdom, but Jehovah's kingdom. "Thy kingdom come" was their ceaseless prayer. The Christ, then, when he should come, would be their ruler, the King, of the kingdom which God, they believed, was committed to establish, eventually, in the world; a kingdom of which Jerusalem would be the holy capital.

Nathanael held this view, as all the other disciples did. As an Israelite of his time, he could have held no other. And when he recognized Jesus as the Christ, it followed in-

evitably that he should also recognize him as "King of Israel."
"Thou art the Son of God, the King of Israel," he said.

But the point is that when Nathanael acknowledged Jesus
as the King of Israel, he, the Israelite indeed, confessed himself to be a subject of his king. A king implies subjects in
his kingdom. The king commands; his subjects obey. So
when Nathanael addressed Jesus as King of Israel, it was
equivalent to an oath of allegiance; he acknowledged his own
duty of obedience. Jesus was his king; the will of his king
would hereafter be his own will.

So the faith of Nathanael was a practical faith, to issue at
once into action. The nature of faith has been the subject of
vast argument in the schools of the Church. But all those
heavy books have no more to do with the soul's simple trust
in God than the *Congressional Globe* has to do with patriotism. Real faith always issues in conduct. What we repeat in
our Creed is not our faith. What we really believe, what we
really see as our vision of truth, is what we express in our
daily lives. If we really believe in Christ, we will do what he
wants us to do.

This is what Jesus meant to Nathanael; he was the Son
of God, he was the King of Israel; and he ought to mean the
same to us. He ought to mean more to us, after nineteen
hundred years of Christian endeavor and experience.

And he does mean more. Our idea of God has developed
far beyond the ideas of the old Israelites. We demand more
of God than Nathanael ever could. But, while our idea of
God expands, we find the character of Jesus always adequate
to express the character of God. It is as if he himself expands with the expanding world, although what really expands is our recognition of him. We now know that if there
is anything divine in this world, it is the spirit of Christ. The
spirit of Christ is the fullest revelation of God we possess:
if there is a God, that is what God is—what we see in Christ.

Another point: Christ reveals the character of God to us;
but he also reveals man to men. He reveals to us what man
may be. In him we see the highest type of religious and
moral excellence we are able to conceive. Again, as our ideals

of manhood expand, we find Christ filling them. If we would realize the possibilities of our being as men, we know of no other method of doing so than by cultivating within ourselves the spirit of Christ.

And a third point. Christ means more to us than he did to Nathanael, because the functions of the Christ, the Messiah of the Jews, have come to embrace much more. He once meant the highest national aspirations of a small, despised people; he now stands to us for the highest social good of the whole round world. We are beginning to see in Christ's second commandment—he left us only two—the simple remedy for current society of all its ills. We are beginning to see in the second commandment, simple as it seems, the magic formula by which the Spirit of Christ is slowly building the jeweled walls of the City of our dreams, the perfect Society, the New Jerusalem.

But society is cured, and the city-walls are built, only as each Christian maintains in his private life the confession of Nathanael, Saint Bartholomew:

"Lord, who knowest what is in my heart, thou art God to me, my Lord and my God. Forms of thought, vast and vague, sit on the throne of the green hills and clothe themselves with the glory of the sun; but because thou knowest what is in my heart, thou art God to me, my Lord and my God.

"Voices call to me, voices seductive or imperious; whether they are voices of devils or voices of archangels it is often hard to tell—but thou, because thou knowest what is in my heart, thou art my Master and my Guide, and whatsoever thou biddest me, that will I do."

(*After 1932.*)

CHAPTER 30

Render Unto Caesar the Things That Are Caesar's

"Render unto Caesar the things that are Caesar's, and unto God the things that are God's."

Mark xii:17.

THIS FAMOUS SAYING has perhaps been most famous because of the adroitness with which the Speaker evaded by it a cunning trap which had been set for him by his enemies. But it contained also an implied rebuke for those who had set the trap, as well as a principle of conduct by which his followers might avoid the snares which life would spread for them to the end of the world. So it is addressed also to us.

"Render unto Caesar the things that are Caesar's, and unto God the things that are God's."

Our Lord stood, when he said it, in the great court of the Temple, surrounded by the people who were that day the sand upon which his popularity was built. That popularity it was now his enemies' scheme to force him to lose, or else to save at the risk of falling into the hands of the Roman government. And so they approached him, moving with the slow dignity of the Pharisees, clothed in those dark and heavy garments which the poet Dante, thirteen hundred years in the future, was to change into lead when he clothed in them his hypocrites down in hell. So very deferentially they approached him, and they addressed him in very fair words:

"Sir," they began, "we know that thou art a teacher of the truth—oh, yes—and we know that thou speakest the very truth without fear of any man. Wilt thou tell us, then, whether it is right to pay the tax to Caesar, or is it not? Ought we to pay it, or ought we not?"

248

Beyond the Temple court, shouldering up against it insolently, was Caesar's castle. It was the visible presence of the power that compelled the tax, and it is not altogether a fancy to imagine that castle was listening to hear what the Teacher might say. Around about him were the people who hated the tax as they hated the castle, and they too were listening very intent to hear the Teacher's reply.

"Have you, by chance," he asked, "a piece of the tribute money?" And someone dug a silver coin out of a purse and handed it to him. And they watched him curiously.

"Whose image is this?" he asked, as he studied it. "Whose head is stamped upon the coin?"

"Why, Caesar's, of course," they answered. "It is Caesar's head upon the coin."

"And this writing around the edge, how does it read, what does it mean?" he asked.

"Why, it is Caesar's name, of course," they made answer. "It is Caesar's name upon the coin."

"Then," said Jesus, "it is Caesar's money. Render therefore unto Caesar the things that are Caesar's—and unto God the things that are God's."

And the Pharisees moved away with slow dignity in their voluminous cloaks, their dignity hiding their humiliation, and their heavy cloaks hiding hearts heavy with gall, ominous of those cloaks of lead that they were doomed to wear through the ages down in Dante's hell.

Yes, it was Caesar's money, and they were using it, just as they were using Caesar's well-paved roads and the good order of Caesar's government. It was Caesar's money, and so it was quite plain that they owed it to him. There was the sting of truth in that. For it is a right which none can deny, the right to claim what is one's own, just as it is a duty which none can refuse, the duty to pay one's debts. Pay what you owe, that was the gist of Jesus' reply, a principle true for all time, a commandment holding good forever. Pay what you owe, render what is due—this is a commandment implicit in all the commandments. It reaches us who are here today, applying as closely to us as to those evil men who listened to our Lord's words in the Temple court. Pharisees or Sadducees, publicans or sinners, or whatever we be, this answer of Jesus enters like a radio message into that inmost office of our souls where we manage the business of our daily living and keep the books of our conscience—as keep them we must, whether as honest men or as forgers and defaulters.

"Render unto Caesar the things that are Caesar's, and unto God the things that are God's." If we are honest men we must keep this law. And so it becomes very important for us to define precisely what are the things that are Caesar's, and what are the things that are God's, in order that we may know how to pay to each exactly what is due.

In the first place, then, what are the things that belong to Caesar? Yes, they are very many. We see that clearly, when we wake up to the fact. For above all things else we are all of us debtors, under immense obligations to the world in which we live, spending Caesar's money all the time. And bills are arriving every hour in our mail. Collectors every hour are ringing the bell at our door. Lawyers are threatening continually foreclosure of mortgages upon pledges given in our name to insistent creditors, creditors insistent but utterly just. For Caesar dwells not only on the Palatine. He issues his decrees not only from under the Capitol Dome. The entire environment in which we live is Caesar. The society in which we move so busily is Caesar. Civilization is Caesar, and all our life consists in paying back, in some sort, freely or reluctantly, what we owe to him.

For all that we have, and all that we are, we owe to the accumulated wealth—material, moral, and intellectual—painfully gathered together by long generations of men in the past, back to the Old Stone Age. All the buildings of the world, town halls and churches, schools and libraries, fortresses and factories, palaces and tenements, all the high towers of trade, all the roads of brick and iron, all the telegraphic wires, all the engines and machines and manifold inventions of speed, and all the books and newspapers, all the art and music, all the philosophies, sciences, institutions, all the civil codes and social etiquette—it all is Caesar's money, with the image of humanity stamped upon the face of it, and with the name of humanity inscribed around its edge. It is not our own, heirs of all the ages as we are; it is not our own except to use and to pay back. And we pay it back by using it in humanity's business of interchange and development and discovery; by adding something in the way of interest to humanity's capital; by fulfilling those obligations and by cultivating those relations which the incalculable advantage of being members in the ancient society of men has entailed upon us. Incalculable is this advantage, and indispensable is this capital, for without them the human race would still be orang-outangs in the forest. The walls of our civilization are built out of men's lives, mortared together with blood and sweat and tears, and all of us who live in it have gone into debt by living in it, and we owe the greatest possible service to our race just because of our privileged sojourn here.

But suppose that we, such debtors, on the road to the bank to pay our bills, should stop on the corner of the street, and, in company with other loafers, risk and squander Caesar's money, matching pennies and shooting craps! And yet that is what we all of us are doing, more or less, in one shape or another, every day.

And now, in the second place, what are the things that are God's? Is there another world separate from God's world? Is there another range of duties quite separate from Caesar's tax? Then what are the things that are God's? We need very much to know. Are things that are Caesar's and things that are God's so neatly defined and exactly distinguished that one's income-tax belongs to Caesar, and the Forward Movement belongs to God? Is going to the polls to cast a vote to be classed as Caesar's tribute, and is attending church, for example, to be ranked as tribute to God?

When Jesus said, "Render unto Caesar the things that are Caesar's," when he laid it down as duty to give back to Caesar his own, he placed fidelity to all these obligations upon the conscience, and, beyond all dispute, things of conscience are things that belong to God. The things of God, therefore, include the things of Caesar. Caesar himself is God's man. "The powers that be are ordained of God," declared Saint Paul. And so, as our own prophet of wide vision once saw, "Assyria is God's hammer, Cyrus is his shepherd, Egypt is his garden, and Tyre is the jewel in his hand."

The whole wide world, then, all Caesar's empire, Europe, Asia, Africa, and the United States of America, they all are God's anvil, on which he beats out experiments and purposes in human living. So that the things of God are things of duty, and all the things that are Caesar's, from the ruling of a State to the sweeping of a floor, they all become things that are God's when they are done as by God's laws—as they ought to be done.

So the things that are God's include everything that we do. All our life may be translated into terms of duty, may it not? For it is impossible to imagine any act that does not involve a question of duty, fitting, as it inevitably must, into the cogs of other lives and producing unlooked-for results. This most intricate interplay of duties belongs to the sphere of human associations and relationships. We are taught that the kinds of duty are two: duty towards God, and duty towards our neighbor; to which there is added a third sometimes, duty towards one's self. But truly all three are one, and cannot be unraveled. For duty towards one's self is grafted on duty to man and God; and duty towards man involves duty to self and God; and duty towards God cannot be separated from duty to self and man. The three are one. But the stage of duty most evident to us is the stage of human living, the stage of human neighbors, the stage where human selfishness and human duties clash.

Here very many of the duties performed are duties exacted of us. There is a constant pressure from outside to compel us to do as we ought. We live inside of a barbed-wire fence, quite fortunately, and cannot do just as we like. So when we rebel against many duties whose irksomeness we deplore, and when we feel many duties to be grievous drudgery, we are paying Caesar's tax just as the old Jews paid theirs, not knowing that a tax paid to Caesar was a tax paid to God.

Duties are the necessary grooves in which human existence runs. We often hear men and women say, "I want to live my own life!" But what they really mean, most often, is to be released from the restraints of duty, free to follow their impulses and their pleasure. But we none of us can be trusted to live our own lives—not yet. It is as if a locomotive on the track should say, "I hate this slavery; I want to live my own life!" and so should jump the straight iron rails and start off across the fields. A locomotive off the track is living its own life.

It is as if a star should say, "I hate this limitation to the curves of gravity, and I will live my own life!" And so it swings out of its orbit for a flight down the Milky Way. And all the cords of its being are loosened, till it becomes a mere cloud of vapor, with no heart and no heat, trailing its ineffectual substance over millions of miles of space, tangled among moons and spurned by suns, that joke of the stars, a comet. A comet is a star living its own life.

It is as if a group of cells in a man's body should decide, as they actually do, how tragically often, "We hate this subordination to ends we do not understand, and we will live our own life!" And so those cells build a new center of government, diverting telegraph nerves and blood streams to their new law, expanding ardently and flaunting red banners of revolt, until the new organism becomes a Satanic flower, wonderful and beautiful from the standpoint of a cancer—for that is what it is: a perfect cancer—but destruction to the body of the man in which it lives its own life.

A cancer is a group of cells in the body living their own life.

But no individual can live his own life apart from other lives. This *is* our own life, to live in conjunction with other lives. We are like the cells of the body, each with its own function in relation with other cells, and all subordinate to the transcendent movements of the whole. It is as if we human beings were the cells in the body of a great Being unknown, and the satisfaction we feel in duty done is the glow of health in the universe. At least this is evidently true, that happiness for man depends upon the most perfect subservience to duty. Doing of duty in physical things means health of body, surely. And doing of duty on higher levels is the necessary way to health of mind and health of soul. "Do the duty that lies nearest to thee"; this rule covers all conduct. It also solves all perplexities. It was Thomas Carlyle who said, "Do the duty that lies nearest to thee, and thy next duty is already made clear." Duty is the narrow way, duty is the strait and difficult gate that leads, nevertheless, into a wide and open space where we shall "know the doctrine"—that is, where we shall have knowledge of the truth that shall make us free.

To be free! It is humanity's ancient dream! Men, how many men! have died for that magic word, never knowing, never realizing, what freedom actually means.

To be free! that is what we all most passionately want! The restlessness that agitates our days; the discontent that beats against the locked doors of our life and frets in dreams all night against our limitations; the strange urge to do right when we are pulled to do wrong; the fears arising from the dark below to challenge hopes like stars above; the fetters on feet that try to run, and the shackles on hands that reach outward and up; the inextinguishable longing for some Land of Heart's Desire, some kingdom wherein to rule and to create;—it is a mystery why beings like us, why beings made as we are, should have such a spirit, the spirit of freedom, mixed with our earth, so heavy and so gross and so enslaved.

Is it not because something divine is stamped upon our substance? Is it not because the image of God is impressed upon our souls? Is it not because his name is inscribed upon our hearts? We ourselves are God's money. Let no one doubt it nor deny. We are God's money, and we owe ourselves to him. We must pay ourselves to him.

Chapter 31

Laodiceans

Rev. iii:14-20.

OUR SECOND LESSON this morning is a short letter written by that Saint John who wrote the Book of Revelation at the end of our New Testament. This letter was addressed to a Christian Church in the city of Laodicea. Its purpose was to rebuke a fault in that Church, a fault so reprehensible as to deserve an extreme retribution. "I will spew thee," says the Amen, the Witness faithful and true, "I will spew thee out of my mouth." This fault was the fault of lukewarmness, the fault of being neither cold nor hot.

"You imagine that you are rich," the letter declares, "but really you are very poor. You are proud of your fine woolen garments, but really you are naked. And you think that you are happy and have need of nothing, but I tell you that you are blind and have need of sight, and that you are wretched and miserable and have need of repentance and new life."

So we get a glimpse, in this sharp little letter, of a prosperous community quite satisfied with itself. Might it not be of interest, therefore, to see what we can find out about this city of Laodicea where these lukewarm Christians dwelt— these Christians neither cold nor hot?

Laodicea was above all things a commercial city. Its situation made it so. It stood, fortified with walls and towers, upon low hills at the opening of a valley which led up from the western plains to the great central plateau of Asia Minor. Through this city and on up the valley ran the great trade road from the sea-port of Ephesus, one hundred and fifty miles away, on to Antioch and Babylon. And other lesser

roads, branch-roads, met the main road at this point. Laodicea, therefore, was the guardian and gate-keeper of the
entrance to the wealthy Orient. Through it of necessity
flowed a constant stream of traffic. Travelers like Cicero
stopped here to get their bank-checks cashed. Merchants
came to buy or sell. Soldiers, marching often back and forth,
hardly could fail to leave their money in the wine-shops and
theaters of the enticing town.

And Laodicea had a lucrative trade of its own. For the
sheep of the valley produced a soft black wool, highly esteemed, which was woven into cloth for export. Moreover,
Laodicea was famous for what we should now call patent-
medicines, among which, in particular, was an eye-salve wide-
ly known and considered very efficacious. We have reference
to these things in Saint John's letter, in the white garments—
contrasted with the local, worldly black—and in the true
ointment for the eyes which the Christians were urged to
buy.

So, from the few hints contained in this letter, we may derive a fairly consistent picture of our Laodiceans: well-to-
do, practical people, with common sense and with no vices
to speak of, or these would most certainly have been thrown
up to them by the uncompromising Saint John; a comfortably
settled, self-satisfied people, with money in the bank; only, if
they were Christians, they were such with divided interests,
Christians without enthusiasm, Christians—in Saint John's
rigorous eyes—fit for no place but the garbage-can.

And yet, perhaps we might allow a fellow-feeling for these
despised Laodiceans. Perhaps we might reflect that Saint
John is a very severe judge. Reading his Book of Revelation
through, we may see that his religion, boiled down by the
fire of persecution, had become a very fierce religion, intol-
erant and revengeful, like an intense and burning acid. The
line between the World and the Kingdom of Heaven was to
him a sharp and decisive one, and the slightest compromise
became a deadly sin. But perhaps the Laodiceans had more
Christian stamina than Saint John thought. Anyway, history
tells us that the Church of Laodicea had its bishops and its

holy martyrs, it entertained a Church Council, and it was the leading Christian congregation of that district for several centuries.

Nevertheless, the adjective "Laodicean," ever since the publication of Saint John's letter, has meant something quite different from merely being a citizen of that busy, money-making town. It has received a special meaning and that an opprobrious one. It expresses the disposition of a person not unreservedly committed to a cause; a half-way person, adapting himself to opposite sides and so without zeal for either; undecided, unreliable, lukewarm, neither hot nor cold. This is what the word "Laodicean" has come to mean. Thomas Hardy has entitled one of his novels *The Laodicean*, making the name stand for the heroine of his story, a young woman who, in certain situations, seemed not to know her own mind.

And the word, as we now use it, signifies a very real thing, of course. Human nature, when not excitingly spurred up, tends to relax into easy grooves, accommodating itself to circumstances, and more apt to make terms with opposing forces than to fight them. But fortunately the world is so constituted that such states of stagnation cannot long endure. If men may not be allured by ambition or pride, or by bright visions of beauty or truth, into adventures of enthusiastic activity, there are always the goads of necessity, and the shocks of calamity and death, to drive men along difficult roads of destiny which they, assuredly, would not otherwise choose.

Now a strange thing has come to pass. Voices are everywhere proclaiming, in various terms of discontent, that the entire Christian Church has become the Church of Laodicea, and we are Laodiceans, all of us. And this condemnation is not from outsiders alone—far from it. The statement is also made by many within the Church itself, and not always in a spirit of fault-finding. There is a thoughtful little book written by an English scholar, entitled *The Lost Radiance of Christianity*—the "lost" radiance! And the present activity known as "The Forward Movement" seems to be an organized endeavor to arouse a departed enthusiasm.

The voices of criticism and complaint are in many keys. Why did not the Church prevent the Great War? Why did the Church even bless it—bless even the rape of Ethiopia? Why does not the Church once and for all bring about a World-Peace? Why does not the Church heal cancers in our civilization, a civilization so proud of itself? Why does the Church build costly monuments to pride, while so many people live in pig-sties. Why does the Church pour money into feeble efforts abroad, while at home the heathen swarm around its very doors? Why does not the Church purify our politics, cleanse our society, and find some means of lifting fellow-creatures out of their mud and misery?

The implied answer always is, because our Christianity is the lukewarm Christianity of the Church of Laodicea.

It is not my purpose to do more than mention these accusing questions. Even if they are justified, we hear them quite often enough. On the contrary, having allowed a possible extenuation for the old Laodiceans, I would rather suggest a thought or two which a modern Laodicean might propose in his own defense.

In the first place, it does not follow that because an outburst of energy no longer maintains its original violence, the sum of energy has therefore lessened; it is only expended over a broader space. When an irrigation stream issues from its containing reservoir, it is with concentrated force, but it soon divides itself into many distributing canals and flows softly through fields and gardens, to be transformed into flowers and fruits. So, in the manner of a parable, Christianity's beginning may be likened to a torrent rushing down a sluiceway, with an impetus to carry it along, gently now, through many minor channels over the earth, to water desert places and change them, ultimately, into orchards and farms, where men and women work and children play.

Instead of being an independent phenomenon, like a geyser, Christianity becomes a disseminated thing, like a blessed dew or rain. Religion must never be taken as an object apart from common life, but as an essential something to be mixed with it. Religion is expressed by the way we live.

And this will be the second point in the Laodicean's plea: that Christianity is fundamentally a matter of the common life. It ferments and becomes a poison when separated from it. It may have its Pentecosts, in which men speak for a very little while in tongues not their own; and it may have its Delectable Mountains, from the top of which, now and then, men gain, in Saint John's fashion, far-away glimpses of something like a Glory and of something like a Golden Gate; but its special glory is the power it has of entering into all the works and days of our common life, charging them with richer values, as water once was turned into wine.

Society is Christian only in proportion as its members are Christian; and if we lament our society's defects, at least we may realize, if we take the trouble to read the history of society as it was in centuries past, that the principles and spirit of Christianity have been steadily permeating all spheres of human living, making men more merciful, and more conscious of obligations to one another, and more sensitive to ideals.

To exhibit our religion there is little use in setting off fireworks in our front-yard; the necessary thing is to show, in every-day living, Saint Paul's fruits of the Spirit: "love, joy, peace, patience, kindness, courtesy, loyalty, gentleness, and self-control." And all these things are things that belong to the common life.

We might remember, too, the declaration of the old Hebrew prophet: "He hath showed thee, O man, what is good; and what doth the Lord require of thee but to do justly, and to love kindness, and to walk humbly with thy God?"

Finally, let us turn again to Saint John's letter, and read his concluding words: "Behold, I stand at the door and knock," says the Witness faithful and true. "If any man hear my voice and open the door, I will come in to him, and will sup with him, and he with me."

This has a pertinence in this connection; for the Laodiceans, in a city so constantly welcoming travelers, must have been a people much given to hospitality, and distinguished visitors must often have knocked at their doors.

It is a parable for all peoples and all times. A divine visitor knocks at the door of every dwelling in which the ordinary human currents of toil and triviality and trouble flow, although with compensating intervals of laughter and of rest. And if Saint John's divine visitor comes in and sits down at the common table and takes the common food, then something miraculous happens. The table is no more common, the food is no more what it was. Those who sit around the table feel closer in affection than they ever were before. Life itself means something different and better, for their ordinary, commonplace meal has now become a sacrament— the Supper of the Lord.

June 21, 1936.

CHAPTER 32

The Transfiguration: Prayer

"And Jesus took with him Peter and James and John, and went up into the mountain to pray. And as he was praying, the fashion of his countenance was altered, and his raiment became white and dazzling. And behold, there talked with him two men, who were Moses and Elijah, who appeared in glory, and spoke of his departure which he was about to accomplish at Jerusalem."

Luke ix:28-31.

THE STORY OF the Transfiguration is one of the most difficult in the New Testament. That is, it is one of the most difficult to conceive of as an actual historical happening upon this earth, as we know the earth. To think of a man's countenance suddenly shining with an inner light, is possible, so radiantly the soul sometimes illuminates the human face; but to think of the very garments of the man as sharing in that brilliancy, becoming white like snow, is difficult. Moreover, to think of two men centuries dead as appearing in recognizable form to talk with one of earth's inhabitants, is so difficult that we will not credit any account of such an appearance nowadays, except as a subjective phenomenon, belonging to psychology. And, last, to think of a bright cloud as settling down from above to give utterance to a Voice, a Voice making articulate words in the name of God himself, this is most difficult.

And the familiar picture of this scene, as the great painter Raphael imagined it, has served to make it still more unreal to our thought; for he has represented the three characters of it, Jesus and Moses and Elijah, not as standing upon the solid earth at all, but upon the clouds of heaven. Evidently

261

the artist himself could not see the story as history, but as vision.

Now to spend time and thought over the mere spectacular details of the story of the Transfiguration, to discuss their probability and to theorize about their origin, this is not only fruitless, for we arrive nowhere, but it diverts us furthermore from the essential facts of the story, which remain untouched and vital, no matter what method of interpretation may be applied to the pictorial form of it.

The essential facts are these: Jesus was now definitely committed to a course which made the authorities his enemies. His deliberate disregard of the common rules for keeping the Sabbath; his association with the lower classes of the community, the publicans and sinners; his independence of forms of piety like fasting; his assumption of authority in the matter of forgiveness of sins—these things seemed to be, in the eyes of respectable people, the actions of a rebel against the very safe-guards of society. His own view of the Messiah's mission and career was one which few of his people could understand. His disciples themselves were slow to understand. The Israelites wanted a political ruler who could rid them of the Romans; he wanted to teach them how to live the heavenly life in any earthly condition—slaves could be his followers. They wanted a Christ who would be the cap-stone of their artificial class-system; he felt himself anointed to proclaim brotherhood to all mankind. They wanted a Christ who would look at things only on the outside, as they themselves did; he could see only the inside of things—their true value in the sight of God. And he had been trying to teach them his insight and his spirit long enough to perceive that the outcome must probably be, for him, the prophet's bloody death.

And now he had gone apart into a mountain place to pray; and, as he prayed, light fell upon the scope and end of his ministry, just as, in the waters of Jordan, light had fallen upon his own relationship to men and to God, and so had led him forth upon that ministry. And both times light had come to him in prayer.

262

He saw clearly, as he prayed, how his teaching was the outcome, the fruit, the fulfilment, of Moses' teaching— Moses had but led up to him. And he saw clearly also how his gospel was what Elijah and all the prophets had foreseen afar. And Moses and the prophets all agreed in this, that the Way of God is the Way of the Cross: to have, a man must give; to conquer, a man must submit; to grow, a man must suffer; to live, a man must die.

And from this point in the life of Christ, the Transfiguration, he set his face like a flint to go up to Jerusalem, to die. He tried to prepare his disciples for the fate that awaited him there. They shrank from the picture that he drew, and would not, could not, understand. But his own heart was fixed; he had seen into the deeper things of God, there on the Transfiguration Mount. The light of that vision revealed the shadow of the Cross stretching the whole length of Palestine, from Calvary at Jerusalem even up to the feet of Jesus, when he stood with Peter and James and John on Hermon's slope. But that shadow was transfigured to his sight; no longer was it the dark omen of dreadful doom; it was the path of victory, opening a way for his beloved people to the Presence and the Love of God.

This is what our Lord saw while he prayed. So the theme of the Transfiguration story we may take to be this: the transfiguring, the transforming, power of prayer.

Man has been called the animal that laughs; but far more significantly might he be called the animal that prays. Stop and think of it a moment: an animal, involved in strife like other animals, in all its own perplexities and extremities instinctively crying out to Something Invisible, Something Above, for help. That is a wonderful thing. For we say that an instinct implanted by Nature argues the existence of something answering to that instinct. So man, kneeling in prayer, makes inevitable an opposite pole, God, listening to that prayer.

And so man always has prayed; when he went hunting, he prayed; when he planted his field, he prayed; when he set sail on the stormy sea, he prayed; when disease struck himself or his child, he prayed; when his loved ones disappeared into the Place of Silence, he still followed them with a prayer. Loss, danger, pain, death, these things were always lying in ambush for him, and against them he always tried to make an alliance with the invisible world.

And how frantic were his appeals to make the invisible gods attend; to make them hear; to make them see; to make them compassionate! What cries, what supplications, what vows, what fires, what clouds of incense, what blowing of trumpets and beating of drums; what slaughter of oxen and lambs; what cutting of one's own flesh with knives; what sacrifice of the first-born son!

And yet, if the invisible gods ever saw; or if the inaudible gods ever heard; or if an unknown heart ever grew compassionate, no clear proof of it ever came to men.

Until, at last, man was ready—or at least he was partly ready—for a new kind of prayer: a kind of prayer which submitted to the laws of this world in which he found himself, and the scope of which he so little understood. He himself, he began to perceive, was made for something larger than his own will and his own pleasure, and he learned to say to the invisible God, "*Thy* will be done."

This prayer implies an oath of allegiance to the laws of nature—which are God's will in nature; we will pray to him by investigating them, and knowing them and obeying them. We no longer pray against typhoid fever; we purify the water supply. We no longer pray for rain; we inaugurate an irrigation system. Or, if we do bring forth a sacred relic and use our ancient prayer for rain, we do not in our heart of hearts believe that it will be effectual, or we should carry our umbrellas to church. It is proof of spiritual growth that we are learning to adapt ourselves to use the earth as God made it. "Subdue it!" said God to Adam. And Adam will never subdue it by whining to God to help him out of every difficulty.

But difficulties exist, and remain after all our labor with them. Disappointments, failure, sudden disaster, loss, enmity, treachery, disablement, disease, death; there is still the constant recurrence of obstacles which disturb our happiness and our peace; obstacles which no human power can possibly move out of our road. What can we do about them except pray? And it is in the instinct of our souls to pray. But how shall we pray? The old way was to pray for the laws of nature to change, and to ask God to change our fate; the new way, the Christian way, is to pray for the grace to endure what we cannot change.

So this will suggest to us the real nature of prayer. It is not an Aladdin's lamp, or a magic ring, or a miraculous ointment; that is the child's way of regarding prayer. It is the endeavor to realize the words of a new ideal, "Thy Kingdom come!" But the Kingdom of Heaven is a thing of the soul; it is something within; our Lord himself has said it. So prayer is the endeavor to become conscious of another state, or another plane of existence than our earthly one. We no longer try to storm the invisible walls of heaven, but we try to realize them. We want to feel ourselves citizens of the celestial city here and now, as well as inhabitants of earth. We want consolation and recompense for the hostilities of earth and the insults of time. We want a refuge in defeat from our enemies—some of whom, we suspect, are within our very selves. And so we pray for some miracle to occur, within our very selves. We pray, we wrestle sometimes, alone, as Jacob did, with some heavenly antagonist, who seems to withhold words of blessing which he might pronounce, if he only would. But alas! he is not able to bless us beyond our own capacity; and to see, to hear, to feel something more clear of our native land, the birthplace of the soul, we must have senses, new senses, developed within us, other than our crude fleshly eyes and fleshly ears and fleshly hearts.

Now prayer is the forcing-process—as far as we know, the only one—for the development of new organs of preception and appreciation of knowledge of the things of a spiritual world. Prayer is absolutely necessary for the maintenance of a Christian life, and for the growth of the soul. Relax prayer, and the things of the world immediately become more insistent, and more important to us—we drop toward the animal again, and spiritual things begin to fade away.

Now this kind of prayer, the endeavor to open the soul to the influences of the spiritual world, is evidently not a kind of prayer which depends upon the utterance of words; it is more like an act of the will determining an attitude of the soul. By an act of the will we hold the mind on a certain level; we keep the background of our consciousness open—like a window always open towards Jerusalem. And this must be the kind of prayer which Saint Paul meant when he said, "Pray without ceasing." Of course no one could begin to keep this rule if Saint Paul had literal words in mind. Saint Paul must mean a kind of prayer which is possible while we are doing our every-day work. And this kind of prayer can only be a prayer-like state of mind, by which every thought, every word, and every deed of ours have a certain quality; and that quality is the quality of issuing forth out of a fixed purpose of living as God wants us to live. That is not impossible. At least we can gradually bring it about. Our stated times of prayer are not intended to be our only praying; on the contrary they are simply to key us up to the mood of prayer which we aim to make permanent in all our days. We can all the time be desiring God's will to be done. We can all the time be in the mood of forgiving and asking to be forgiven. We can all the time be on our guard against temptation, no matter what we are doing, so that no attack can be made more quickly than we can have our rifles up and be ready to resist. We can make our daily lives one continual Lord's Prayer, because we can make the substratum of our conscious life the three essential virtues, faith and hope and love.

And thus we see this habit of prayer gradually transforming the world around us. The reason is, of course, within ourselves; we grow to look upon the world in a different way. We walk down the city street: how strange it is now, and how interesting, how beautiful! The people passing by, they are transfigured. We see them, now, as brothers, sisters, and we say, "God bless them every one!" And possibly we shall see rags that shine, and silks and laces that turn to tatters. No longer are they, in our eyes, just a crowd pouring along on sordid, trivial errands—they are pilgrims, on their way to the Holy Land; souls on their way to heaven. "God bless them, every one!"

The solid business blocks, tower-high, rising like cliffs above the river of traffic below—they shall not browbeat us now with their show of material power. No, our souls shall see the dust of them blown along a deserted river-bank— some time. In the perspective of a soul, they are like frost on a window-pane. And that is the perspective implied in prayer, no less; the transfiguration of time.

And of all the happenings of our daily life, nothing shall seem trivial or of no account. In God's world nothing shall be common or unclean. The trials, fears, perplexities, embarrassments, humiliations, disappointments, which constantly befall—they may still be hard, but they are not intolerable. Each one is a lesson to learn, each one has a strength or a grace to give.

This world is the soul's school-room, athletic ground. It is also an unexplored continent, full of wonders; it is also the field of adventure and achievement, forests to pass, rivers to map, peaks to climb. It is the Land of Miracle, where mountains are rooted up and cast into the sea. It is also the Garden of Eden, and the New Jerusalem. It is all this and more, to the eyes of the soul, as we learn to see outward things by an inner light—the light which never was on sea or land —the Transfiguration Light, the light which is kindled in Prayer.

CHAPTER 33

The Man Nobody Knows

"Jesus saith unto him: 'Have I been so long time with you, and dost thou not know me, Philip?'"

John xiv:9.

A FEW YEARS ago a jaunty book sprang forth from the press and flaunted this title in the face of the world, *The Man Nobody Knows*. Very likely you have read it. That was a provocative title, because the world has an impression that it knows every man worth knowing. A man whom nobody knows is usually assumed to be a man whom nobody cares to know. There are so many of them; so very many that we lump them all together and call them "the masses." Psychology is coldly interested in the type, and statisticians are interested in the number, but the individual is lost in the sameness of the crowd. However, here was a finger pointed at an individual, and curiosity sold the book far and wide. Everybody wanted to know the particular man whom nobody knew. And then it was discovered that the man whom nobody knows is none other than the central Man of Christendom, its Lord and its Savior, Jesus Christ. Could it be true that no one of the millions of his followers knew him? Could it be true that here was someone at last who was really acquainted with him, and really could introduce us to him? It concerned us, vitally, to find this out. And so, eagerly reaching for this information and reading the book, we learn that the Christ so long unknown is now revealed to us as the ideal Business Man, the Great Hustler, the Efficient Supreme Advertiser. Come, all ye who are weary and heavy-laden, meet the First Rotarian!

In such wise some read and scoffed. But no doubt others

read and said, "Yes, it is he!" It would surely be a sorry task
to attempt to spoil the portrait that any man might draw
of his Lord. It is his very own, and for that reason sacred.
It is not only his right, it is also his duty to defend it. But
when the artist assumes that the Lord Jesus Christ is a figure
unknown to all who do not recognize him in such a special
portrait, he ignores a world outside of his own contracted
studio, a world where other eyes have other vision.

For here is one who sees his Lord walking through the
spring-time fields and marking as he goes how King Solomon in all his glory was not arrayed as the flowers there, and
he writes a book and calls it, *The Poet of Galilee.*

And here is a literary man of England who studies the
perfect art of the parable of the Prodigal Son, and he writes
a book out of his appreciation and calls it, *Jesus, the Man
of Genius.*

And here is one whose attention is riveted upon the out-
door life and the physical activity of the Lord, enthusiastic
also over the way he wrestled with Satan and threw him, and
he writes a magazine article, calling it "Jesus, the Great
Athlete."

And here is one who scrutinizes the movements of Jesus
as he challenges conservative wrongs and drives the traders
out of the Temple Court, and he writes a book to proclaim
that Jesus is the Great Social Reformer.

And here is one who remembers that Jesus was a carpen-
ter and exhorted men to count the cost and to be careful
about its foundations before beginning to build a house or
a tower, and so to him Jesus is, pre-eminently, the Master-
Workman.

And there is a medieval picture of Jesus representing him
as wearing the triple crown of the pope upon his head, while
he gives to the king of France the royal diadem. As posses-
sor of the keys of the Kingdom of Heaven, he is also Pontifex
Maximus and Pastor Pastorum, the King of Kings, the Im-
perial Roman Catholic.

But here is another Christian who sees most significance
in Jesus rejecting in the wilderness the kingdoms of the

world and the glory of them: the Jesus who said to Saint Peter himself, "Get thee behind me, Satan!" and to him Jesus is another Luther. He is the First Protestant.

And then there are the fervent medieval centuries that gazed, hypnotized and intense, upon the tragic focus of the Cross, and to them, above all things, Jesus was the "Man of Sorrows and acquainted with Grief."

And perhaps, during these terrible years we live through now, the figure of the Lord that most appeals to us is that of the Warrior of the Apocalypse, on his great white horse, his blood-red banner streaming afar as "he treadeth the wine-press of the fierceness of the wrath of God." Does not our heart burn within us whenever we hear the marching hymn, "The Son of God goes forth to war"?

What has he not been, indeed, to men, the "Man whom nobody knows"? What is he not, indeed? He is the Play-mate of Children, and he is the Avenger with his terrible swift sword; he is the Good Shepherd, and the dreadful Judge on the Day of Wrath; he is the Light of the World; he is the Bread of Heaven; he is the Way, the Truth, the Resurrection, and the Life; he is the Alpha and Omega, the First and the Last. Does it not seem as if the Man No-body Knows is, in fact, after all, the Man whom Everybody Knows?

At any rate it appears to be a truer name, "The Man whom Everybody Knows." Everybody seems to recognize him, at least, in spite of the fact that everybody recognizes a different character. Different, and yet the same man; for of course each one sees the same man, but with different eyes. And of course the difference is made by something behind the eyes, in the depths of each one's nature.

And here, in each one's nature, is indeed the man whom nobody knows, the Unknown Self that is regnant there. "Know Thyself," the old Greeks said; but they might have said, as well, "Explore the deep sea, explore the wide sky." We ourselves are doing just that, in this our day, in our study of psychology, although along the edges only; and the dim coral forests inhabited by strange monsters, and the

fields of starry space through which music and language
fly on currents of diffused lightning, suggest very analogous
discoveries, discoveries analogously limited and discoveries
analagously wonderful, in the mysterious regions of the human mind.

But there is one thing that Everybody knows to exist in
the Unknown Self within him, always there in the background of consciousness, and the most important element
there, for it represents that which makes a man human, and
the germ out of which his manhood grows. It is the picture
of his ideal man; it is the picture of the man he would like
to be. No man is human without it: some idea, vague or
clear, of the better man he would like to be.

This ideal figure in the soul of Everyman is at once our
hope and our despair; the inspiration of our labor and our
war, and also the paralysis of our endeavor. It is at the center
of our discontent and pain, because it proves to be so difficult to make our vision come to life.

But now into this difficult world of ours arrives the
Gospel, the "Good News." And Good News it truly is, for
therein is presented the figure of an Ideal Man who also is
a real man, one who lived a real human life on our earth.
This accomplished ideal comes face to face with the ideal
in Everyman's soul, and a miracle occurs. For the two are seen
to have been created for each other. In the first place, Everyman sees the Christ of the Gospel in the shape of his own
vision of a perfect man. His own particular values color
the human glass he sees him through, and the Christ is his
own Christ, the Christ he knows—becoming thus the Man
that Everybody knows.

On the other hand, by some divine transfusion or induction, the ideal figure in Everyman's soul is charged with life
and power, and begins to rule the lawless passions, the dis-
cords and inertias that before had kept it prisoned and ineffectual. It becomes itself transfigured, reflecting more and
more the qualities of its example. In Saint Paul's words,
the Christ of history, the Christ outside, now becomes the
Christ within, the "Christ in us, the hope of glory."

271

In other words, the ideal within us acquires a divine personality which is both ourselves and not ourselves. It may even be said to be an extension of the process of the Incarnation, the Word becoming flesh. But this mystery of God becoming man has further implications. It affects also our view of nature. For when Christ with his humanity went back into the Being of God, he added to our thought of the universal presence of God that of a universal human heart. And straightway all nature becomes alive to us with a fulness which it did not have before. Saint Paul must have felt this when he declared that all creation groaneth and travaileth together in the pain of waiting for a great consummation yet to come. But a creation that groaneth and travaileth is capable also of having other moods. Creation sings and is glad on a spring morning, just as it mourns in November. "The pines commune and have deep thoughts," so Rober Browning said. The beauty of nature and the response to beauty in the human soul, have a relationship so intimate and so full of meaning that it is only to be conceived of in terms of personality. The universe of which we are a part is not a machine; it is rather the organ of a mind. And mind communicates with mind. So that Everyman may make reply to the Mind of nature, recognizing there the Man that Everybody knows, each in his own degree and fashion:

> "Thy voice is on the rolling air;
> I hear thee where the waters run;
> Thou standest in the rising sun,
> And in the setting thou art fair."

But this divine identification will be most clear and frequent along the roads of humankind. Everyman's chief interest is in his fellow-travelers, and it is among them that he will look most eagerly for signs of the divine. It was a true instinct that led the great painters to choose so often the subject of Mother and Child, and to put them in scenes familiar—a soft Italian landscape, perhaps, with Lorenzo the Magnificent, perhaps, as one of the three adoring kings. For Bethlehem is everywhere.

Christ is, himself, an individual, with his own place in human history, but we are following a sense, too, in which he is all humanity. And so each time that Everyman is torn with temptation, in sore distress what choice to make, the trodden streets and the familiar walls around him melt into a lonesome wilderness, with wild beasts lurking in the shadows of the rocks, and with his only weapons against the Tempter certain sacred words he treasures in his heart.

And Christ's miracles of healing reappear. Never in all the history of the race has disease been so tracked into its hiding-places, through veins and nerves and caverns of the mind; never has disease been so defied by scientists and saints; never have so many sick been enabled to rise, so many lame been made to walk, so many blind and deaf been made to see and hear; never have so many devils been cast out of human souls and been made to dissipate into harmless air.

I once heard a man say that whenever he sits down at a table for a meal he always thinks of the Lord as sitting at the head of it. Every meal thus becomes a Supper of the Lord. And so all bread becomes the bread of a sacrament. Nor is he doing despite to the altar thus; rather, the altar's sacrament has given a fuller meaning to all men's meat and drink: just as our Lord, in living a human life, has made all human life a sacrament.

Then if human life becomes thus transfigured, that element of it that is so hateful and so hated, human suffering, becomes along with life a sacrament. The immeasurable pain and grief and loss of earth becomes another thing when we realize that Christ himself has entered all humanity, and endures divinely what we so humanly endure. Saint Paul, again, can rejoice, even, in his own great tribulation, when he reflects that it is a part of the passion of the Cross. The world's agony, this day, is a part of the passion of the Cross.

And, finally, that thing so dread and so dreaded, human death, itself becomes along with life a sacrament. Our Lord received it, and called it a cup that he had to drink. And there is no ray of light, anywhere, on death's impenetrable gloom, but this one fact: namely, that our Lord, himself, could die. And straightway the face of death becomes his face, because he is the Resurrection and the Life. And the ultimate disaster which Everyman so shudderingly knows and fears, becomes the veil of a hope which Everyman may know. For, behind it, we still may hear our Lord Christ say the same words he spoke to Philip:

"Have I been so long time with you, and dost thou not know me, O thou of little faith?"

November, 1942.

CHAPTER 34

The Streets of the City

"And the streets of the city shall be full of boys and girls playing in the streets thereof."

Zech. viii:5.

THIS CITY IS old Jerusalem under a new name. Earlier in the chapter it is called by the prophet the City of Truth. Manifestly it is no local Jerusalem that is meant, anchored in space and walled by time. It is a city in the air above Jerusalem. Its name is the City of Truth: that is, it is the true city, the ideal city, the vision of what a city should be. But a city does not consist of houses; it consists of people living in houses together. The houses are an accident. So that the true city is the true society, the ideal society, the vision of what Society should—and what Society shall in time—grow to be.

There are other pictures of the Perfect City, the Perfect Society, in the Bible, painted by prophet-artists who used their strongest colors to depict the splendor of what they saw; walls of jasper, gates of pearl, streets of shining gold; a river clear as crystal flowing through, and a Tree of Life extending boughs wide-spread as the earth; a music of ten thousand harps, and a court of angels and a multitude of men in festal garments surrounding a great white throne.

Pictures all, their very concreteness may hide from us the reality which they were meant to tell. Their Oriental extravagance may dazzle our sight so that we do not catch the outlines of the truth behind.

But here is a picture which all can understand; a picture which all are bound to love for the humanness of it; a picture which appeals to all the world. It is the picture of a city full of children playing in the streets of it,—an ideal city, of course, with no automobiles, and with no surly signs, "Keep off the grass."

Now perhaps the conception of an Ideal Society full of play may seem to us a conception too trivial; but on the other hand, perhaps, what is too trivial may be our conception of play, just as we may have too trivial a conception of work.

Our Ideal Society is a modern equivalent for what we are familiar with as the Kingdom of Heaven, which was the old Hebrew name for it. And into the Kingdom of Heaven, so we are told with authority, no one is able even to enter who becomes not as a little child. The Ideal Society, then, will be the society of a people who are children—children in heart. In heart, and not in mind, or else the Kingdom of Heaven would be a community of morons. But the life of a child is above all things a life of play—if devils are not allowed to tamper with it. And so is it not suggested, at least, that the life of the Ideal Society will be a life running along the lines essential in play?

At any rate, let us look at the essential elements of play, and try to see whether we can maintain their transference to the Ideal Society.

The first element of play will surely be its spontaneity, its freedom. The entire nature of a child is expressed in his play. He is full of coiled springs urgent to be let loose, and now he is free in play to let them loose in his own way. And his vitality bubbles up and overflows and expands itself in all kinds of easy natural activities. He will not walk; he runs and dances. He will not tamely talk; he sings and shouts—if you allow him. His entire sorrow in life lies in those irritating conventionalities of the grown-up world which interfere with his free expression of himself.

Life must keep moving, or it is not life; and life, like water, loves best to explore its own channels through woods and meadows, with many a wayward turn and many a laughing waterfall. Water must feel it hard to be shut up in iron pipes and measured out through faucets, or made to fill

tanner's vats and operate mill-wheels. That is work; the water is no longer free to express anything but solution and the law of gravitation.

So human life finds its first opportunity in childhood, and makes the most of it. Its scope is very limited, in view of what human life is destined to become; but such as it is, there life feels itself free, and unfolds itself with a joy which suggests that freedom is the demand of all true life.

The second essential element of play is action along lines of imagination. Now imagination is perhaps the most divine power in us, because it is creative. So in play certain conditions are assumed as a basis for its activities, certain things are imagined, that is, and then are dealt with as realities. The child takes the materials of his observation, everything he has got glimpses of in the wonderful new world into which he has arrived, and with them he constructs the scenery and furniture of the stage on which he proceeds to act. His playmates will all help in this, each contributing what he can of knowledge and of fancy, and each acting his own part—along with such heroes and heroines of history as have fallen from the table-talk of their elders, and along with the fascinating inhabitants of Fairy-Land. Children write letters to Santa Claus, and often talk with invisible personages bearing strange names. They fight with Indians, and go riding with Rough-Riders, and explore African forests, and are cast away on desert islands. Give the children a garret during the winter, and leave them alone, and presently a city is built there, with a civilization—since wars are frequent—and with a history, since a sequence of momentous events flows on from day to day. I know a sad and lonely garret in the dust of which are the memories of Babylon and Troy.

In one form or another, the imagination is always active in play, because it is necessary to provide a sufficient field for the self-expression which the expanding human being craves for itself. No room in any house, no house itself, no known neighborhood, is big enough for it.

So these two elements, freedom and imagination, will

suggest to us a definition of play. Play is self-expression for its own sake, play is self-expression for the sake of joy in the process.

We have taken a glance at play in childhood, simply because childhood presents it in its most perfect form. But the thing itself never dies out of a human being's life—unless, alas! the human being petrifies, and becomes ready, before death, for a museum or a tomb. When we no longer desire to play, then we may know for a surety that we are growing old.

It remains, then, our greatest pleasure in existence to feel our life forces working freely in spontaneous ways; to be able to do the things we like best to do, unconfined by walls of grim necessities. We count that happiness, and so it is. We may be resigned to poor and inadequate imitations of freedom, but, nevertheless, the craving is still unquenchable, to give our entire self its exercise, and to stretch ourselves, at intervals, loose from the bandages of drudgery.

In games, like football, or bridge, or checkers, or chess, we invent difficulties which we deem it a credit to overcome. In theaters we watch imaginary human situations develop into climaxes. In music we find most plastic material for imagination to mould into all devices of enchanting forms. In symbolic pageantries and in memorial celebrations, we aim to lift a day or an hour into some nobler mood. In a thousand ways we seek to escape from the slavery of work into the freedom of play. The honor paid to an elected Queen of Beauty in an American city is not altogether silly; it is the people's worship of the Goddess of Liberty.

Happy is that man whose work so fits into his nature that he is able to exert in it his best capacities, and so to feel that he expresses himself in it to some approximate degree. Then what does he call his work? He calls it play! And that represents then the man's best work, because the most of himself is in it, the work that he can call his play. To be sure, it is the hardship of the grown-up life that such a fortunate aspect of work is not often realized; although nothing is more certain than that we might make it so, far

278

oftener than we do. But the door of escape, again, from the narrow rounds of actuality is that same ivory door of imagination:—the very same door through which Saint John the Divine looked into heaven.

We can throw a halo around any prosaic monotonous task which will make it shine with dignified meanings; we can give it a value in the thought which will make it seem worthy of our exertion upon it. An unholy thing it is that we should be obliged to spend any precious hours upon things of no account;—but let us once assume that the things of no account are important factors in some large result, at least in the way we attack them, and we have justified ourselves to our own souls.

Now this endeavor for freedom, and this endeavor to extend the arena of our life through imagination, all this is the assertion of the play-spirit within us. So all our work is mixed with play in some form, and each is necessary to the other. Work without play is slavery; and play without work soon becomes satiety, like a dinner of cake and sugar.

If all this is true in our life as we know it, and it surely is, then is it too far to go to say that the play-spirit has its essential part also in the Ideal Life, the Ideal Society, the Kingdom of Heaven?

We desire above all things to be free, to have the chance to express ourselves in all the lines of our nature. Freedom means just this, and it means no less: the unhindered activity of every part of us, according to the laws of our being; no part blocking another part, no part acting selfishly and independently for itself. This is freedom, and nothing else is freedom, the harmonious working together of the whole man. But there is only one attitude of a man's soul which will guarantee this freedom, and that is the attitude of submission to some supreme Unity which exists behind all our life. And this attitude of submission to some supreme Source of life, has an old, old name: we call it Religion.

But this wider vision of freedom demands a still wider field to act upon. Earth itself is now not wide enough, nor high enough. Our soul reaches out for an Over-Soul in nature, and then our heart, with sublime audacity, invites that World-Soul in to be a dweller within itself. And we stake all our destiny upon this inconceivable Comradeship, and we proceed to fashion all our conduct, if possible, into forms worthy of such a transcendent assumption. And we assume new relations to earth, and we assume new relations to men— relations assumed, indeed, but they prove themselves true in the experiments of living which we base upon them. But how is this anything else than the very highest effort of the imagination: to launch upon an invisible ocean, to reckon by invisible stars, and to aim for the port of Heart's Desire, the City invisibly built beyond the sea, out of the ruins of earth? What a triumph of freedom! and what a creative enterprise!

So, to express ourselves spontaneously in those activities for which we were made: to do right naturally because all our nature wants to do right—this is what we know as salvation; and to commit ourselves to the attainment of the soul's best hope, to set ourselves to the proving of things unseen— this is what we know as faith; and to love because to love is the soul's true function—this is the greatest of the Christian graces. And these things are things of Religion, things belonging to the Kingdom of Heaven, the city of Truth.

If a man sets out to develop every part of himself, to grow in every root and fiber and branch of himself, all at once and inevitably he finds his life religious: he cannot help doing so, because the elements of religion are a part of him.

Religion, then, is that which makes us truly free. Selfishness is the real prison of life; sin is the real slavery, hindering us from due development and from our best activity. Too long and too often have men conceived of Religion as confinement, repression, and constraint. On the contrary it is the only thing that can make us free. Real Religion is not the acceptance of a creed, nor is it the following of a schedule of rules, nor is it the performance of elaborate ritual. It is the growing of a living human soul.

Again, Religion is that which expands the whole sphere of life, and expands, at the same time, the soul to fill it, although never able to overtake the widening horizon. Religion opens windows in the dimness of our doubts and fears. Religion adds the sky to our back-yard. It adds to our prosaic existence among things the zest of adventure among realities to be realized only as we seek for them. It is the true Quest of the Holy Grail.

And who would ever shrink from the name of Religion, who would ever shrink from the freedom and the glory of the true religious life, if men, blinded by the physical views of things which require so many centuries and so much bitter pain to get out of our eyes, if men had not so long made the name of Religion include so much that is narrow and gloomy and harsh and cruel and inhuman?

But down through all the ages, through all the blood of slain beasts, dumb victims slain in religion's name; through all the deserts where lonely hermits scourged themselves for heaven's sake; through all those prison cloisters where men and women tore their human hearts out for Christ's sake; through all those infernal fires kindled on earth by Christians for the same Christ's sake, and those piteous fires kindled in hell for the damnation of babes; through Holy Leagues and Holy Wars, through blasphemous Te Deums and Satanic orthodoxies, and through all those atrocious codes that made gloom a virtue and joy a crime;—through all these horrors the song of the children has never ceased, since the prophet heard it in the Heavenly City's streets:

> "O serve the Lord—with gladness;
> And come before his presence—with a song."

May 13, 1943.

—1—

And Paul said unto them: "Have you received the Holy Ghost since you believed?" And they said unto him: "We have not so much as heard whether there be a Holy Ghost." Acts xix: 2.

It is told of a bird that it once went flying to and fro in the sky, inquiring, "Where is the air?" And it is told of a fish that it once went swimming about in the wide Atlantic, inquiring, "Where is the sea?" Even so the Ephesians said to Saint Paul: "The Holy Ghost? We have never so much as heard whether there be a Holy Ghost."

But we in our Church could hardly make a like complaint. We very often say or sing an ascription of praise to the Father, the Son, and the Holy Ghost. And we very often, in a solemn Creed, affirm our belief in the Father, the Son, and the Holy Ghost. Yes, we hear often enough, one might think, that there exists a Holy Ghost.

This divine name, so bound together with two other divine names in the Gloria and the Creed, has a place now in the religious belief of men of which it shall hardly be dispossessed. They are welded together now in a permanence hardly to be dissolved, although it required long strife to weld them so, and even human blood, indeed\

282

Chapter 35

The Holy Ghost

"And Paul said unto them: 'Have you received the Holy Ghost since you believed?' And they said unto him: 'We have not so much as heard whether there be a Holy Ghost.'"

Acts xix:2.

IT IS TOLD of a bird that it once went flying to and fro in the sky, inquiring, "Where is the air?" And it is told of a fish that it once went swimming about in the wide Atlantic, inquiring, "Where is the sea?" Even so the Ephesians said to Saint Paul: "The Holy Ghost? We have never so much as heard whether there be a Holy Ghost."

But we in our Church could hardly make a like complaint. We very often say or sing an ascription of praise to the Father, the Son, and the Holy Ghost. And we very often, in a solemn Creed, affirm our belief in the Father, the Son, and the Holy Ghost. Yes, we hear often enough, one might think, that there exists a Holy Ghost.

This divine name, so bound together with two other divine names in the Gloria and the Creed, has a place now in the religious belief of men of which it shall hardly be dispossessed. They are welded together now in a permanence hardly to be dissolved, although it required long strife to weld them so, and even human blood, indeed.

The formula stands as a monument over ancient battle-fields, commemorating victories in doctrine. For Christianity today is Trinitarian. There is no question today, practically, where questions once were burning. To be a Christian today is, almost as a matter of course, to accept as fundamental the doctrine of the Trinity. It is a heredity now, accepted

283

unchallenged, like the law of gravitation or the Copernican theory, so that, in the language of our theology, we are all Trinitarians. That is, we all believe in, or concur in, or submit to, a conception of God as three-fold in nature and aspect, a Trinity in Unity, three Persons in one God: the Father, the Son, and the Holy Ghost.

This is what we say with our lips. It is what we sing in our Glorias and repeat in our Creeds. We accept it and assent to it and believe that we believe it, the fundamental doctrine of the Holy Trinity. We do not doubt that it is the rock upon which the temple of our religion is built.

We say this continually with our lips, and we see it symbolized in triangles and clover-leaves and in three circles interlaced, but one might ask how the mind translates these hieroglyphic signs, and what meaning is commonly found in these three more definite, but still symbolic, words.

We have a certain magnificent conception of the Father, as the Creator and Sustainer of the universe. We have a far more intimate and vivid conception of the Son, because we see him in our Lord Jesus Christ, as God becoming man. In fact, our religious horizon is filled from East to West with the transcendent manhood of him in whom our aspiring God-worship and our loyal hero-worship have united and become one. Thus the Father and the Son occupy distinct spheres in our minds, and yet we are able even, in a wavering way, to hold an idea of them as being One, and as forming one God.

But when we come to the third Person of the Trinity, the Holy Spirit, we enter immediately a region of such vagueness that if it were not for the constant presence of the Name in our Glorias and our Creed, and for the special festival at which we commemorate the Holy Spirit on Whitsunday, we might fancy the possibility that men might so leave the Holy Spirit out of account that finally he might drop out of memory and out of mind, and men might say at last with the old Ephesians:

"The Holy Ghost? We have never so much as heard whether there be a Holy Ghost!"

284

Suppose Saint Paul should land on our shores in a fourth Missionary Journey. He finds the country full of churches dedicated to his Lord, in which he hears the Christian Creed repeated constantly. But there is something on his mind, and he asks us, as he asked the old Ephesians: "Have you received the Holy Ghost since you believed?"

"Oh, yes," we should probably reply, "we received the Holy Ghost when the bishop's hands were laid upon our heads in Confirmation."

And then Saint Paul might ask: "But how do you know? Did you feel the Holy Spirit in your soul? Did you receive the gift of tongues—the gift of miraculous speech? Did you have a vision, or, above all, did you prophesy, as the prophet Joel foretold?"

Then what should we say? Did we actually experience any extraordinary emotion or exhibit any new ability to prove that the Holy Spirit had entered into us in a form in which he had not been there before? So perhaps we should answer Saint Paul like this:

"More things are wrought in our soul than we are conscious of. It is by faith that we know we received the Holy Ghost."

This answer may satisfy Saint Paul, but his question sets us thinking. Suppose we recall those symbols which are used in the New Testament to describe the Holy Spirit's activities in our world.

We think immediately—the very word "Spirit" suggests it—of the wind which our Lord told Nicodemus is like the Spirit. Nicodemus the Rabbi had come to Jesus by night to talk with him. Now every night in Jerusalem a wind blows up from the sea and walks up and down the streets, crying outside the windows, sometimes like the singing of David to his harp, and sometimes like the ravings of a wild old prophet foretelling doom. Such a wind must have been keening outside the window as Jesus and Nicodemus talked together that night.

"Hark!" said Jesus unto him. "The wind bloweth where it willeth, and thou hearest the voice thereof, but canst not tell whence it cometh nor whither it goeth. Even so is the Spirit."

No one can see the wind, except in the things which it does. We hear it on tiptoe behind us, we feel it brushing past us as it runs on ahead. We hear it mourning under the eaves or singing over the wires. We see the dead leaves blown into spirals and chased across the campus, and we see the tall trees bowing courteously, or perhaps wrathfully, as an invisible presence passes by. And we know that a wind is at work or at play, although we see it not. Even so is the Spirit. Invisible in itself, it is perceived only in its movements. We cannot tell whence it cometh nor whither it goeth. Not seeing any speaker, we yet may hear a voice—perhaps a still, small voice, perhaps a battle-cry.

The second form that may occur to us, symbolizing the Holy Spirit, will be that likeness of a dove which floated down upon our Lord at his baptism.

Wings have long been used to show pictorially the independence of spirit over the law of gravitation. It is hardly conceivable that when primitive artists represented angels with wings, they intended to affirm a literal anatomical fact. No, the wings were only a symbol, indicating that the beings who wore wings were spirits not bound to earth by laws of earth. Men and the beasts must move about laboriously and slowly, with the weight of material bodies holding them down; but spiritual beings roam at will in a world of air and sky, and only wings can present such an idea to the eyes and imagination of men.

So, if spirits are represented with wings, then the Spirit of spirits, the Holy Spirit, will hardly lack them. Perhaps that is the reason, or part of the reason, why a dove is described as coming down out of the skies, to set the seal of the spiritual world upon the earthly career of our Lord at his baptism.

If the Holy Spirit is invisible, like the wind, its dwelling also is above the earth, having wings. It is gentleness personified, like a dove. Out of mystery—out of heaven—it floats down gently, like a dove.

And the third manifestation of the Holy Spirit which comes to our minds will be, of course, that of the flames of fire that settled upon the brows of the disciples as they waited for the promise of their Lord at Pentecost.

What a wonder is a flame of fire! A thing half matter, half spirit, we might well believe! Visible, indeed, as a color, but elusive as a wind. Impalpable, impossible to seize or to get hold of, yet destructive of everything which it itself seizes on. Immaterial itself, yet of irresistible power over matter. It tears down, it dissolves, it melts, it dissipates, it separates like a judgment, it utterly destroys, like a penalty, all forms of matter. Wood and stone, metal and adamant, green forests and stubborn mountains—they all are wax in the breath of the fire.

So what an appropriate symbol, or vehicle, of the Holy Spirit fire will be! Fire is immaterial—even invisible, for the yellow and red are but the fluttering robes of an unseen potency. Immaterial and invisible, yet irresistible, as thus is the fire, even so is the Spirit. Invisible, seen only in effects, like the wind; gentle and of nature ethereal, like the dove; and yet irresistible, all-conquering, like the fire.

Wind and wings and fire! An unseen force, on the plane behind and above matter, the absolute master of all forms of matter—even so is the Spirit.

Wind and wings and fire! What is there in our observation of the phenomena of the world which will answer to this outline description of the attributes of the Spirit, as we may approach it by symbols? There is only one thing which at all answers to it; but there is one thing, and that is Life. Life is invisible, seen only in the wonderful forms in which it moulds matter. We know not whence it cometh, nor whither it goeth. Of all imaginable operations of energy throbbing in rhythms of gentleness—in cells and seasons and planets' orbits beating and pulsating like wings—life is the gentlest. And yet, of all imaginable puttings-forth of power, life is the most ultimately irresistible.

Herein we have found the sphere of the Holy Ghost, although it is only what our Nicene Creed has been asserting all through the centuries: it is the sphere of life. "And I believe in the Holy Ghost, the Lord, and the Giver of life."

And straightway the Holy Spirit in the Trinity possesses a kingdom, in our conception of It, which is definite enough for the mind to take hold upon as a concrete object of thought; definite enough and yet offering such endless exploration as to suggest the infinite; a kingdom beautiful enough and wonderful enough for all that we can imagine as divinity. As the Father is the Universal Center and Source, and as the Son is the Universal Man, so the Holy Spirit is the Universal Life.

It was the Spirit that brooded over the face of the waters in the beginning, and like the gradual transformations within an egg, so, under the potent, vivifying influences of the Holy Spirit, operations of life drew forth out of chaos all the vast work of creation and the great Seven Days: continents and geologic ages; creeping things and flying things; sun and moon and stars, and Man.

In the physical realm the manifestations of life are manifold: all the marvelous unfoldings of the springtime; the processions of the seasons; flower and fruit and the fall of the leaf; birth and growth and death and birth again; the strange weavings of instinct and heredity; and the struggle of Evolution up its spiral stair—all these things are activities of the Holy Spirit.

Above this, but intertwined most intimately with it, lies a mental realm: a world of thought, where human minds find unceasing interest in exploring their environment and making of it material for a new creation, where human minds erect structures of thought in which to dwell. Whether it be myths or magic or folk-lore, whether it be Parthenons or Iliads or symphonies, or maps of stars or systems of science or institutions of society, a creative impulse never sleeps, keeping men forever building and unbuilding and building up again. And all these things are activities of the Holy Spirit.

Above the mental realm of life, but most intimately related with it, lies another, which we call the spiritual realm. It surely is the most important of all, because the way we live in it determines the happiness we find in living in the other two. Here we have to do with a movement of life called Conscience, inexorably urging a difference between right and wrong. Here we have to deal with a movement of life which draws us toward ideals of being, higher than those we already know. And here, finally, we find that group of gentle virtues—self-control, humility, patience, loyalty, goodness, kindness, joy, peace, love—which Saint Paul calls "the fruits of the Spirit."

To see these things, anywhere upon this earth, is to see the operations of the Holy Spirit. Artificial labels make no difference; the signs of the Holy Spirit are always the same. And to feel these things stirring within one's own soul—yes, even to feel no more than a bitter, despairing endeavor to drag one's self along on an upward path—to know any of these things within you is to know of a truth that the Holy Spirit, the Lord and the Giver of life, is within you.

But all these things were in the world before Pentecost. Men from earliest days felt within their souls unaccountable fears of an invisible region behind their world, strange shrinkings from wrong-doing, groping impulses toward self-sacrifice—movements within them like the rising of a wind, or the fluttering of a dove, or the springing of a fire. And men have thirsted for something unknown, as the hart desireth the waterbrooks; they have crudely sinned and repented, they have crudely believed and hoped and loved, from the beginning. They have done all these things, manifesting the presence of the Holy Ghost in human living, even while, like the Ephesians of old, they had not so much as heard whether there was a Holy Ghost. Just as, from the very beginning, birth and growth and change and death and resurrection have always gone on, so sin-sense and repentance and faith and hope and love have been struggling like living seed-germs in the dark soil of matter ever since the world began. For the Holy Spirit has been from the beginning in every atom of the world; and spiritual life, as well as mental life and physical life, has always been striving after its due expression.

Expression life must have, since it is life. And although the Spirit's efforts toward equilibrium are often like a Day of Judgment; its coming like a rushing, mighty wind; its wings no longer doves' wings but eagles' wings, darkening all the sky; its fire setting continents in flames; yet it is always the same Spirit, whether Comforter or Avenger—always, since the world began, the Lord and the Giver of Life.

The Holy Spirit has been in the world ever since the world began. And yet the prophet Joel speaks thus in the name of God:

"And it shall come to pass in those days that I will pour out my Spirit upon all flesh; and your sons and your daughters shall prophesy; and your old men shall dream dreams, and your young men shall see visions; even upon the servants and upon the handmaids in those days will I pour out my Spirit."

And yet all men, all the time, have lived and moved and had their being in the Spirit.

It is as if the bird in the sky, looking for the air, should suddenly come to know the air as the very medium supporting its wings; the air then would suddenly seem to be poured around it.

It is as if the fish in the Atlantic, searching for the sea, should suddenly come to realize that the sea was its very home; the sea then would suddenly seem to be poured around it.

So to the blind man receiving his sight, the light must seem to come pouring into his dark world, filling its spaces with wonder. It is a matter of standpoint. The Spirit is poured upon the children of men when the windows of their souls are opened to the surrounding light; and they suddenly see themselves not as isolated atoms in a soulless creation, but as brothers of men and as sons of God and as heirs of eternal life.

This is the dream that old men dream, and this is the vision that young men see. And the days which the prophet foretold are now; the time is now. The very conflict which blots out the sun and turns the moon into blood is a proof of it. Dreams and visions are clashing with material things outworn. And if the dreamers of dreams and the seers of visions still perceive men as trees walking, their precious discovery is that there is such a thing as sight. They sense a wider horizon. And if the very servants and handmaids speak in unknown tongues, and fill the temple-courts with clamor and discordant noise, it is still a blessed thing that they are trying to prophesy at all. Tomorrow they will have a clearer speech.

In the strife between the old and the new, many doubts arise. But perhaps the young man must have his doubts before he sees his vision. Down by the ford of a river one night, a young man named Jacob, tormented with doubts and fears, wrestled until the break of day with a strong antagonist whom the dawning light revealed as the angel of the Lord. And in the rising sun the angel blessed the persevering fighter, and gave him a new name—Israel: God's hero.

In such guise the angels of the Lord often come, compelling struggle. It is the price that life demands. It is the price we all must pay for the gift of the Spirit, the price of worthiness: a price imposed upon us by Him who created us, the God who "maketh his messengers the winds, and his ministers the flaming fire."

(*June, 1943.*)

CHAPTER 36

The Servant of Yahweh

(A Fragment)

WHEN THE TWENTIETH century shall look back upon the nineteenth and estimate what it has done for knowledge, it will doubtless head the list of the nineteenth century's achievements with the discovery and formulation of that method in nature which we term Evolution. In science that evolutionary process has been defined to be "the gradual working of physical laws upon an earlier condition of matter." But such is the light which the application of this theory has thrown upon the relations of recorded facts,—such is the order which it has brought about in the former chaos of observed phenomena,—that it has been used as a working hypothesis in all directions and extended to universality. Life in every department, we now declare, carries on its operations according to the laws of Evolution; and we will redefine the method in order to adapt it to its infinite domain. "Evolution," we will say, "is the process by which potentiality becomes actuality."

So, believing in the unity of God, and therefore in the unity of his universe, wheresoever we perceive a phenomenon of whatsoever kind, we shall know that it is the product of forces working upon possibilities already existent in certain elements, and so we shall be able, in some sort, to trace a way backward through fossils and ruins, and write a history of a living thing.

We deal thus with the development of man's body, his mind, his civilization, the planet upon which he lives, and the stars in his sky. Shall we deal in like manner with his religion? Undoubtedly. And we shall find in his religious history the same advancement from stage to stage; the same roots of growth running back from any given attainment to what has gone before; the same influence of environment upon the outward expression of an inner, vital impulse. But shall we deal in like manner with Christianity? The only answer is yes, undoubtedly; for, by divorcing Christianity from God's method of creation as science and philosophy perceive it in every other department, we introduce duality into nature, and unreality into our religion. Our observation of facts may be imperfect and our logic may be faulty, but things have reality to our minds only as attested by the sense and reason. The method of the senses and of reason in all other departments has led to the sublime theory of Evolution. If religion draws away in scorn from its application to herself, she draws away from our credence finally, and follows the Greek gods and goddesses into the region of myths, leaving us but the flutter of her flying garments in a mood of dreams, and the pathos of her broken altars along the highways of our life.

Now as to the record of our Christian religion's development, we possess such a record in the fullest and richest form. Our Bible is that record, the story of the evolving heart and mind and soul of man. And just as science finds ripple-marks and glacier-scratches, foot-prints on ancient beaches and fern-leaves stamped in rock; stone axes and broken vases and golden ear-rings, mounds of funeral ashes and a few upthrust columns of carven stone; and as science reads in these remains the story of a million years' development, and paints for us anew therefrom successive races of animals strange and manifold; forest-age and ice-age and water-age; and then successive populations of men, climbing up through plane after plane of savagery, until a Parthenon crowns a hill and a Sophocles sings in a plain;—even so in the Bible lies stratum after stratum of fossil-words and fossil-metaphors; hints of ancient custom and ancient thought; fragments of ancient history imprinted on Babylonian brick; and forms of beauty lovelier than the fern-leaves, preserved imperishably in prophet's rhapsody and poet's song. Almost anywhere may be picked up a bit of wisdom, of potency sufficient to transform a life; without delving into it for doctrine, without subjecting it to the processes of the scholar, we easily find in it all things necessary for salvation. But it also furnishes endless material for the scientific investigator, who, seeing in this rich mass of literary remains the forms which a persistent current of life has secreted and shaped and left behind, applies to it his working hypothesis of a law of growth, and deduces therefrom philosophies and histories, making ancient civilizations take form again, and ancient peoples live again, showing a never-ending struggle upward in submission to a plan which they knew not of, now unfolded in a long panorama of order and design. Wonderful unity with itself, wonderful harmony with all nature the Bible presents, when it is studied in a manner which the magnificent theory of Evolution suggests.

So, looking along the ordered progress of Jewish history, considering the ideal which always went before that nation like a pillar of cloud by day and a pillar of fire by night, it is proposed that we should pause for some thought upon that most striking phenomenon in the changing forms of that ideal, the picture of Israel's promised Messiah as the Servant of Yahweh, put to suffering and shame; the people's Savior, who accomplishes his mission by his humiliation and death. Yet this ideal of the Servant of Yahweh is the climax of Israel's ideal of the Messiah. But how contrary it appears to all preconceived notions of what a people's hope might center upon: a hero who dies, a king who is reckoned among transgressors, a savior who saves by his very suffering and failure. This seems to be a conception isolated and unique, to be explained only by a theory of an inspired fore-knowledge and a supernatural insight.

But we have set out upon a line of meditation in which we are to regard particularly that aspect of the Bible which is its progress from things old, and out of things old, to things new, according to a method which seems to be God's method in all nature. According to this method we deem that, when we gaze upon any phenomenon whatsoever, we may see in it a stage of development, the outcome of a process of growth. So, before we pronounce this conception of the Servant of Yahweh one isolated and unique, let us see if it might not fall in order as, in some sort, an outcome of the Law of Evolution; the ultimate flower of a tree of inspired upward reach after a saving ideal, which grew ten thousand years in order to bloom in that one consummate form; the flower of a seed which fell just outside of Eden amid the thistles and thorns, and which grew under the rain and sun which were Israel's varying fortunes of prosperity and woe. Our thought will be simply a line of meditation, a suggestion; it will attack no doctrine of inspiration or prophecy; it will intrude upon the field of neither the theologian nor the scientist, which would be but presumption where space and time and opportunities for research are so limited. It will simply be a line of fancy indulged in for an hour by one to whom the world seems more divine the more clearly it is all seen to come under one method and one plan; and to whom the idea of the Servant of Yahweh means more as a product from within than as an interjection from without.

With such disclaimer of all irreverent or over-ambitious or iconoclastic intent, let us look for the seed from which the idea of the Servant of Yahweh grew. And here we find it, the shell of it, at least, imbedded in the allegorical record of humanity's beginnings:

"The seed of the woman," said God to the serpent which tempted man to sin, "the seed of the woman shall bruise thy head, and thou shalt bruise his heel."

Just what this hieroglyphic story stands for in actual event and literal history is a riddle beyond all guessing. That there is a certain admixture of symbolism even the most unimaginative of scholars will hardly deny; but the bounding-line between figure and fact every attempting hand draws differently. The Garden of Eden, the apple, the serpent, the fall of man, —these simple outlines embody a record which, whatever it may mean as to facts of history, at least unmistakably means this as to the summing up and philosophy of facts of history:

that man in God's image, set to keep the Garden of Eden, indicates man's proper place of sovereignty in creation; that he loses his lordship by disobeying the law of creation—the law even here may be inferred to be the law of service; that he pays a long penalty of pain, but at length conquers the fatal tendency to wrong choice in himself, and takes possession of the office in the universe which God in the beginning designed him to take. Whatever else Eden may mean, it means man's ideal state. Whatever else the apple may mean, it means the recognition of a right and wrong choice. Whatever else the serpent may mean, it means the impulse to use creation for one's own self. And whatever else the fall of man may mean, it means man's humiliated sense of the distance between what he is and what he ought to be. And here at this point, contemporaneous with this sense of humiliation, enters the primeval prophecy and promise: "Sin will hurt man, but man shall overcome sin." And all theology, the Trinity, the incarnation, the atonement, the resurrection and eternal life, all are embraced in this first great sweep of the pencil of prophecy. Man's sense of an outer source from which he himself sprang, this indicates God the Father; man's sense of man as the climax of creation, this indicates God the Son; and man's sense of obligation to something right, this indicates God the Holy Spirit, speaking within him warningly as a conscience, and hopefully as a promise, and inspiringly as an ideal.

No matter where or how in farthest history, the first glimmering conception kindled in the soul of primitive man that there was a difference between *ought* and *ought not*, when he did the *ought not* he ate the fruit of the tree of knowledge of good and evil. That first glimmering conception held within itself the germ of all that followed: in the *ought not* was man's downward possibility; in the *ought* was man's upward possibility, the pattern in which he was made and the power to become ultimately like it. It is all bound together; the voice within man which told him of a right and wrong, and which pierced him with his shame when he chose the wrong, this voice foretold to him also his ultimate victory over wrong.

So there stands the first prophecy in the consciousness of humanity in the dawn of time; vague and undefined, but a formative point of life in humanity's ethical history; humanity created for a place of power, and responsible; humanity abusing its privilege and wandering far afield; humanity feeling that someway it should at last, through pain of toil, of child-bearing, and of conflict, attain its destiny in spite of all; a sense of its divine origin and of a behavior unworthy of it, and a confidence in an ultimate return and restoration,—to such end the blessed Spirit of God began to whisper into humanity's inner ear as soon as humanity began to listen; and humanity wrote out the wondrous revelation in a beautiful picture story on the walls of its earliest Temple— the story of the Garden of Eden, which we have now preserved, like a precious Elgin-marble slab, in our book of Genesis.

* * * * * *